Presenting Windows® 98 One Step at a Time

Presenting
Windows® 98
One Step at a Time

Brian Underdahl

IDG Books Worldwide, Inc.

An International Data Group Company

FOSTER CITY, CA · CHICAGO, IL · INDIANAPOLIS, IN · SOUTHLAKE, TX

Presenting Windows® 98 One Step at a Time

Published by
IDG Books Worldwide, Inc.
An International Data Group Company
919 E. Hillsdale Blvd., Suite 400
Foster City, CA 94404
www.idgbooks.com (IDG Books Worldwide Web site)

Library of Congress Catalog Card No.: 97-74703

ISBN: 0-7645-3191-3

Printed in the United States of America

10 9 8 7 6 5 4 3 2 1

1E/RV/QZ/ZX/FL

Distributed in the United States by IDG Books Worldwide, Inc.

Distributed by Macmillan Canada for Canada; by Transworld Publishers Limited in the United Kingdom; by IDG Norge Books for Norway; by IDG Sweden Books for Sweden; by Woodslane Pty. Ltd. for Australia; by Woodslane Enterprises Ltd. for New Zealand; by Longman Singapore Publishers Ltd. for Singapore, Malaysia, Thailand, and Indonesia; by Simron Pty. Ltd. for South Africa; by Toppan Company Ltd. for Japan; by Distribuidora Cuspide for Argentina; by Livraria Cultura for Brazil; by Ediciencia S.A. for Ecuador; by Addison-Wesley Publishing Company for Korea; by Ediciones ZETA S.C.R. Ltda. for Peru; by WS Computer Publishing Corporation, Inc., for the Philippines; by Unalis Corporation for Taiwan; by Contemporanea de Ediciones for Venezuela; by Computer Book & Magazine Store for Puerto Rico; by Express Computer Distributors for the Caribbean and West Indies. Authorized Sales Agent: Anthony Rudkin Associates for the Middle East and North Africa.

For general information on IDG Books Worldwide's books in the U.S., please call our Consumer Customer Service department at 800-762-2974. For reseller information, including discounts and premium sales, please call our Reseller Customer Service department at 800-434-3422.

For information on where to purchase IDG Books Worldwide's books outside the U.S., please contact our International Sales department at 415-655-3200 or fax 415-655-3295.

For information on foreign language translations, please contact our Foreign & Subsidiary Rights department at 415-655-3021 or fax 415-655-3281.

For sales inquiries and special prices for bulk quantities, please contact our Sales department at 415-655-3200 or write to the address above.

For information on using IDG Books Worldwide's books in the classroom or for ordering examination copies, please contact our Educational Sales department at 800-434-2086 or fax 817-251-8174.

For press review copies, author interviews, or other publicity information, please contact our Public Relations department at 415-655-3000 or fax 415-655-3299.

For authorization to photocopy items for corporate, personal, or educational use, please contact Copyright Clearance Center, 222 Rosewood Drive, Danvers, MA 01923, or fax 508-750-4470.

ABOUT IDG BOOKS WORLDWIDE

Welcome to the world of IDG Books Worldwide.

IDG Books Worldwide, Inc., is a subsidiary of International Data Group, the world's largest publisher of computer-related information and the leading global provider of information services on information technology. IDG was founded more than 25 years ago and now employs more than 8,500 people worldwide. IDG publishes more than 275 computer publications in over 75 countries (see listing below). More than 60 million people read one or more IDG publications each month.

Launched in 1990, IDG Books Worldwide is today the #1 publisher of best-selling computer books in the United States. We are proud to have received eight awards from the Computer Press Association in recognition of editorial excellence and three from *Computer Currents'* First Annual Readers' Choice Awards. Our best-selling ...*For Dummies*® series has more than 30 million copies in print with translations in 30 languages. IDG Books Worldwide, through a joint venture with IDG's Hi-Tech Beijing, became the first U.S. publisher to publish a computer book in the People's Republic of China. In record time, IDG Books Worldwide has become the first choice for millions of readers around the world who want to learn how to better manage their businesses.

Our mission is simple: Every one of our books is designed to bring extra value and skill-building instructions to the reader. Our books are written by experts who understand and care about our readers. The knowledge base of our editorial staff comes from years of experience in publishing, education, and journalism — experience we use to produce books for the '90s. In short, we care about books, so we attract the best people. We devote special attention to details such as audience, interior design, use of icons, and illustrations. And because we use an efficient process of authoring, editing, and desktop publishing our books electronically, we can spend more time ensuring superior content and spend less time on the technicalities of making books.

You can count on our commitment to deliver high-quality books at competitive prices on topics you want to read about. At IDG Books Worldwide, we continue in the IDG tradition of delivering quality for more than 25 years. You'll find no better book on a subject than one from IDG Books Worldwide.

John J. Kilcullen

John Kilcullen
CEO
IDG Books Worldwide, Inc.

Steven Berkowitz

Steven Berkowitz
President and Publisher
IDG Books Worldwide, Inc.

*Eighth Annual
Computer Press
Awards ≥1992*

*Ninth Annual
Computer Press
Awards ≥1993*

*Tenth Annual
Computer Press
Awards ≥1994*

*Eleventh Annual
Computer Press
Awards ≥1995*

IDG Books Worldwide, Inc., is a subsidiary of International Data Group, the world's largest publisher of computer-related information and the leading global provider of information services on information technology. International Data Group publishes over 275 computer publications in over 75 countries. Sixty million people read one or more International Data Group publications each month. International Data Group's publications include: **ARGENTINA:** Buyer's Guide, Computerworld Argentina, PC World Argentina; **AUSTRALIA:** Australian Macworld, Australian PC World, Australian Reseller News, Computerworld, IT Casebook, Network World, Publish, Webmaster; **AUSTRIA:** Computerwelt Österreich, Networks Austria, PC Tip Austria; **BANGLADESH:** PC World Bangladesh; **BELARUS:** PC World Belarus; **BELGIUM:** Data News; **BRAZIL:** Annuário de Informática, Computerworld, Connections, Macworld, PC Player, PC World, Publish, Reseller News, Supergamepower; **BULGARIA:** Computerworld Bulgaria, Network World Bulgaria, PC & MacWorld Bulgaria; **CANADA:** CIO Canada, Client/Server World, ComputerWorld Canada, InfoWorld Canada, NetworkWorld Canada, WebWorld; **CHILE:** Computerworld Chile, PC World Chile; **COLOMBIA:** Computerworld Colombia, PC World Colombia; **COSTA RICA:** PC World Centro America; **THE CZECH AND SLOVAK REPUBLICS:** Computerworld Czechoslovakia, Macworld Czech Republic, PC World Czechoslovakia; **DENMARK:** Communications World Danmark, Computerworld Danmark, Macworld Danmark, PC World Danmark, Techworld Danmark; **DOMINICAN REPUBLIC:** PC World Republica Dominicana; **ECUADOR:** PC World Ecuador; **EGYPT:** Computerworld Middle East, PC World Middle East; **EL SALVADOR:** PC World Centro America; **FINLAND:** MikroPC, Tietoverkko, Tietoviikko; **FRANCE:** Distribuique, Hebdo, Info PC, Le Monde Informatique, Macworld, Reseaux & Telecoms, WebMaster France; **GERMANY:** Computer Partner, Computerwoche, Computerwoche Extra, Computerwoche FOCUS, Global Online, Macwelt, PC Welt; **GREECE:** Amiga Computing, GamePro Greece, Multimedia World; **GUATEMALA:** PC World Centro America; **HONDURAS:** PC World Centro America; **HONG KONG:** Computerworld Hong Kong, PC World Hong Kong, Publish in Asia; **HUNGARY:** ABCD CD-ROM, Computerworld Szamitastechnika, Internetto online Magazine, PC World Hungary, PC-X Magazin Hungary; **ICELAND:** Tolvuheimur PC World Island; **INDIA:** Information Communications World, Information Systems Computerworld, PC World India, Publish in Asia; **INDONESIA:** Nikkei Personal Computing, OS/2 World Japan, SunWorld Japan, Windows NT World, Windows World Japan; **KENYA:** PC World East African; **KOREA:** Hi-Tech Information, Macworld Korea, PC World Korea; **MACEDONIA:** PC World Macedonia; **MALAYSIA:** Computerworld Malaysia, PC World Malaysia, Publish in Asia; **MALTA:** PC World Malta; **MEXICO:** Computerworld Mexico, PC World Mexico; **MYANMAR:** PC World Myanmar; **NETHERLANDS:** Computer! Totaal, LAN Internetworking Magazine, LAN World Buyers Guide, Macworld Netherlands, Net, WebWereld; **NEW ZEALAND:** Absolute Beginners Guide and Plain & Simple Series, Computer Buyer, Computer Industry Directory, Computerworld New Zealand, MTB, Network World, PC World New Zealand; **NICARAGUA:** PC World Centro America; **NORWAY:** Computerworld Norge, CW Rapport, Datamagasinet, Financial Rapport, Kursguide Norge, Macworld Norge, Multimediaworld Norge, PC World Ekspress Norge, PC World Nettverk, PC World Norge, PC World ProduktGuide Norge; **PAKISTAN:** Computerworld Pakistan; **PANAMA:** PC World Panama; **PEOPLE'S REPUBLIC OF CHINA:** China Computer Users, China Computerworld, China InfoWorld, China Telecom World Weekly, Computer & Communication, Electronic Design China, Electronics Today, Electronics Weekly, Game Software, PC World China, Popular Computer Week, Software Weekly, Software World, Telecom World; **PERU:** Computerworld Peru, PC World Profesional Peru, PC World SoHo Peru; **PHILIPPINES:** Click!, Computerworld Philippines, PC World Philippines, Publish in Asia; **POLAND:** Computerworld Poland, Computerworld Special Report Poland, Cyber, Macworld Poland, Networld Poland, PC World Komputer; **PORTUGAL:** Cerebro/PC World, Computerworld/Correio Informático, Dealer World Portugal, Mac*In/PC*In Portugal, Multimedia World; **PUERTO RICO:** PC World Puerto Rico; **ROMANIA:** Computerworld Romania, PC World Romania, Telecom Romania; **RUSSIA:** Computerworld Russia, Mir PK, Publish, Seti; **SINGAPORE:** Computerworld Singapore, PC World Singapore, Publish in Asia; **SLOVENIA:** Monitor; **SOUTH AFRICA:** Computing SA, Network World SA, Software World SA; **SPAIN:** Comunicaciones World España, Computerworld España, Dealer World España, Macworld España, PC World España, PC Plus Publish, Seti; **SWEDEN:** CAP&Design, Computer Sweden, Corporate Computing Sweden, Internetworld Sweden, it.branschen, Macworld Sweden, MaxiData Sweden, MikroDatorn, Nätverk & Kommunikation, PC World Sweden, PCaktiv, Windows World Sweden; **SWITZERLAND:** Computerworld Schweiz, Macworld Schweiz, PCtip; **TAIWAN:** Computerworld Taiwan, Macworld Taiwan, NEW ViSiON/Publish, PC World Taiwan, Windows World Taiwan; **THAILAND:** Publish in Asia, Thai Computerworld; **TURKEY:** Computerworld Turkiye, Macworld Turkiye, Network World Turkiye, PC World Turkiye; **UKRAINE:** Computerworld Kiev, Multimedia World Ukraine, PC World Ukraine; **UNITED KINGDOM:** Acorn User UK, Amiga Action UK, Amiga Computing UK, Apple Talk UK, Computing, Macworld, Parents and Computers UK, PC Advisor, PC Home, PSX Pro, The WEB; **UNITED STATES:** Cable in the Classroom, CIO Magazine, Computerworld, DOS World, Federal Computer Week, GamePro Magazine, InfoWorld, I-Way, Macworld, Network World, PC Games, PC World, Publish, Video Event, THE WEB Magazine, and WebMaster; online webzines: JavaWorld, NetscapeWorld, and SunWorld Online; **URUGUAY:** InfoWorld Uruguay; **VENEZUELA:** Computerworld Venezuela, PC World Venezuela; and **VIETNAM:** PC World Vietnam.

3/24/97

CREDITS

Acquisitions Editors
Andy Cummings
Ellen Camm

Development Editor
Katharine Dvorak

Technical Editors
John Preisach
Keith Underdahl

Copy Editors
Kyle Looper
Nate Holdread

Production Coordinator
Katy German

Book Design
Seventeenth Street Studios

Graphics and Production Specialists
Mario Amador
Linda Marousek
Mary Penn
Ed Penslien
Andreas F. Schueller

Proofreader
Rebecca Page

Indexer
Ty Koontz

ABOUT THE AUTHOR

Brian Underdahl has been a full-time author since 1989 and
has authored or co-authored a broad range of titles. He has
also written articles for several publications including *PC World*
and several newsletters. The following list includes just a few of
the books Brian has authored: *Windows NT Workstation 4.0
Advanced Technical Reference, Windows NT 4.0 Installation
and Configuration Handbook, Special Edition Using Windows NT
Workstation 4.0, Special Edition Using 1-2-3 97, Excel Expert
Solutions,* and *Quick Memory Management Techniques.*

Be content. You have put your head inside a Wolf's mouth and taken it out again in safety; that ought to be reward enough for you.

Aesop

PREFACE

If you use a computer, chances are that computer runs Windows 95. As the most prevalent operating system on modern PCs, Windows 95 is everywhere. Soon, however, you'll be hearing a lot about Windows 98—the successor to Windows 95. Windows 98 is the next upgrade for Windows 95-based PCs, and this book tells you all about the important changes Windows 98 brings to your desktop.

Okay, I'll let you in on a little secret—this book is intended to give you a preview of Windows 98, and Windows 98 hadn't been released yet when I wrote the book. How did I manage to write about Windows 98 before it was released? I wrote this book using *beta* versions of Windows 98. Beta versions are test copies manufacturers make available to a group of people willing to risk their computers, along with their sanity, so that most of the bugs can be found and corrected before software is officially released to the public. Because I used several beta versions of Windows 98 while writing this book, there are bound to be some small differences between some of the figures and the final retail version of Windows 98. We've done our best to watch out for every change during the beta testing, but I know that some last minute changes will occur just before Windows 98 is released. Having said that, I'll also tell you that those small differences won't matter much to you. What you're really interested in is a great preview of Windows 98, and that's what you find here.

In this book I teach you all the essentials so that you can quickly learn everything you need to know about Windows 98 in a few simple lessons. I won't waste your time, either. I've created a series of focused, hands-on lessons that will help you become comfortable with using Windows 98. In these lessons I focus on the needs of the new Windows 98 user.

As an experienced author and trainer, I've had the opportunity to learn what real people want when learning about a topic such as Windows 98. I've seen the frustration of both new and experienced PC users who just wanted to know how to get a job done with the least amount of fuss and aggravation. In writing this book I distilled the knowledge I've gained through these experiences into the essence of Windows 98 training. I'm certain you'll learn more in less time and with far less aggravation from this book than you can from any other method.

Who This Book Is For

I've written this book for you, a beginning to intermediate PC user. You don't want a lot of technical jargon—you want to learn how to use your PC and Windows 98 as quickly and painlessly as possible. You also want a book that's straightforward, and one that doesn't make you feel stupid and confused just because you don't already know all those strange little buzz words computer people tend to throw around. I understand how you feel, and I make certain you learn what you really need to know.

How This Book Is Organized

This book is broken down into a series of easy-to-follow lessons, with each lesson building on the knowledge you gained in the earlier lessons. Each lesson focuses on a number of related topics to help you easily learn Windows 98.

JUMP START: WHAT'S NEW IN WINDOWS 98?

This section gives you a quick start by showing you the most important new features in the Windows 98 beta. Here you get a quick glimpse of the major changes between Windows 95 and Windows 98. You' see why people are so excited about new features such as the Active Desktop, which brings the Internet right to your computer screen.

LESSON 1: GETTING STARTED WITH WINDOWS 98

In this first full-blown lesson I expand on what you learned in the Jump Start and show you how you can find files, use shortcuts, get help right from Windows 98, and automatically run your favorite programs.

LESSON 2: CHANGING THE APPEARANCE OF WINDOWS 98

In this lesson I show you how to have some fun with Windows 98 by customizing its appearance. This lesson is more than just fun, however, because you learn how to make some simple changes that actually make Windows 98 easier to use.

LESSON 3: WORKING WITH FILES

Here you learn how to manage your files and organize your folders. You see how long filenames can be a real help in keeping track of your work, and you see what you can do if you accidentally erase a file.

LESSON 4: WORKING WITH DISKS

This lesson shows you how to work with both your diskettes and your hard disks. You learn how to format diskettes so that you can store data, how to make certain your disks don't contain errors that could destroy your data, and how to improve performance. You even see how to increase the capacity of your disks using tools built into Windows 98.

LESSON 5: LIGHTS, ACTION, MULTIMEDIA!

Working all the time is no fun, so this lesson gives you a chance to play around with the multimedia capabilities of Windows 98. You see how to use both sound and video to make your PC a bit more exciting.

LESSON 6: INSTALLING AND UNINSTALLING PROGRAMS

In this lesson you learn how to add new programs to your PC, as well as remove old ones you no longer need. In addition, you see interesting pieces of the Windows 98 beta that probably aren't installed on your system, and you learn how you can add or remove DOS programs, too.

LESSON 7: LET'S GET CONNECTED TO THE INTERNET

If it seems like the whole world but you is on the Internet, here's your chance to see what all the fuss is about. After this lesson you'll be surfing in no time!

LESSON 8: JUST THE MAIL AND FAX

You need to communicate to stay current, so this lesson shows you how to set up and use both e-mail and fax with the Windows 98 Messaging System. You see how to organize all your mail in one central location, and you learn how to create and send e-mail over the Internet.

To conclude this book, I provided information that helps you install the Windows 98 beta, answers to the bonus study questions that are included with each lesson, and a glossary of Windows 98 terms.

The Conventions Used in This Book

I've tried to make it easy for you to use this book by including several easy to understand features. For example, when you see

the text that follows contains a special tip intended to give you some "inside information" that can save you time or frustration.

When you see

the text that follows explains a special note about the subject. Notes tend to be a bit more technically oriented than the rest of the text, but the information they contain is important if you want to know "why" rather than simply "what."

When you see

the text that follows discusses important new Windows 98 features that are of special interest to anyone who's used Windows 95 in the past.

Another special element you see is the command arrow (➢) separating a series of menu selections you need to choose in order to complete a command. For example, File ➢ Open means click the File menu and select the Open command.

Speaking of commands, text you need to type appears in **bold** characters. You should type the exact characters shown in bold text.

Text messages that appear on your screen are shown in a special font like this: `This is a message from your computer.`

The figures in the book are labeled with callouts that direct you to the exact step or process they illustrate. Also, the figures are placed right next to the text in which they are referenced. You won't have to flip pages back and forth to compare a figure with the text.

The One Step at a Time CD-ROM

The CD-ROM that accompanies this book includes the exclusive *One Step at a Time On Demand* interactive software. This software coaches you through the exercises in the book while you work on your computer at your own pace. You can use the software on its own, or concurrently with the book. In addition, the software includes the entire text of the book so that you can search for information on how to perform a function, learn how to complete a task, or make use of the software itself.

Feedback

Please feel free to let us know what you think about this book and whether you have any suggestions for improvement. You can send your questions and comments to me and the rest of the *Presenting Windows 98 One Step at a Time* team on the "Contact Us" page of the IDG Books Worldwide Web site at `www.idgbooks.com`.

ACKNOWLEDGMENTS

An author is but one part of a whole team of people who create a book. Without all of the members of that team, the book would never be finished. I'd like to thank the following special people who helped so much on this project:

  Ellen Camm, Senior Acquisitions Editor; **Andy Cummings**, Acquisitions Editor; **Walt Bruce**, Publishing Manager; **Katharine Dvorak**, Development Editor; **Nate Holdread** and **Kyle Looper**, Copy Editors; **John Preisach** and **Keith Underdahl**, Technical Editors; **Katy German**, Production Coordinator; and the rest of the wonderful production staff.

  Sorry about your PC, John, but we told you not to play those CDs!

CONTENTS AT A GLANCE

CONTENTS

Jump Start

20 MINUTES

GOALS

This Jump Start is intended to get you off to a fast start with Windows 98 by showing you the most important new pieces in the Windows 98 beta:

- Internet Explorer 4

- The Active Desktop

- System Information utility

- System File Checker

- Windows Tune Up Wizard

- Task Scheduler

- TV Viewer

- Imaging

- FrontPad

- Web Publishing Wizard

- NetMeeting
- Virtual Private Networking

GET READY

Because this book is a preview of the Windows 98 beta, you probably don't have the Windows 98 beta installed and ready to use. If you have the Windows 98 beta but don't already have it installed on your PC, you probably want to take a short detour to Appendix A, "Installing Windows 98 Beta," near the back of this book. If you don't have the Windows 98 beta or are waiting for the commercial release of Windows 98, just sit back and follow along for a preview of what you'll find when you do get a chance to install Windows 98 on your system.

HOW DID THIS BOOK COME ABOUT?

Did you know that software is tested extensively before it's released to the public? *Beta* testing is used to make certain that most of the inevitable problems in new software are found and corrected before the software is sold. Most computer book authors do a lot of beta testing simply because it's the only way to have books ready when the software is released. If we didn't work with beta versions of new software, no books would be available until long after the software reached the stores.

Windows 98 is an *operating system*, which is just a fancy way of saying it's the software your PC needs to load before it can do anything. Without Windows 98 (or another operating system) your computer doesn't know how to do anything except sit there and take up desk space. Testing an operating system is also some of the most complex work software manufacturers ever perform, if only because a new operating system has to work with many different existing computers and all sorts of application software.

A brand new operating system like Windows 98 is also exciting. Because virtually everything you do on your PC is affected by the operating system, you want to know how Windows 98 will affect you. That's why I wrote this book—so you can get an advanced look at Windows 98 and get ready for the changes it brings.

WHAT'S NEW IN WINDOWS 98?

Just as Windows 95 did a couple years ago, the Windows 98 beta brings many interesting and exciting changes to your desktop. In the following sections I give you a sneak preview of the changes I feel are the most interesting to you.

The Windows 98 beta also ushers in a number of smaller changes—some of which you'll notice, and some which you probably won't notice. These smaller changes may not be as exciting as something like the Active Desktop, but who can argue with subtle differences like better stability, improved online help, and better display drivers? These small changes may not make a lot of news, but they'll certainly make using Windows 98 much more enjoyable!

One last comment before you begin: The sneak previews you see in this Jump Start section are really only teasers. Each of the major new Windows 98 features is covered in much greater depth in the lessons that follow the Jump Start.

■ Internet Explorer 4

You're never far from Internet Explorer 4 when you're using Windows 98. Internet Explorer 4 is pretty much everywhere in Windows 98, which means you can go just about anywhere, too. Internet Explorer 4 replaces both your Web browser and Windows Explorer with a single Explorer for everything. Want to see what's on your hard disk? You use Internet Explorer 4. Want to visit a Web site on the Internet? You use Internet Explorer 4 for that, too. Want to read some documentation on your company intranet? You guessed it, it's Internet Explorer 4 again!

What's it like to use Internet Explorer 4 to browse your computer's folders and files? The figure on the right shows how a folder full of JPEG images appears when viewed as a Web page. When you view your folders as Web pages, passing the mouse pointer over an object displays a description of the object, and a single click opens the object. If you've browsed the Internet, then you'll feel right at home in Internet Explorer 4's Web page view.

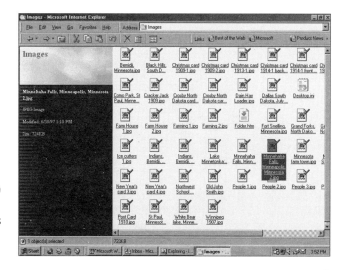

You learn a lot more about Internet Explorer 4 in Lesson 7, "Let's Get Connected to the Internet." Where in the world will you go with Internet Explorer 4?

■ The Active Desktop

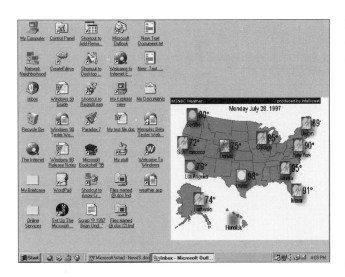

Your Windows 98 desktop acts a little differently than the old, dead Windows 95 desktop. The Windows 98 beta incorporates the *Active Desktop* to make your desktop come alive with active content, such as weather maps that automatically update using the Internet. Want more than just a weather map? How about stock tickers, up-to-date headline news, or the latest sports scores? These are just some of the many possibilities for your Active Desktop—you choose what you want on your Active Desktop. The figure at left shows the weather map I have on my desktop.

Lesson 2, "Changing the Appearance of Windows 98," tells you all about adding items to your Active Desktop. What neat accessories will you add?

■ The new utilities

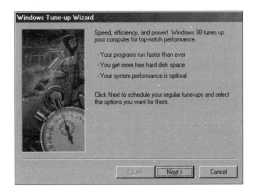

Who could get excited about the bunch of new utility programs in the beta version of Windows 98? Any users who have ever tried to figure out why their computers crashed, who ever wondered why programs that used to work suddenly quit working, or who wished their computers weren't so slow, that's who! Oh sure, you're probably thinking, "This is going to be boring, technical stuff." Well, I'm not sure about you, but I know what's really boring—sitting on hold waiting for some surly technician who's supposed to help you get your computer working again. What's even worse is when you finally do get to talk to someone, and he or she says they can't help you because *their* software obviously isn't causing the problem.

The most important new utilities in the Windows 98 beta include the System Information Utility, the System File Checker, and the Windows Tune Up Wizard. Trust me on this—there will come a time when one of these utilities will save your day. The figure on the left is just a teaser—to learn more about the important new Windows 98 beta utilities, you have to read Lesson 2, "Changing the Appearance of Windows 98."

■ Task Scheduler

When was the last time you took out the garbage—no, not that garbage—the extra garbage on your hard disk that's slowing down your computer? If you're a little behind at taking care of some of the maintenance chores that keep your PC running at top efficiency, don't feel like you're alone. There are lots of little things people forget to do, and taking the time to maintain your PC probably isn't at the top of your list. How would you like a little help?

The Windows 98 beta has a nifty built-in feature that you only got with Windows 95 if you spent extra to buy the Plus! add-in—the Task Scheduler. The Task Scheduler helps you out by making sure all those little maintenance tasks get done for you. You still have to deal with your own empty soda cans, but you won't have to feel bad about forgetting your PC's maintenance needs. The figure to the right shows an example of a Task Scheduler list of scheduled events.

You can find out more about scheduling events in Lesson 3, "Working with Files."

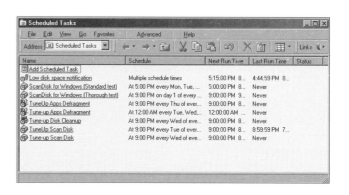

■ TV Viewer

The old question "What's on TV?" may never mean quite the same thing after you try out the Windows 98 TV Viewer. This new application may seem a bit ahead of its time, but who ever thought computers would come as far as they have in such a short time? With the TV Viewer you can view local television schedules, search for particular shows, have your PC remind you when your favorite show will be on, and with the right equipment, even watch high-definition TV right on your PC's monitor.

The figure on the right shows how TV Viewer displays your local TV viewing schedule. You can learn more about TV Viewer in Lesson 5, "Lights, Action, Multimedia!"

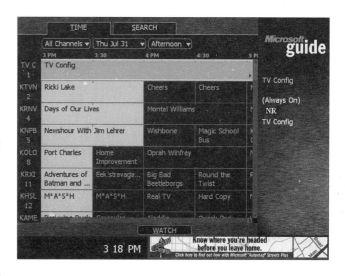

■ Imaging

Who couldn't use a better image? The Windows 98 beta includes Imaging, a new graphics program created by Kodak, which promises to help you view, print, and annotate nearly any type of PC-based image file. This may not sound too exciting, but when was the last time you tried to add some notes to a fax someone sent to your PC? Imaging makes it easy!

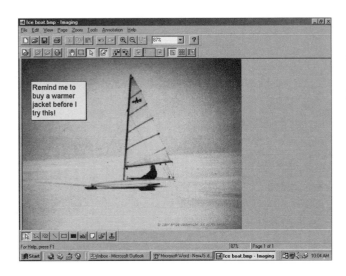

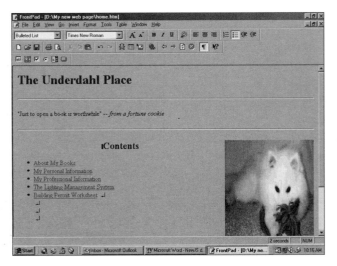

The figure on the left shows how easy it is to add a note to an image you've opened in Imaging. You can find out quite a bit more about Imaging in Lesson 5, "Lights, Action, Multimedia!"

■ Creating a Web site

If you've ever wanted to let the world know you exist, the Internet sure seems like the place to do it. The problem is, where do you begin? How can you create your own Web pages and publish them on the Internet? Doesn't that take all sorts of skill, fancy tools, and a lot of hard work?

Not anymore. The Windows 98 beta gives you all the tools you need to create and publish your own site on the World Wide Web. FrontPad is an easy to use Web page creator that even includes several wizards to do most of the hard work for you. After you've created your masterpiece, the Web Publishing Wizard takes over and handles all the sticky little details of making it possible for everyone to actually see your home on the Internet.

Want to create a Web page like the figure at left? If so, you definitely want to learn more about FrontPad and the Web Publishing Wizard in Lesson 7, "Let's Get Connected to the Internet."

■ Communicating for free on the Internet

You might say I've left the best for last. How would you like to get something for nothing? It would be even better if you could really use that "free" something. Well, prepare yourself for NetMeeting and Virtual Private Networking—two new features in Windows 98 that can save you some real money.

NetMeeting enables you to use the Internet for free, private long-distance calls. If you have the right equipment, NetMeeting also enables you to perform video conferencing, share an electronic whiteboard, or even share applications over your Internet connection. Virtual Private Networking makes it possible to feel secure connecting your network to the Internet by allowing only authorized users access. With NetMeeting and Virtual Private Networking on your side, the world becomes a little smaller and a whole lot more secure.

The figure on the right shows NetMeeting, but until you try it out in Lesson 7, "Let's Get Connected to the Internet," you won't really know how much more you can do with NetMeeting.

END OF THE JUMP START

This warm-up has given you a quick "jump start" to Windows 98. There's quite a bit more to learn, but now that you've been teased a little, you should be ready for a closer look at Windows 98. Now it's time to have some fun learning more about Windows 98!

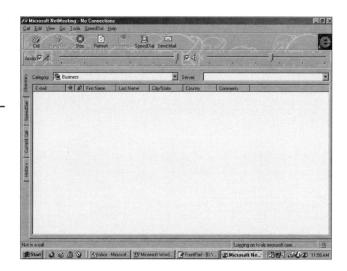

Getting Started with Windows 98

50 MINUTES

GOALS

The goals of Lesson 1 reinforce many of the skills you already have. The major goals of Lesson 1 include the following:

- Learning how to explore your computer
- Using shortcuts and icons
- Starting programs with the Start menu
- Getting help when you need it

GET READY

The most important things you need to do to prepare for Lesson 1 are to be at your PC and to make certain the system is on and Windows 98 is started. To print help topics, you also need to have a printer attached to your system and powered on. Finally, you need one formatted diskette that has enough space for a small file.

When you finish the exercises, you will have learned how to perform the following tasks: open Windows Explorer using two different methods, find your files and delete old ones, create shortcuts, edit a shortcut name, choose an icon for your shortcuts, run programs with the Start menu, use the Start menu document list, change the Start menu, use the Send To command, use pop-up help, use the help window, and finally, print a help topic.

If you're ready, it's time to begin with the exercises.

EXPLORING YOUR COMPUTER

To work effectively and efficiently, you need to know how to find files on your computer. Both program and document files can be buried quite deeply in the folders on your hard disk, and if you can't find them, you can't use them. Old, unneeded files may be even worse than lost files. You need to know how to remove files you no longer need to make room for newer files and to prevent your PC from slowing to a crawl while Windows 98 struggles to write to a hard disk that's bloated with obsolete data. Finally, you need to know what to do when you accidentally delete the wrong file.

Windows 98 is a graphical operating environment that makes it much easier to explore your computer than if you were using a nongraphical operating system such as MS-DOS. In fact, Windows 98 is often called a *Graphical User Interface* or *GUI* ("gooey"). In contrast, MS-DOS uses a *command line interface* or *prompt*. What this means to you is pretty simple — a computer running Windows 98 is a lot easier to use than a computer that just displays a DOS prompt.

Your Windows 98 screen shows you much more information than you would see in any nongraphical operating system. Windows 98 also provides easy access to a whole range of tools through simple mouse clicks. When you combine these two benefits, you realize one of the great advantages of Windows 98 — you don't have to remember a lot of commands to use Windows 98. In fact, you could use Windows 98 for years and never type a single command. As the following exercises illustrate, however, a few simple commands can often be quite useful.

The tool you use to explore your Windows 98 computer is the Windows Explorer. If you've used an older version of Windows, you probably used the File Manager on occasion. Windows Explorer is probably best described as File Manager on steroids. Even though Windows Explorer is very powerful, it's also very easy to use.

There are several ways to start the Windows Explorer; each method produces slightly different results. You can use these differences to help you accomplish different goals.

Exercise 1: Using right-click to open Windows Explorer

To use the first method for opening the Windows Explorer follow these steps:

1. Right-click the Start button and then click Explore.

When Windows Explorer opens, it displays the contents of the Start menu folder.

TIP

When you are using a menu that you displayed by right-clicking on something, you can use either mouse button to make selections from the menu. You can click on Explore with either the left or right mouse button.

When you take a close look at the Windows Explorer window, you notice that a lot of information is displayed. At the top of the screen is the *titlebar,* which says Exploring - Start Menu, telling you exactly which folder is open. At the far right side of the titlebar there's a button with an × on the face — the close button. Clicking the close button closes Windows Explorer.

The menubar (below the titlebar) contains several menus that drop down and display their commands when you click one of the menubar choices. The toolbar buttons are shortcuts to some of those commands. Hold the mouse pointer over the toolbar

Open folder icon   Menubar   Vertical scrollbar
Folders pane   Titlebar   Toolbar   Close button

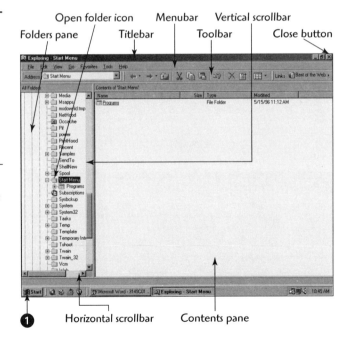

Horizontal scrollbar   Contents pane

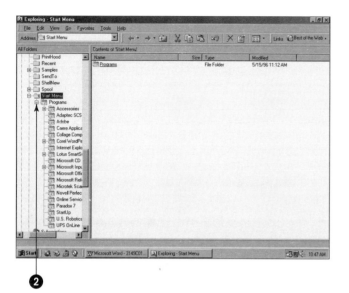

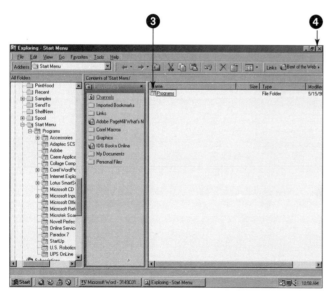

buttons for a bit without clicking, and Windows 98 pops up a short description of the button.

The Windows Explorer window has two panes. The left-hand pane displays the folders and the right-hand pane displays the contents of the open folder. You can tell which folder is open by looking at the icons in the left-hand pane—the open folder has an icon that looks like an open folder, while all the other folder icons look like closed folders. Notice the little square boxes to the left of some of the folder icons. If no square box is shown, the folder doesn't contain any additional folders. If there is a square box that contains a plus sign (+), the folder contains additional folders you can't see right now because the folder is collapsed. The plus sign changes to a minus sign (-) when the folder's contents are completely visible.

2. Click the plus sign next to the Programs folder to expand the Programs folder display.

Each computer is likely to have different items in the Programs folder, so you probably won't see the same items shown in the figure—unless you're using my computer!

NEW IN WIN 98

If you select View ➤ Explorer Bar, you can add a third pane to the Windows Explorer window. This extra pane can include buttons to connect to your favorite Web sites, channels, search options, or your favorite folders on your PC. The accompanying figure shows the Favorites Explorer Bar added to the Windows Explorer window.

To view the contents of a different folder, click the icon of the folder you want to view. If necessary, click on the arrows at the ends of the scrollbars to bring the folder you want into view.

3. Click the Programs folder icon to display the contents of the Programs folder.

The Programs folder contains all the items you see when you choose Programs from the Start menu. Later, you learn how to use this information to modify the Start menu.

4. Click the Close button at the upper-right corner of the Windows Explorer window to close Explorer.

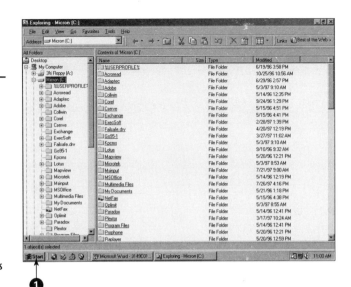

Exercise 2: Using the Start menu to open Windows Explorer

You can also start Windows Explorer using the Start menu:

1. Click the Start button to display the Start menu.

2. Click Programs ➢ Windows Explorer to display the Windows Explorer window.

Can you distinguish the difference between opening Windows Explorer by right-clicking the Start button and by using the Start menu? When you use the Start menu to open Windows Explorer, the window displays the contents of drive C rather than the contents of the Start menu folder. This view is more useful most of the time because you can more easily see all the folders on your hard drive when you start from the *root directory*—the ultimate parent of all the folders on a disk.

There's one more way to open Windows Explorer, but before you have a look at it, close the Windows Explorer by clicking the Close button at the upper-right corner of the Windows Explorer window.

Exercise 3: Opening Windows Explorer where you want

Wouldn't it be handy to tell Windows Explorer which folder to open so you wouldn't have to search through the list of folders each time? Well, guess what? It's pretty easy to do, and once you learn how, you know something that most Windows users don't know! Here you are in your first Windows 98 lesson and already you're becoming an expert.

The key to controlling Windows Explorer is to create a shortcut that tells Windows Explorer just what you want to do. To tell Windows Explorer to open the Windows folder automatically, follow these steps:

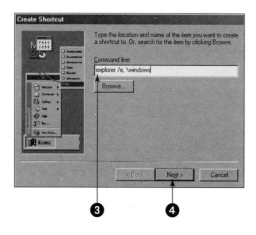

3   **4**

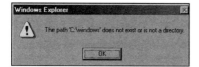

1. Right-click an empty place on your desktop.

2. Select New ➤ Shortcut.

3. Type this text in the Command line text box: **explorer /e,\windows** (if your Windows folder happens to have a different name than Windows, you have to substitute the correct name in the command).

4. Click Next to continue.

5. Type this text in the Select a name for the shortcut text box: **My Explorer view**.

6. Click Finish to place the shortcut on your desktop.

Test your shortcut by double-clicking the new My Explorer view icon on your desktop. If you see a message like the one in the accompanying figure, then your Windows directory probably isn't named windows. Use the Windows Explorer to find out the correct name and then start over at Step 1.

If you did everything correctly, double-clicking your shortcut should produce results similar to the figure on the following page. Notice that because my Windows directory is called Win95, I had to enter the command as **explorer /e,\win95** in Step 3. It doesn't matter whether you use upper- or lowercase letters when you enter the command; Windows 98 ignores any differences in the case of the letters.

NOTE

Yes, it's true. My Windows 98 folder is called Win95. The reason for this is pretty simple — I upgraded my PC from Windows 95 to the Windows 98 beta, but renaming the Windows folder isn't an easy task. If you simply rename the Windows folder, most of your programs and possibly Windows itself will stop functioning. Even if your Windows folder has an outdated name, it's better to leave the old name than deal with the major problems involved in making a change.

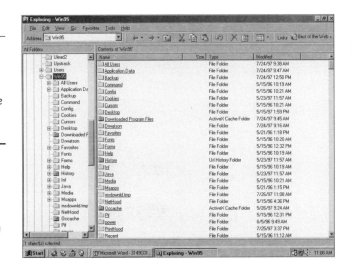

TIP

To enter a folder name that contains spaces, enclose the entire name in quotation marks. For example, type **explorer /e,"\windows\start menu"** *to create a shortcut that works just like right-clicking the Start button and choosing Explore.*

Exercise 4: Finding your files

Your hard disk holds hundreds if not thousands of files. Finding specific files in all the chaos of folders on a typical PC can be very frustrating — unless you know what you're doing, of course. Fortunately, Windows 98 has a powerful file-finding tool to help you out. In this exercise you learn how to take advantage of this tool.

Before Windows 98 came along, PC users were very limited in how they could name their files. Filenames used a maximum of eleven characters, which were split into an eight character name and a three character extension. Because the extensions were normally used to indicate a file's type, you really only had eight characters available for naming any file. This restriction often led to some creative file naming, and also meant that filenames were often so cryptic that it took a real genius to remember what each file contained. Was that letter to the bank named LT2B626.DOC or was it BK011796.DOC? Windows 98 changed all that by allowing you to use up to 255 characters in a filename. Now you can name the letter to your bank "Letter to bank regarding loan 6-26-97.DOC" or something similar.

TIP

In practical terms, filenames are usually limited to fewer than 255 characters because the complete name of the file (which includes the drive letter, the names of the folders containing the file, and the extension) is limited to 260 characters.

USE FILENAMES TO FIND YOUR FILES

Although long filenames make it easier for you to recognize your files, they also add a major complication to working with your files. If you use spaces in a filename, Windows 98 can have a difficult time determining just what you mean when you try to find the file.

TIP

Several of the following examples assume you have a file named My test file.doc on your desktop. You can create such a file by right-clicking a blank area of your desktop and selecting New ➢ Text Document. Type **My test file.doc** *as the name of the document, and click Yes to change the file type.*

As an example to illustrate this, try the following exercise:

1. Click the Start button to display the Start menu.

2. Select Find ➢ Files or Folders to display the Find dialog box.

3. Type the following text in the Named text box: **my test file.doc**

4. Click Find Now to search for files that match. After your PC stops searching, your screen should look something like the accompanying figure.

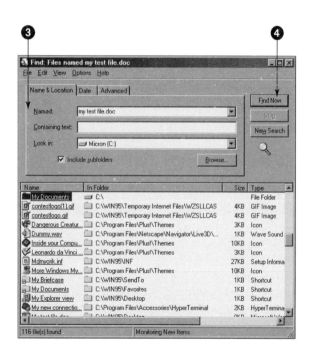

On my system, the search found 116 files. How many did it find on yours? Although Windows 98 actually found the file you specified, it also found quite a few files that didn't seem to match what you were trying to find. That's because Windows 98 couldn't tell if the name you typed was a complete filename or a group of names—any of which it should match. In other words, Windows 98 looked for files with any of the words you typed in their filenames. Can you determine why Windows 98 found all the files shown in the figure? At least one of the words you typed is contained in each of the filenames (yes, even Mdmyorik.inf has one of the words—just look a little closer and you see it).

Now try a new search that focuses more directly on just what you want to find. This time, though, give Windows 98 a little help by telling it that you're entering a complete filename, not a series of names:

1. Click New Search to clear your old results.

2. Click OK to confirm that you want to begin a new search.

3. Type this text in the Named text box: **"my test file.doc"** (be sure to include the quotation marks).

4. Click Find Now. When your PC stops searching, your screen should look like the accompanying figure.

By enclosing the filename in quotation marks, you told Windows 98 to find only the files that matched exactly. In this case, Windows 98 found only one file, but if you had more files with the same name in different folders, those files would appear in the results list, too.

You can further limit the search by careful use of some of the Find dialog box options. For example, if you remove the check from the Include subfolders checkbox, Windows 98 looks only in the current location shown in the Look in text box. Usually, though, you want to leave this checkbox selected so your searches aren't limited to the current folder. You can also click the Browse button and then select where to begin the search. Use this option only if you have a pretty good idea where you want to locate a specific copy of a file when you know several exist.

USE DATES TO FIND YOUR FILES

You can also find files based on when they were created or last modified. In this exercise you search for files created or modified on a specified date, June 24, 1997:

1. Click the Date tab in the Find dialog box to see the date options.

2. Click New Search to clear your old results (if you don't clear your old search, Windows 98 tries to find all files that match the old search and your new search conditions—you want to use only the new conditions in this case).

3. Click the Find all files created or modified button.

4. Click the between button and type **6/24/97** in both boxes.

5. Click Find Now. Your screen should look similar to the accompanying figure when the search is complete.

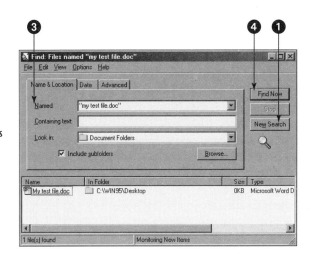

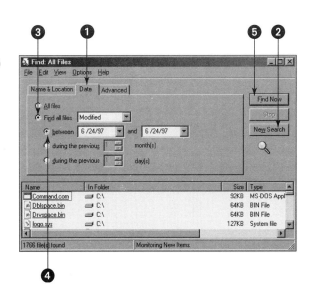

The number of files dated 6/24/97 that Windows 98 finds depends on a number of factors. June 24, 1997 was the date used on the beta release of Windows 98. If your computer is very new, many of your Windows 98 files may have a later date.

TIP

If your searches don't seem to produce the desired results, make certain you select the correct location in the Look in list box on the Name & Location tab. By default, Windows searches only document folders.

You can also find files that were recently created or modified by clicking either the during the previous month(s) button or the during the previous day(s) button and specifying the number of months or days.

USE ADVANCED TECHNIQUES TO FIND YOUR FILES

If none of the filename, location, or date options pin down your search well enough, Windows 98 still has more useful tricks to offer. You can look for files by type, by specific text messages, or even by size. By itself, Windows 98 knows about many file types, but when you install new programs it learns even more file types. You can search for things like applications (programs), help files, sound files, animated cursors, or a whole raft of other types. In this exercise you find all the application files on your PC:

1. Click New Search to clear your old results.

2. Click the Advanced tab in the Find dialog box to see the advanced options.

3. Click the arrow next to the Of type list box and select **Application**.

4. Click Find Now. Windows 98 displays results similar to the accompanying figure.

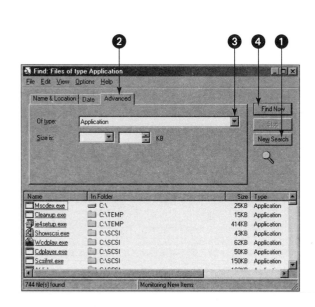

Although Windows 98 lists a large number of your files as applications, don't make the assumption that you can simply double-click any of them and have a new, undiscovered program to play with. Quite a few of the files listed as applications really aren't programs you can run. Many of them are there to help another program, and some of them could cause damage if you're not careful. If you're not sure about one of these files, don't try to run it!

You can also search for files by entering text in the Containing text box on the Name & Location tab, but don't be too surprised if you don't find just what you expect. If you specify a fairly common word, many files among the hundreds on your hard disk will probably match. Also, files are often stored in a format other than plain text, so you might not find a file using a text search even if the file exists. If a text search doesn't produce the results you want, try a different type of search.

Exercise 5: Deleting old files

There's an old axiom in the computer world: "Data expands to fill the available space." Even though the size of hard drives in PCs today is larger than ever before, you'll eventually run out of room if you don't remove old files you no longer need. Long before you run out of room on your hard disk, however, you encounter degraded system performance due to the clutter of old files. Do your house cleaning to keep your computer running efficiently.

Before you simply delete old files, you should consider whether you may need them in the future. Sometimes it makes more sense to move old files to diskettes and store them away rather than deleting them. That way you can always recover your data if it suddenly becomes important again. Notice, though, that I said your data. I didn't say program files. Data is the information you created through hard work. You can always restore your program files using the original distribution diskettes or CD-ROM, so there's no reason to waste your time saving those types of files.

Okay, so you've decided to get rid of an old file you no longer need, and you just can't wait to begin. Here goes:

1. Move the mouse pointer to the icon on your desktop labeled My Explorer view (see the accompanying figure to see how these icons appear).

2. Hold down the left mouse button and move the mouse pointer to the icon labeled Recycle Bin.

3. Release the left mouse button.

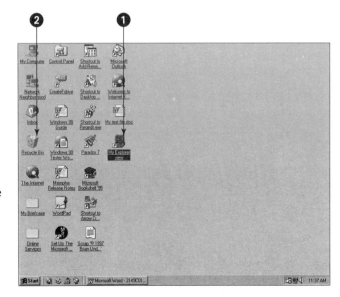

Holding down the left mouse button while you move a selected object as you did in Step 2 is called *dragging*. Releasing the object as you did in Step 3 is called *dropping*. In this exercise you dragged and dropped the My Explorer view icon from your desktop into the Recycle Bin. This is the easiest way to remove files you don't need from your desktop, but most files aren't on your desktop; you need a way to delete those other files, too. In the following exercise you use Windows Explorer to delete files:

1. Click the Start button to display the Start menu.

2. Click Programs ➢ Windows Explorer to display the Windows Explorer.

3. Click the Desktop folder to display its contents in the right pane.

4. Right-click the My test file icon to display the pop-up menu.

5. Click Delete in the pop-up menu to display the Confirm File Delete dialog box.

6. Select Yes to delete the file.

7. Click the Close button at the upper-right corner of the Windows Explorer window to close Explorer.

Windows 98 almost always gives you choices, so it should come as no surprise that there are alternate ways to delete files, too. You can click the Delete button on the Windows Explorer toolbar to delete any files you've selected, or you can use the File ➢ Delete command to do the same thing. You can even drag and drop files to the Recycle Bin folder, but this may not be easy if the Recycle Bin folder isn't visible.

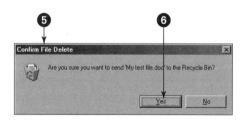

Exercise 6: Oops, recovering files from the Recycle Bin

I bet you wonder why it was called the Recycle Bin, don't you? Why not just call it a trash can? The Recycle Bin is named that way to let you know that sending files to the Recycle Bin isn't just a one-way street. Everyone makes mistakes, and the mistake of deleting the wrong file could be very costly. The Recycle Bin is there to save you from these types of mistakes.

In Windows 98 you can choose to use a double-click or a single-click to select and activate items on your desktop and in the Windows Explorer. To switch between the two options, open My Computer or Windows Explorer and select View ➢ Folder Options. Select Web Style to use a single click or Classic Style to use double-clicks. You can also choose Custom to select a combination of options. Click OK and then the Close button to activate your changes and close My Computer.

GETTING YOUR FILES BACK

To recover the two files you just deleted, complete this exercise:

1. Double-click the Recycle Bin icon to display the Recycle Bin contents. You may want to drag the edges of the Recycle Bin window to make it easier to see the contents.

2. Hold down Ctrl while you select the My Explorer view and My test file icons. If these two are the only items in the Recycle Bin, you can use Ctrl+A as a shortcut to select everything in the Recycle Bin.

3. Click File ➢ Restore to move the two files from the Recycle Bin back to their original location on your desktop.

4. Click File ➢ Close or the Close button to close the Recycle Bin.

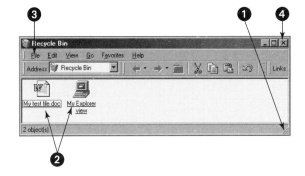

You safely restored your two files back to your desktop and didn't lose the work it took to create them. These two small files wouldn't be difficult to reproduce, of course, but at some point you'll probably accidentally delete a file that would take a lot of work to redo. Fortunately, the Windows 98 Recycle Bin is there to help.

Files you delete at the Windows 98 DOS prompt aren't placed in the Recycle Bin and cannot be recovered once deleted. Always delete files using Windows Explorer so that you have a second chance.

TAKING OUT THE TRASH

Eventually, even the Recycle Bin can get too full. When that happens, it's difficult to find the things you want to restore amid all the trash. In extreme cases, you could even lose files you really wanted to restore, too, because when the Recycle Bin gets full, Windows 98 automatically throws out the oldest items to make room for more deleted files. To save yourself from these problems all you need to do is take out the trash by emptying the Recycle Bin now and then.

1. Restore any files currently in the Recycle Bin that you want to save. Remember, after you empty the Recycle Bin, there's no going back!

2. Right-click the Recycle Bin icon to display the pop-up menu shown in the figure on the left.

3. Select Empty Recycle Bin.

4. Click Yes to confirm that you want to delete the files remaining in the Recycle Bin.

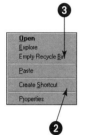

TIP *You can prevent files from filling up the Recycle Bin by holding down Shift while you delete them. This prevents these files from being placed in the Recycle Bin, but it also prevents you from recovering them, so use this tip with extreme caution!*

USING SHORTCUTS AND ICONS

There's probably nothing worse than doing something the hard way time after time when you know there's probably a shortcut that can save you time. In Windows 98 you can take advantage of many existing shortcuts, and you can create your own shortcuts, too. Why wade through several levels of menus or dig through a whole series of nested folders when you can easily create a shortcut right on your Windows 98 desktop?

Shortcuts and icons really make life with Windows 98 a lot easier. Instead of typing a command to start a program or open a document, you can simply double-click the mouse button. *Icons* are small pictures that represent a program or document. The Trash Can icon, for example, is used for the Recycle Bin. You can think of *shortcuts* as copies of those icons you use to access a program or document. Shortcut icons have a small arrow in their lower-left corner to remind you that they're shortcuts, while icons that are not shortcuts don't have the arrow. There's an important difference between shortcut icons and normal icons—you can delete shortcut icons without deleting the program or document, but if you delete a normal icon, you do delete the program or document. In the figure on the right, the icon for My Explorer view is a shortcut to Windows Explorer, and you can delete the shortcut without deleting Windows Explorer. The icon for My test file.doc is a normal icon, so if you delete it, you delete the document, too.

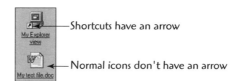

Shortcuts have an arrow

Normal icons don't have an arrow

Exercise 7: Creating shortcuts to programs or documents

It's a good idea to create shortcuts to some of your favorite programs and maybe even to documents you use often. One woman I know keeps shortcuts to forms she frequently uses on her desktop so that she can always open the form with just a double-click. I keep shortcuts to programs rather than shortcuts to documents on my desktop because I don't reuse the same documents very often, but I do use the same programs quite a bit. You may find that a mix of program and document shortcuts works best for you.

There are two primary ways to create desktop shortcuts. Earlier you created a shortcut to Windows Explorer by right-clicking the desktop, selecting New ➢ Shortcut, and then entering the command to start Windows Explorer where you preferred. Although this method certainly works—your shortcut ran Windows Explorer just as you expected—it has one major shortcoming. Before you can create a shortcut manually, you already have to know the correct command necessary to run the program you want. As bad as this sounds, it's even harder to create a shortcut to a document. A document shortcut not only has to start the correct program, but it has to load the document, too. Fortunately, there's a much simpler way to create shortcuts—your old friend drag and drop. Here's how you can create a shortcut to WordPad using drag and drop:

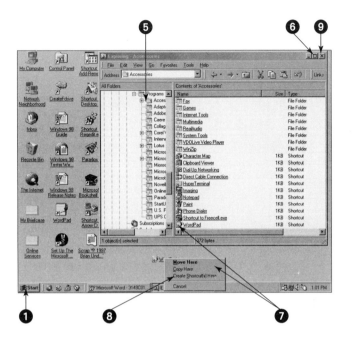

1. Click the Start button.

2. Click Programs ➤ Windows Explorer.

3. Click the plus sign (+) to the left of the Windows folder to expand the view of the folders.

4. Expand the Start Menu and Programs folders, too.

5. Click the Accessories folder to display its contents in the right-hand pane.

6. Click the Restore button, the second button from the right in the Windows Explorer titlebar, to reduce the size of the Windows Explorer window so that you can also see your desktop. The Restore button changes appearance slightly when the window size is reduced, and it is then called the Maximize button.

7. Point to the WordPad icon, hold down the right mouse button, and drag the pointer onto your desktop. This displays the menu shown in the figure on the left.

8. Click Create Shortcut(s) Here.

9. Click the Windows Explorer Close button.

Now that you've created a desktop shortcut to WordPad, you can start WordPad without going through several levels of the Start menu. It's certainly much easier to double-click the WordPad shortcut icon on your desktop than to wade through the menus, isn't it? Your WordPad shortcut icon isn't just a one-trick pony, though. Try this to see what I mean:

1. Point to the icon for My test file.doc.

2. Hold down the left mouse button and drag the icon onto the Shortcut to WordPad icon.

3. Release the mouse button to drop the document onto the Shortcut to WordPad icon.

When you drop the document onto the WordPad icon, you're telling Windows 98 to open the document using WordPad. You can use this same trick to open any text document or Microsoft Word document.

Exercise 8: Creating shortcuts to your frequently used folders

You can make opening your most frequently used folders just as easy as running your favorite programs by creating shortcuts to those folders. Once you have created shortcuts to your folders, a quick double-click shows you everything in the folder, giving you quick access to the programs and documents in the folder. You've opened the Accessories folder pretty often in the exercises, so that folder seems like a good candidate for a desktop shortcut. Here's how you can create a shortcut for the Accessories folder:

1. Click the Start button.

2. Click Programs ➢ Windows Explorer.

3. Click the plus signs (+) to the left of the Windows folder, the Start Menu folder, and the Programs folder to expand the view of the folders.

4. If the Windows Explorer window is covering the entire desktop, click the Restore button to reduce the size of the Windows Explorer window so you can see your desktop.

5. Point to the Accessories folder icon in the left pane, hold down the right mouse button, and drag the pointer onto your desktop.

6. Click Create Shortcut(s) Here.

7. Click the Windows Explorer Close button.

To test your new folder shortcut, double-click the Shortcut to Accessories icon. Open the Accessories folder shown in the figure on the right. You may have different items in your Accessories folder than appear in mine, but your shortcut still provides you with quick access to anything in the folder.

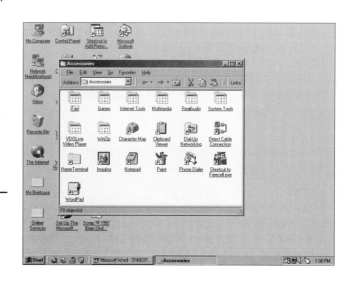

Exercise 9: Editing a shortcut name

When you create a shortcut, Windows 98 automatically creates a name that begins with Shortcut to and ends with the program, document, or folder name. You're probably more creative than that and can think of names you'd rather use. The name doesn't have to say `Shortcut to`, and it doesn't have to use the real name of the program, document, or folder either. You can use whatever name you prefer. Crowded desktops especially benefit from short, to the point names. Here's how you can rename the Shortcut to Accessories icon to My stuff:

1. Right-click the Shortcut to Accessories icon.

2. Click Rename.

3. Type this text: **My stuff**.

4. Press Enter.

There's another, slightly trickier way to rename icons. Click the label Shortcut to Accessories once, pause, and click the label again. You can then type the new label and press Enter. This method is a little harder to master than the right-click method because clicking the second time too quickly opens the program, document, or folder instead of editing the name.

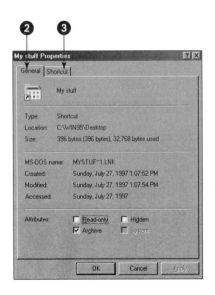

Exercise 10: Choosing your own shortcut icon

You don't have to accept the default icon that Windows 98 uses when you create a shortcut. Although the default icon is intended to provide visual feedback about the purpose of the shortcut, you can have some fun by customizing shortcuts to use a different icon. Here's how you can choose a different icon for the My Stuff shortcut:

1. Right-click the My Stuff icon.

2. Select Properties to display the My Stuff Properties dialog box. The General tab shows you basic information about the shortcut and enables you to change the attributes for the shortcut— don't change any of these settings!

3. Click the Shortcut tab.

4. Click Change Icon to display the Change Icon dialog box. In the figure on the following page I moved the Change Icon dialog box so that you can see both dialog boxes at the same time.

5. Click the icon that shows a desktop and lamp, located in the third row of the Current icon list box

6. Click OK first in the Change Icon dialog box and then in the My Stuff Properties dialog box to change the icon (there is a slight delay before the icon changes).

You won't find as many optional icons for some shortcuts as you did for the My Stuff shortcut. Shortcuts to programs and documents use icons built into the program rather than Windows 98's set of icons. Still, some programmers do have a sense of humor and include optional icons that are more fun than the default icons. One database program, for example, pokes a little fun at its name with optional icons, including one with a pair of ducks and another with a pair of docks.

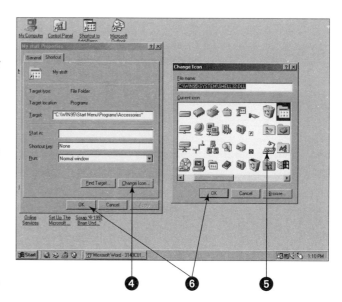

USING THE START MENU

By now you should be pretty accustomed to accessing the Start menu. You've used it several times in previous exercises, and the following exercises teach you a few tricks you haven't seen before as well as reinforce some of the things you've already learned. The Windows 98 Start menu has a major advantage over desktop shortcuts — the Start menu is often much easier to access than the desktop. Even when you're running a program that covers the whole screen, you can usually get to the Start menu with a single click of the mouse. You can also use the Start menu to automatically start programs whenever you start Windows 98, and to ease the task of editing many types of files.

TIP

If you can't see the Start button, you can still open the Start menu by pressing Ctrl+Esc. Some newer PCs also have a Windows key ▦ that displays the Start menu.

Exercise 11: Running a program from the Start menu

You probably won't find all of your programs on the Start menu. There just isn't room for everything, and you probably have some programs that you don't use often enough to want to have them on the Start menu. But just because a program doesn't appear on the Start menu doesn't mean you can't easily run the program. In this exercise you learn to use the Run command that appears on the Start menu.

The Run command also provides you added flexibility compared to selecting a program icon from the Start menu or the desktop. When you use the Run command, you can add additional information—known as *arguments* or *parameters*—to control how the program runs. For example, you can run a program and specify which document to open in a single command. In this exercise you see how you can use the Run command to open Windows Explorer and display a slightly different view than you've seen before:

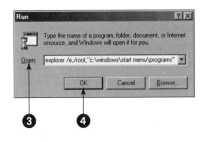

1. Click the Start button.

2. Click Run.

3. Type this text in the Open text box (remember to use the correct name if your Windows directory has a different name than `Windows`): **explorer /e,/root,"c:\windows\start menu\programs."**

4. Click OK to run the Windows Explorer. Your screen should look like the figure on the left.

Can you see how this Windows Explorer view is different from the ones you've seen before? By adding the `/root` argument, you told Windows Explorer to treat `c:\windows\start menu\programs` as the *root*, or parent, of the view. None of the folders on drive C are visible except those branching off `c:\windows\start menu\programs`. In this example you entered the command to run Windows Explorer, `explorer`, and then three arguments that told Windows Explorer how you wanted the program to run: `/e`, `/root`, and "`c:\windows\start menu\programs.`"

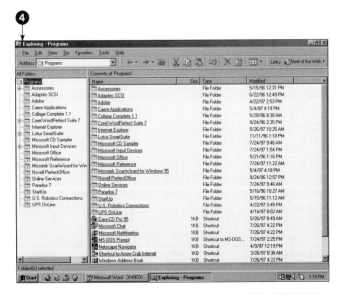

Use the Run command when you need to specify additional arguments you don't normally use—for example, when you need to specify a special command-line argument to enter an administrative mode in an application program so you can access commands not available to ordinary users.

The Run command remembers the last 25 or so commands you entered. To see the History list, click the down arrow at the right side of the Open text box. You can then select any of the listed commands to repeat.

Exercise 12: Using the Start menu document list

The Start menu document list is a handy listing of the documents you've used most recently. You can use the list to gain quick access to any of the documents.

■ Opening a document from the list

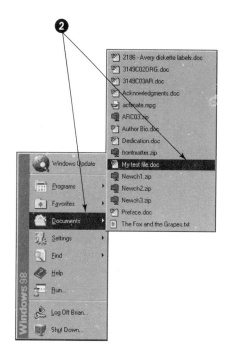

To open one of the documents you've recently used, follow these steps:

1. Click the Start button.

2. Click Documents ➢ My test file.doc. Your documents list probably has different documents than those shown in the figure simply because the list changes every time you open new documents.

■ Removing documents from the list

Unfortunately, you're not the only one who can look at your Start menu document list to see your list of recently used documents. Do you really want your boss to know you've been working on your resume? Sometimes it's not a good idea to have certain documents appear on the Start menu document list. Here are two ways to remove documents from the list:

1. Right-click a blank space in the Taskbar (at the bottom edge of your screen).

2. Click Properties.

3. Click the Start menu Programs tab.

4. Click Clear to remove everything from the Start menu document list.

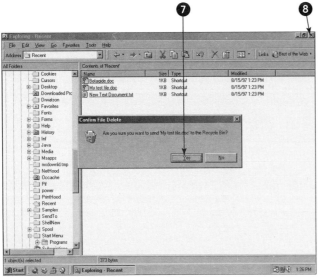

5. Click the OK button to close the dialog box.

Although this method of clearing the Start Menu document list is effective, it has one shortcoming—everything is removed from the list, even those items you'd rather keep for easy access. Perhaps a selective method of removing documents from the list would be more useful. Here's a way to remove some of the items from the Start Menu document list without removing everything:

1. Double-click the My test file icon to open the file, and then click the Close button to close WordPad so that My test file.doc once again appears in the list of documents.

2. Right-click the Start button.

3. Click Explore.

4. Click the Recent folder (which is a bit above the open Start menu folder).

5. Click My test file.doc.

6. Click the Delete button.

7. Click Yes to confirm the deletion.

8. Click the Close button.

You can select as many documents as you like in Step 4 by holding down Ctrl as you select each document.

Exercise 13: Changing your Start menu

You probably use the Programs section on your Start menu more than almost any other component of Windows 98, so it only makes sense to customize this section for your needs. Your Start menu Programs section begins with a collection of items added automatically when you install Windows 98. When you install new programs, they probably end up there, too. Pretty soon you can have a real mess, and your Start menu is hard to use because it contains so much junk while lacking some things that would be quite useful.

You can modify the Programs section by adding new items or removing ones you don't want. The layout of this section is predetermined—folders are arranged alphabetically at the top with programs arranged alphabetically below the folders.

Because numbered items sort above items starting with letters, you can control the layout of items in the Programs section by renaming them with numbers before the names.

In this exercise you learn how to add a program to the Programs section. The program you add—Program Manager—isn't too useful in Windows 98, but you can have a little fun with it making your friends think you have a strange version of Windows installed. Program Manager makes Windows 98 look almost like Windows 3.*x*. Follow these steps:

1. Right-click a blank space on the Taskbar.

2. Click Properties.

3. Click the Start menu Programs tab.

4. Click Add.

5. Type this text in the Command line text box:
c:\windows\progman.exe (don't forget to use the correct name for your Windows directory).

6. Click Next to continue.

7. Make certain the Programs folder is selected and click Next to continue.

8. Type this text in the Select a name for the shortcut text box:
Program Manager.

You could leave the name as progman.exe, but a descriptive name helps you remember what the entry actually is.

9. Click Finish to place the new entry on your Start menu. You don't need to close the Taskbar Properties dialog box right now.

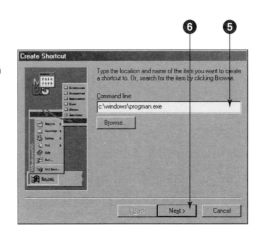

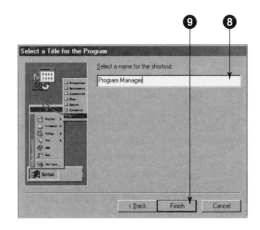

To test your work, click the new Program Manager item on the Programs section of your Start menu. You should see the Windows 3.x-style Program Manager window with each of the Start menu folders in a separate window. Click the Program Manager window Close button to close Program Manager.

Removing an item from the Start menu is just as easy. In this exercise you remove Program Manager from your Start menu—you can always add it back later if you really want to. Here's what you need to do:

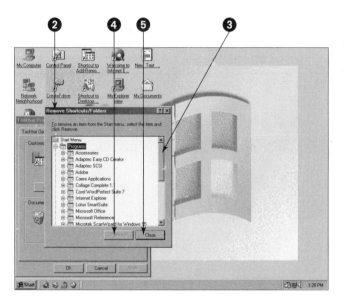

1. If the Taskbar Properties dialog box is not still open, right-click a blank space on the Taskbar and select Properties to reopen it.

2. Click Remove to display the Remove Shortcuts/Folders dialog box.

3. If necessary, use the vertical scrollbar to scroll down until you can click Program Manager.

4. Click Remove. If the Remove button is grayed out, you haven't selected an item you can remove.

5. Click the Close button on the Remove Shortcuts/Folders dialog box, and then the Close button on the Taskbar Properties dialog box.

Exercise 14: Running applications at startup

You've probably noticed that the Start menu Programs section includes a folder called StartUp. Anything you place in this folder automatically runs whenever you start Windows 98. You might use this feature to make certain your word processing software automatically starts if word processing is your main use of your PC, for example. Some programs, like Microsoft Office, place items in the StartUp folder without even asking you.

Use the same procedure for adding an item to the StartUp folder as you did to add Program Manager to the Start menu. The only step you need to change is the step where you select the location for the shortcut—it should be in the StartUp folder rather than in the Programs folder.

1

Exercise 15: Using the Send To command for frequent operations

It's always nice when something you have to do often is pretty easy, isn't it? In Windows 98 there are many little helpers just waiting to make your life easier. In this exercise you learn how one often-overlooked technique can save you a bit of time copying files to a diskette. You should develop the habit of saving copies of your critical files to diskettes to protect you from losing data in the event something goes wrong with your computer. This exercise shows you just how easy it can be to make a quick backup of an important file. The technique works equally well on the Windows 98 desktop or in Windows Explorer.

1. Insert a formatted diskette into drive A. You need to make certain the small plastic write-protect slider is pushed toward the center of the diskette so the hole is covered—otherwise your PC won't be able to copy anything to the diskette.

2. Right-click My test file.doc.

3. Click Send To ➢ 3 1/2 Floppy (A) to copy the file to the diskette.

It couldn't get much easier than that, could it? A couple of clicks and you've got a backup copy of your document.

By the way, if you try this exercise a second time, you see a message similar to the message in the figure on the right. In this case it's pretty clear that both the existing file, the one already on the diskette, and the new file are the same. They have the same size, date, and time, so you can be pretty sure they're identical. If any of the information differed, you'd have to decide whether you wanted to replace your backup with the new file. You may even want to keep your existing backup copy and copy the new file to a different diskette.

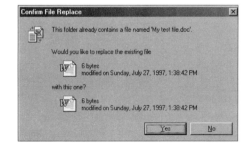

You can make the Send To command even more useful by creating additional shortcuts in the SendTo folder (which you can find under the Windows folder). These shortcuts can point to programs or folders.

USING WINDOWS HELP

Using a computer is frustrating sometimes, isn't it? You know what you want to do, but why doesn't the stupid machine let you do it? Usually the problem is pretty simple — you just don't know how to tell your PC exactly what you want it to do in terms it can understand. Sometimes it's hard to remember that computers are, after all, just machines, and they really don't think. That's why Windows 98 has online help available — to teach you the language your computer understands.

Unless you have a photographic memory, you probably need to look up information from time to time. Once you know how to look up information in the Windows 98 online help system, you can access help with just a few keystrokes and mouse clicks. You can even print some of the more complex help topics to use as a constant reference while you work with Windows 98.

Exercise 16: Using pop-up help

Often all you need is a quick reminder rather than a complete explanation. That's why Windows 98 often displays a little pop-up help window when you point to one of the Toolbar buttons. In this short exercise you see how these *tooltips* work as you try out several Windows Explorer Toolbar buttons.

1. Click the Start button.

2. Click Programs ➢ Windows Explorer.

3. Point to the button at the right end on the Standard Buttons Toolbar until the word Views appears below the mouse pointer, and then click the button. The display changes to a listing of filenames without details, large or small icons, or a listing with full details, depending on the current view.

4. Click the down arrow to the right of the Views button.

5. Find List and click it.

6. Click the down arrow and click Details.

7. Click the Close button.

Exercise 17: Using the Help window

When you need more than just a quick reminder of a button's purpose, it's time to turn to the Help window. Here's how you can open the Help window and find topics:

1. Click the Start button.

2. Click Help to display the Help window.

3. Click Local Help.

4. Double-click the closed book icon next to Introducing Windows. This opens the book and shows you what's inside.

5. Double-click the closed book icons next to Using Windows Accessories, then For Writing and Drawing, and finally WordPad. Each of the question mark icons represents a help document you can jump to by double-clicking the icon.

6. Click the Index tab to display the Index pane.

7. Type this text in the blank text box below the tabs: **ani.**

As you type, the list of topics scrolls up until your screen looks like the figure on the right. You can display any topic by double-clicking the topic or by selecting the topic and clicking Display.

8. Click the Close button to close the Help window.

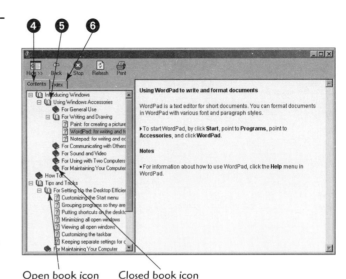

Open book icon   Closed book icon

Exercise 18: Printing a Help topic

There are times when on-screen help is just too hard to use. If you have to perform a number of steps to solve a problem or perhaps even restart your computer, a printed copy of the help information is the only way to go. In this exercise you print the instructions for adding a new folder to the Programs section of the Start menu.

1. Click the Start button.

2. Click Help.

3. Click Local Help

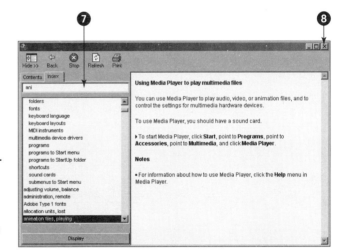

4. If the Index pane is not displayed, click the Index tab.

5. Type this text in the blank text box below the tabs: **adding.**

6. Double-click `submenus to the Start menu` (you may have to scroll down some to find this item).

7. Click Display.

8. Click the Printer button to print the help topic.

9. Click the Close button to close the Help window.

Exercise 19: Getting the Windows 98 Resource Kit for free

Would you like a free bonus just because you read about it in this book? If you have the beta version of Windows 98, I can tell you how to find the Windows 98 Resource Kit—a much expanded version of the Windows 98 online help.

1. Place the Windows 98 beta in your CD-ROM drive.

2. If the blue Windows 98 screen appears, click Browse This CD. If the screen does not appear, click the Start button, select Programs ➢ Windows Explorer, and choose the CD-ROM drive icon in the left pane.

3. Open the Tools, Reskit, and Helpfile folders.

4. Double-click Win98rk.hlp to open the Windows 98 Resource Kit.

The Windows 98 Resource Kit contains quite a bit of information you can't find in the normal Windows 98 help files.

TIP

You may want to copy the Windows 98 Resource Kit files, Win98rk.hlp and Win95rk.cnt, to your c:\windows\help folder and then create a desktop shortcut to Win98rk.hlp. Name your shortcut **Windows 98 Resource Kit.**

SKILLS CHALLENGE: PUTTING YOUR WINDOWS EXPLORER KNOWLEDGE TO THE TEST

It's time to see if you remember what you've learned in Lesson 1. I'll give you some tasks here, but I won't tell you the steps you need to take to accomplish them. Here goes:

1. Open Windows Explorer.

 How do you create a shortcut that opens Windows Explorer with the C:\Windows\Start Menu\Programs\Accessories folder visible in the contents pane?

 How do you create a shortcut that opens Windows Explorer with the contents of your CD-ROM drive visible?

2. Open the Desktop folder.

3. Rename the My Explorer view shortcut to Special Explorer.

4. Add a copy of the Special Explorer shortcut to a diskette in drive A.

 How can you add WordPad as an option to the Send To command?

 What can you do to make it easy to copy files to a specified folder using the right-click menu?

5. Use the Run command to open a Windows Explorer window that has c:\windows as its root.

 What do you do to make Windows Explorer run automatically whenever you start Windows 98?

 How do you find files created during June, 1997?

Problem	Solution
I don't see the Toolbar and buttons in my Windows Explorer window.	Click View ➤ Toolbars and select the toolbars you want displayed.
My Taskbar is missing.	Move the mouse pointer to the bottom of the screen. When the Taskbar appears, right-click a blank space, click Properties, uncheck Auto hide, and then click OK.
When I try to use Send To, I see an error message that says something like `Cannot create file`.	Make certain the write protect tab on the diskette is blocking the hole.
My Windows Explorer window shows icons instead of the full listing shown in the figures.	Click the Views button at the right side of the Windows Explorer toolbar and select Details.

 How can you find out which files were created or modified by a program you installed today?

 How can you find a document file someone created on your computer yesterday if you don't know the name or location of the file?

6. Check to see whether the Recycle Bin is empty.

7. Find out what's new in Windows 98 by looking on the Help window Contents tab.

 How do you find and open the help file called Backup.hlp?

8. Find out what the Help window Index tab says about scraps.

9. Remove My test file.doc from the list of recently used documents.

10. Add My test file.doc back to the list of recently used documents without using Windows Explorer.

How did you do? Some of these tasks were a little harder than others, but you should have been able to figure out how to complete each one using the skills you've learned.

1

WRAP UP

This lesson covered a lot of ground, didn't it? Along the way, you've become familiar with Windows Explorer, your desktop, the Start menu, and Windows 98 help. You've learned some of the basics of how to use Windows 98. I'm sure Windows 98 seems quite a bit easier to understand and use now that you're comfortable and know your way around.

The next lesson is a lot of fun. You learn how to customize the appearance of Windows 98 so your PC won't look just like everyone else's. But don't worry, it isn't all play and no work—you also learn how to make Windows 98 easier to use.

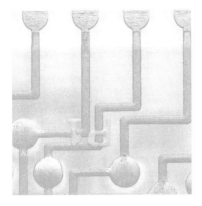

Changing the Appearance of Windows 98

45 MINUTES

GOALS

"One size fits all" rarely works for anyone. That's why restaurants always have more than one item on their menus, why clothing stores sell shirts in different colors, and why you need to know how to customize Windows 98. The simple modifications you learn in this lesson can boost your enjoyment while working with Windows 98, and increase your productivity, too. The major goals for Lesson 2 include:

- Customizing your desktop

- Having fun with the screen saver

- Customizing your Taskbar

- Customizing Send To

- Customizing the mouse

- Customizing the keyboard

- Using the Taskbar clock

- Using the new Windows 98 utilities

GET READY

You don't need much to complete Lesson 2. You need to have the Windows 98 beta completely installed, of course. To change the resolution of your screen, you need at least a Super VGA monitor and adapter—one that supports at least 800 × 600 resolution. Unless you're working on a laptop *PC* (personal computer), having this resolution isn't likely to be a problem. If you are working on a laptop PC, you may not be able to complete one of the exercises because some laptop PCs have a fixed screen resolution. If your laptop PC can't change screen resolutions, you have my permission to skip that exercise—just don't make a habit of it!

To complete some of the exercises, you will also use sample images from the *Presenting Windows 98 One Step at a Time* CD-ROM. These image files may be found on the CD-ROM in the Exercise folder.

When you finish the exercises in this lesson, you will have changed the appearance of Windows 98 in the following ways: the screen resolution, the number of colors shown on your monitor, the size of your desktop fonts, and the wallpaper and background pattern of your desktop. You also will have to set up a screen saver; moved, hidden, and resized the Taskbar; added an item to the Send To menu; created a "lefty" mouse; and adjusted your double-click speed, pointer speed, keyboard settings, and the system clock.

Okay, time to begin. Make certain you're sitting at your PC with the Windows 98 desktop on your screen. Close any programs you may be running—we don't want any unnecessary distractions.

CUSTOMIZING YOUR DESKTOP

I bet you've added some of your own touches to your home, apartment, or office. No matter what the efficiency experts might have to say, not everyone can do their best work without some little personal touches.

You can make quite a few changes to Windows 98 by starting with your desktop. You're just a few clicks away from seeing more on your screen (or less, if you prefer), changing the number of colors on your screen, changing the size of the fonts, selecting your own color scheme, adding some wallpaper, or displaying a pattern on the desktop.

In a highly visual environment like Windows 98, the amount of information displayed on the screen can be pretty incredible, can't it? That's one reason for one of the biggest trends in PCs over the last several years — bigger monitors. With all the titlebars, toolbars, menus, status lines, scrollbars, and so on, you need more room just to do your work. Buying a new, larger monitor, however, doesn't automatically let you see more on the screen. Unless you know how to adjust the display, your larger monitor simply displays the same information in a large size — probably not just what you expected. In the following exercises, you learn how to adjust several different display properties so that your screen suits your needs.

Exercise 1: Changing the screen resolution

Screen resolution is measured using a rather funny-sounding unit of measure — the *pixel* — which is short for a picture element. One pixel is the smallest amount of space, either horizontal or vertical, that can be controlled by your PC. If your display is set for the standard VGA setting of 640×480 (most people drop the word pixel when talking about screen resolution), there are 480 rows each containing 640 columns on your display. If you don't believe me, start counting the dots — you should get to 307,200 by the time you've counted them all!

NOTE *The screen resolution settings available on your PC are dependent on the type of display adapter installed in your system as well as the capabilities of your monitor. Older PCs generally have fewer options available than the newer systems.*

Although 640×480 sounds like a lot of dots, most monitors can display even more. There are two additional common settings, 800×600 and 1024×768. Your PC may have additional options, but these three settings are the most common.

In this exercise you examine your current display settings and try out one of the optional settings. You change the screen resolution using the standard Windows 98 method. Although it's possible that your system includes other tools for changing the screen resolution — for example, a screen-resolution changer provided by your display adapter's manufacturer — we ignore those for now so you can learn how to use the method built into Windows 98.

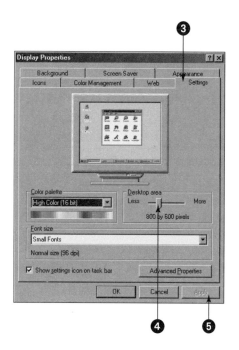

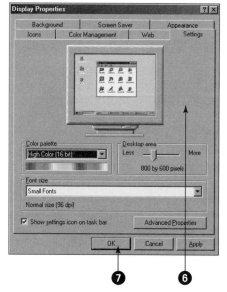

To examine and change your screen resolution, follow these steps:

1. Right-click a blank space on your desktop.

2. Select Properties from the pop-up menu to display the Display Properties dialog box.

3. Click the Settings tab. If your screen is set to 640 × 480, then your display is probably similar to the figure on the left.

4. Drag the resolution slider (in the Desktop area box) to the right until the setting shows as 800 × 600 pixels.

5. Click Apply. You probably see a message that tells you that Windows 98 intends to test the new setting. If so, click OK. If you see a message telling you that you have to restart Windows 98 before the new settings can be used, go ahead and let Windows 98 restart.

6. After your desktop is resized, click Yes within 15 seconds to keep the new setting. If you don't click Yes within 15 seconds, then Windows 98 restores your old desktop size. If your display never shows the new desktop setting you selected, or if your display seems quite distorted at the new setting, your monitor may not be capable of properly displaying the selected resolution.

The figure on the left shows how the screen appears at the new 800 × 600 pixel setting. Compare this figure to the earlier 640 × 480 figure to see how much more is visible at the higher resolution.

7. Click OK to close the dialog box.

NEW
IN
WIN 98

Click the Show settings icon on taskbar checkbox to include the resolution settings icon on your Taskbar. You can use this icon to select a new screen resolution without first displaying the Display Properties dialog box.

When you compare the 640 × 480 and 800 × 600 screens, you can see that everything is a little smaller at 800 × 600. That's because Windows 98 is packing more dots into the same space—the display area of your monitor. This isn't a problem on larger monitors, but you probably don't want to use anything higher than 800 × 600 unless you have at least a 17-inch monitor. It's up to you, of course, but if you set the resolution too high on a small monitor, you may strain your eyes trying to read the display.

TIP

If your monitor seems to flicker at higher resolutions, change back to a lower resolution setting. Some monitors cannot display higher resolutions properly, and the flickering can quickly tire your eyes or even cause headaches. You can usually find out about your monitor's capabilities in the user manual—make certain you use a resolution setting that allows your monitor to use a vertical refresh rate of at least 72 Hz if possible. The vertical refresh rate refers to the number of times per second your screen is redrawn, and too low a rate causes flickering.

Exercise 2: Changing the number of colors shown on your monitor

How many colors do you need on your computer screen? That's not an easy question to answer, because the answer depends on how you use your PC. The first computer displays had only two colors, black and white, which certainly wouldn't work too well for the graphical environment of Windows 98. In fact, Windows 98 requires a minimum of 16 colors but can use many more.

More colors allow pictures to be more realistic. Imagine how much more true to life a photo of a rainbow would appear if the photo had several-hundred color variations instead of, say, 16. Now imagine that the number of colors available jumped into the thousands or even millions. With each jump the picture would look more like a real rainbow and less like a child's drawing. Increasing the number of colors shown on your monitor has the same effect—up to a point. A photo that contains 256 colors doesn't look any better if you set your display to 16 million colors than if you set the display to 256 colors.

Unfortunately, your computer has to move more data and work harder to display more colors. You may not notice the difference on a fast computer, but you might if your PC already seems slow. It takes twice as much information to display a picture in 256 colors as it does to display the same picture in 16 colors; therefore, the number of bits of data required to display different color settings often distinguishes the resolution rather than the number of colors displayed. The following table shows the most common color settings:

Bits of Data	# of Colors
4	16
8	256
15	32,768
16	65,536
24	16,777,216
32	4,294,967,296

Because I don't know your current color setting, I want you to set the display to 16 colors to start the exercise. To do so, follow these steps:

1. Right-click a blank space on your desktop.

2. Select Properties from the pop-up menu that appears to display the Display Properties dialog box.

3. Click the Settings tab.

4. Click the down arrow at the right edge of the Color palette list box to display the list of options. The available options are determined by your display adapter and may not include all the choices shown in this figure.

5. Choose 16 Color as the new color setting and click Apply. Depending on your display adapter, Windows 98 may either offer to test the setting or ask if you want to restart Windows 98. Click OK or Yes as appropriate to continue.

6. Click OK to close the dialog box.

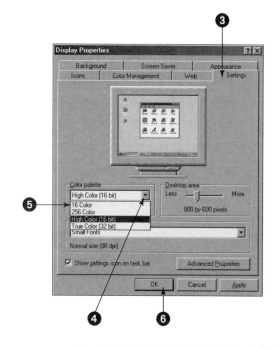

You probably don't notice too much difference on your desktop, but you will if you try to view any pictures that use more than 16 colors. Instead of looking like a normal picture, any image you view while Windows 98 is set to 16 colors looks like a poster. You might try some of the sample images in the Exercise folder on the CD-ROM that accompanies this book to see the difference.

Repeat the exercise, this time setting your display to 256 colors. When your display is set to 256 colors, you can continue to the next exercise.

Exercise 3: Changing font sizes

When you set your display for higher resolution, everything on the screen becomes a bit smaller, including the descriptive text in dialog boxes, under icons, and in menus. If you choose a high-resolution setting or use a fairly small monitor, you may find yourself straining to read the text on your screen. In this exercise you learn how to adjust the font size so the text is easy to read.

To adjust the font size, follow these steps:

1. Right-click a blank space on your desktop.

2. Select Properties from the pop-up menu.

3. Click the Settings tab.

4. Click the down arrow at the right end of the Font size list box to see the two standard options—Small Fonts and Large Fonts. In most cases one of these options should work well.

5. Click Other to display the Custom Font Size dialog box. You can use the settings in this dialog box to reduce or increase the font size by a factor of five.

6. Drag one of the ruler markings left to decrease the font size to 50% of normal (the current size is shown in the Scale fonts to be X% of normal size box). Release the mouse button to see how the sample text appears below the ruler.

7. Drag a ruler marking right to increase the font size to 150% of normal, and release the mouse button to see the change in the sample text.

Drag the ruler markings left or right to change the text size

8. Return the font size to 100% and click OK to close the Custom Font Size dialog box.

9. Click Cancel to close the Display Properties dialog box. This prevents Windows 98 from applying any changes you made to the font size.

Changing the font size does not affect the size of text in most programs. Your word processing program, for example, continues to use its own settings.

Exercise 4: Choosing Windows colors

Want to add some color to your desktop? You can change the colors of virtually every part of your Windows 98 display using the settings on the Appearance tab of the Display Properties dialog box. You can also select from a list of predefined color schemes if you're not feeling quite artistic enough to choose your own colors.

To make some color selections, follow these steps:

1. Right-click a blank space on your desktop.

2. Select Properties from the pop-up menu.

3. Click the Appearance tab. The window in the top half of this tab shows the effects of any color selections you make and can also be used to select individual items so that you can change their appearances.

4. Click the down arrow at the right side of the Scheme list box to display the list of predefined color schemes.

5. Use the down-arrow key to scroll through the choices. As you choose each color scheme, you see how the color scheme appears in the sample window. Choose Windows Standard to return the colors to the normal settings.

6. Click the down arrow at the right side of the Item list box to display the list of items that have colors you can change individually.

You can click an item in the sample window to select it if you're not certain of the item's name. For example, click the text Inactive Window to see that the object is called the

Click an object in this window to select it in the Item list box

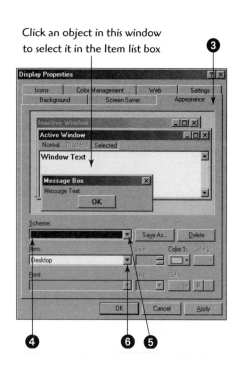

`Inactive Title Bar`. When you select an object such as a titlebar that contains text, the font options become available and you can choose how you want the object's text to appear.

Two items, Icon Spacing (Horizontal) and Icon Spacing (Vertical), can only be selected by choosing them from the list box. You can use these two settings to control how far apart your desktop icons are spaced.

7. Choose Desktop and then click the Color box to display the color palette. You can choose a color for your desktop from this palette by clicking one of the boxes. Select fluorescent green, the third box down in the left column.

8. Click OK to close the dialog box.

TIP

You can use the Save As button in the Display Properties dialog box to save your special color schemes under their own names. It's a good idea to save your favorite color scheme so that you can quickly restore your settings if someone changes your colors.

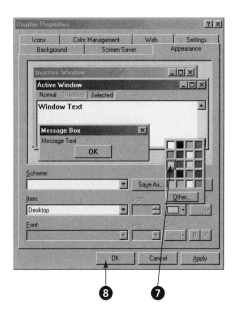

Exercise 5: Hanging some wallpaper

To make your Windows 98 desktop even more interesting, you can display a picture under the icons. You might want to use a sunny scene to brighten your mood during stormy weather, or even a scanned photo of your dog to make your desktop unique.

To add wallpaper to your Windows 98 desktop, follow these steps:

1. Insert the *Presenting Windows 98 One Step at a Time* CD-ROM into your CD-ROM drive.

2. Open the Display Properties dialog box and display the Background tab.

3. Choose Sierra Sunrise.bmp from the Exercise folder on the CD-ROM.

4. Make certain Center is selected in the Display list box—this places a single copy of the image in the center of your desktop. If you select Tile, the image is repeated several times to cover the entire desktop.

5. Click OK to add the wallpaper to your desktop and close the dialog box.

You can use any Windows bitmap image as your desktop wallpaper. Select None to remove the current wallpaper. You can find a few more interesting images in the Exercise folder on the *Presenting Windows 98 One Step at a Time* CD-ROM.

Exercise 6: Using a background pattern

Background patterns change the texture of the desktop background. To add a background pattern, follow these steps:

1. Open the Display Properties dialog box and display the Background tab.

2. Choose Waffle's Revenge from the Pattern list box.

3. Click OK. If you've been following along with the exercises, then your screen probably looks as bad as mine does in the figure on the left.

Feel free to restore your original desktop color, remove the wallpaper, and remove the pattern. Although the selections you made in these exercises didn't really do much to improve the appearance of your desktop, they did show you your options.

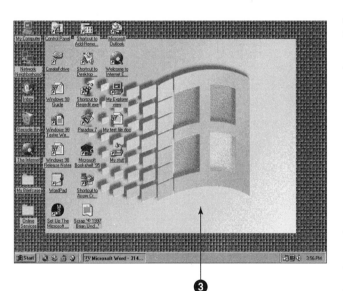

③

Exercise 7: Changing the Monitor Refresh Rate

Windows has the capability to set the refresh rate for many monitors. A higher refresh rate reduces flicker and eyestrain. If your display adapter and monitor are able to support variable refresh rates, and Windows 98 includes support for making this setting with your adapter and monitor, then you may be able to select a higher refresh rate.

If you select too high a refresh rate, you may damage your monitor. The only safe way to determine the highest refresh rate for your monitor is to look in your monitor owner's manual. This is one area where you can cause expensive damage by not taking the time to make certain you know what you're doing before you experiment. The author and publisher take no responsibility if you damage your monitor because you set your refresh rate too high!

To check whether your monitor refresh rate can be adjusted, follow these steps:

1. Open the Display Properties dialog box and display the Settings tab.

2. Select Advanced Properties to display the Advanced Display Properties dialog box.

3. If your display adapter and monitor are adjustable, then the Refresh rate list box shows the available options. Select Optimal to choose the preferred setting. Do not select a setting higher than what is listed in your monitor owner's manual.

4. Click OK to close the dialog box.

Many popular (and expensive) display adapters have faulty display drivers that result in flickering. Unfortunately, display adapter manufacturers generally deny that any problems exist, so PC users in the past have been forced to endure poor display quality. Now that Windows 98 gives you the ability to override the refresh rate setting, you are able to reduce the eyestrain and headaches often associated with PC use.

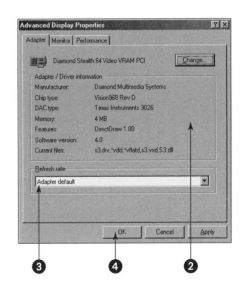

Exercise 8: Using the Icons tab

In Windows 98 a new tab called Icons appears in the Display Properties dialog box. This new tab gives you several options that were available in Windows 95 only if you spent extra for the Plus! add on. You can change the icons for My Computer, Network Neighborhood, and the Recycle Bin. You can also change several other visual settings, as you learn in the following exercise.

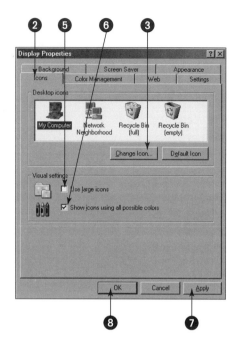

To use the Icons tab settings, follow these steps:

1. Right-click a blank space on your desktop and choose Properties to display the Display Properties dialog box.

2. Click the Icons tab.

3. To change one of the icons, choose the icon you want to change. Then click the Change Icon button to display the Change Icon dialog box.

4. Choose an icon and click OK.

5. If you want your desktop icons to be larger, select the Use large icons checkbox. This option is especially useful if you use one of the higher resolution settings for your screen display. You may want to experiment with this setting to see whether you prefer normal or large icons.

6. Select the Show icons using all possible colors checkbox to make certain desktop icons have the best possible appearance. This setting probably won't have much visual effect, but you may want to deselect this option if your system uses a 486 processor.

7. Click Apply to see your changes.

8. Click OK to close the Display Properties dialog box.

Although you probably won't notice much difference, the visual enhancements you can apply using the Icons tab of the Display Properties dialog box may decrease your system performance by a small amount. If your PC has a slow processor or less than 16MB of memory and you want top performance, then you may want to avoid using these enhancements. Or you may want to test each of the options individually to see if you notice a difference and then decide whether the visual improvement outweighs any slight performance degradation.

Exercise 9: Using the Active Desktop

The most fundamental change in Windows 98 is something Microsoft calls the *Active Desktop*. The Active Desktop essentially makes your Windows 98 desktop similar to a Web page. Icons on the Active Desktop function like the links you see on a Web page—you can activate an icon using a single mouse click rather than by double-clicking the icon.

The Active Desktop can also contain additional items that have direct links to the Internet. For example, you can add a stock ticker or a scrolling news window to your desktop. In this example you add an active weather map to your Active Desktop.

To add items to the Active Desktop, follow these steps:

1. Right-click a blank space on your Windows 98 desktop.

2. Select Active Desktop and make certain View as Web Page is checked.

3. Right-click a blank space on the desktop.

4. Select Properties to display the Display Properties dialog box.

5. Click the Web tab.

6. Select New to display the New Active Desktop Item dialog box.

7. Click Yes to connect to the Internet and visit the Active Desktop gallery. You can also click No, but you'll have to enter the correct address yourself rather than having it added automatically.

8. If necessary, confirm that you want to connect to the Internet. After you've connected to the Active Desktop Gallery Web site, your screen should look similar to the figure on the right. You'll probably see different choices because Microsoft is constantly adding new objects for the Active Desktop.

9. Click MSNBC Weather Map as the item you want to add to your desktop. The Weather Map from the MSNBC Web page loads as shown in the figure on the following page.

10. To add the item to your desktop, click the Add to my Desktop button. This displays the Subscribe dialog box.

11. Select OK to add the item to your desktop.

12. When the download has completed, click the Close button to close Internet Explorer.

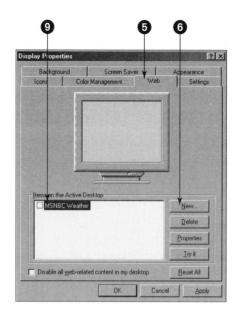

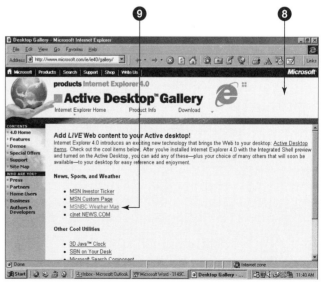

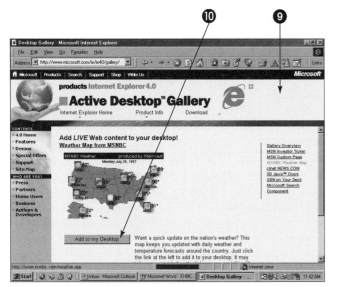

13. If the weather map does not automatically appear on your desktop, right–click a blank space on the desktop and choose Refresh. The figure on the bottom left shows how the weather map appears. If you like, you can drag the corners or edges of the weather map to resize the map.

Items you add to the Active Desktop need to be updated from time to time if they're going to be of any value to you. The update method you use depends on the type of Internet connection you have. If you connect to the Internet using a modem, you probably want to update the items manually. To update the weather map manually, move the mouse pointer into the weather map title bar. When the gray bar appears at the top of the map, click the down arrow at the left edge of the gray bar. Choose Properties and then click the Schedule tab. Click Update Now to retrieve the latest weather data. The Schedule tab also includes additional options you can use to schedule automatic updates.

To remove items from the desktop, remove the check from the item's checkbox on the Web tab of the Display Properties dialog box.

HAVING FUN WITH THE SCREEN SAVER

Screen savers don't really save your screen from anything simply because modern monitors are designed not to suffer damage from what's displayed on the screen. Still, screen savers can be fun and, if you use a password, can protect you from snoops when you leave your desk for a few minutes.

Exercise 10: Setting up a screen saver

In this exercise you learn how you can display moving text as a screen saver whenever you stop using your PC for a few minutes. You also see how to add a password so that no one else can see what's on your screen under the screen saver.

To set up a screen saver, follow these steps:

1. Open the Display Properties dialog box and display the Screen Saver tab.

2. Click the down arrow on the Screen Saver list box and choose Scrolling Marquee.

3. Select Settings to display the Options for Scrolling Marquee dialog box.

4. Type this text in the Text box: **Windows 98 Preview** (I moved the Options for Scrolling Marquee dialog box to the side so you could see the screen a little better).

5. Click OK to close the Options for Scrolling Marquee dialog box.

6. Click Preview to see how your screen saver appears. Be careful not to bump your mouse or touch any of the keys—as soon as you do, the screen saver disappears. This is also the way to restore your screen when the screen saver is displayed later.

7. Select the Password protected checkbox.

8. Click Change to display the Change Password dialog box.

9. Type this text in both text boxes: **idg**

   This is your screen saver password, and it is very important that you remember it exactly. Unless you know your password, you can't restore your screen after the screen saver appears.

10. Click OK to close the Change Password dialog box.

11. Click Apply and then sit back and wait for the screen saver to appear.

12. After the screen saver appears and you've enjoyed reading the message several times, press a key or move your mouse.

13. Type this text to restore your screen: **idg**

14. Click the up arrow at the right side of the Wait box until the time is set to 30 minutes.

15. Click OK to confirm your changes and close the Display Properties dialog box.

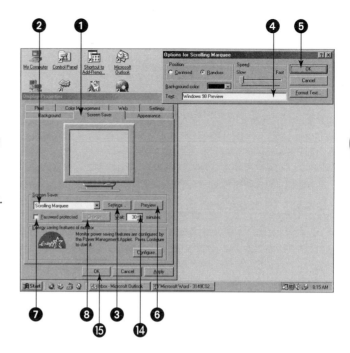

TIP

*To instantly activate your screen saver just before you leave your desk, click the Start button, select Run, and enter the text **Scrolling Marquee.scr** in the Open text box. Click OK to run the screen saver.*

Exercise 11: Using your display's energy-saving feature

Many monitors made in the past few years incorporate energy-saving features that allow them to go into a low-power mode when they receive a special signal from the computer. If your monitor has this feature, you can configure Windows 98 to send the power down signal to your monitor after a specified period of time. Some energy-saving monitors have two low-power modes, but for most monitors the two energy-saving modes are identical. You have to read your owner's manual to see which energy-saving modes apply to your monitor.

To activate the energy saving-features of your monitor, follow these steps:

1. Open the Display Properties dialog box and display the Screen Saver tab.

2. Click Power to configure the monitor power settings.

3. Select a scheme from the Power schemes list box.

4. Select the time in the Turn off monitor list box.

5. Click OK to close the dialog box.

After your monitor has gone into low-power-standby mode, you can reactivate the monitor by pressing a key or moving the mouse. This usually works to reactivate the monitor when it enters shut off mode, too, but your owner's manual tells you if you need to do anything else to reactivate the monitor in case that doesn't work.

The Display Properties Dialog Box

The Display Properties dialog box contains quite a few settings, so we've gathered them all into one place so you can see the various options.

Use the Background tab to set desktop wallpaper or a pattern.

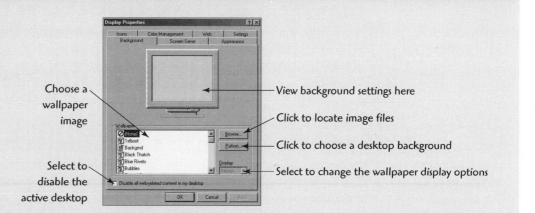

Choose a wallpaper image

Select to disable the active desktop

View background settings here

Click to locate image files

Click to choose a desktop background

Select to change the wallpaper display options

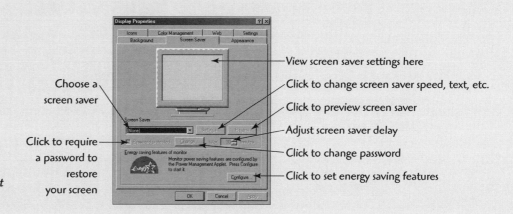

Choose a screen saver

Click to require a password to restore your screen

Use the Screen Saver tab to set up a screen saver.

View screen saver settings here

Click to change screen saver speed, text, etc.

Click to preview screen saver

Adjust screen saver delay

Click to change password

Click to set energy saving features

2

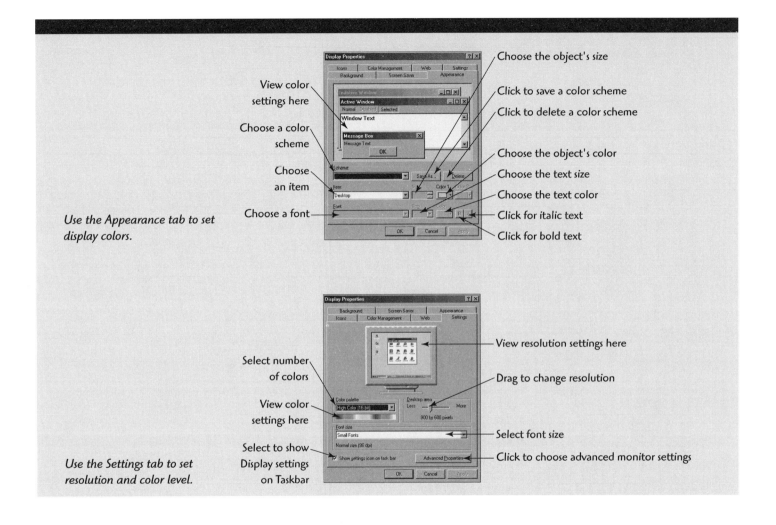

View color settings here

Choose a color scheme

Choose an item

Use the Appearance tab to set display colors.

Choose a font

Choose the object's size

Click to save a color scheme

Click to delete a color scheme

Choose the object's color

Choose the text size

Choose the text color

Click for italic text

Click for bold text

Select number of colors

View color settings here

Select to show Display settings on Taskbar

Use the Settings tab to set resolution and color level.

View resolution settings here

Drag to change resolution

Select font size

Click to choose advanced monitor settings

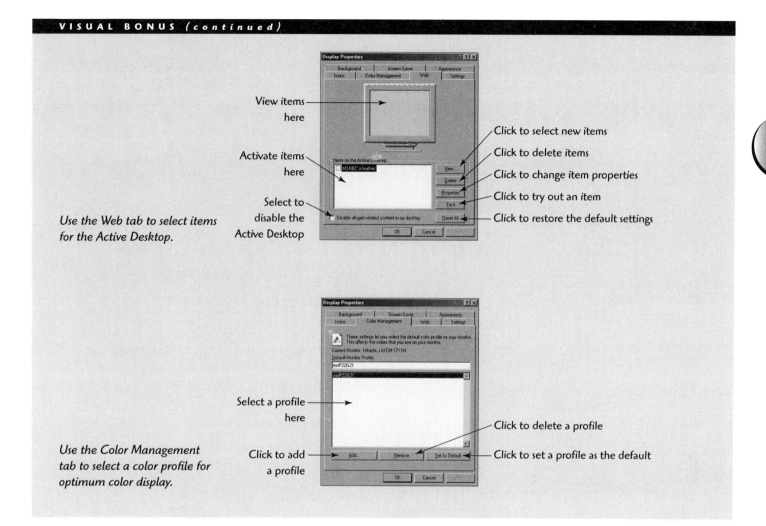

View items here

Click to select new items

Click to delete items

Activate items here

Click to change item properties

Click to try out an item

Select to disable the Active Desktop

Click to restore the default settings

Use the Web tab to select items for the Active Desktop.

Select a profile here

Click to delete a profile

Use the Color Management tab to select a color profile for optimum color display.

Click to add a profile

Click to set a profile as the default

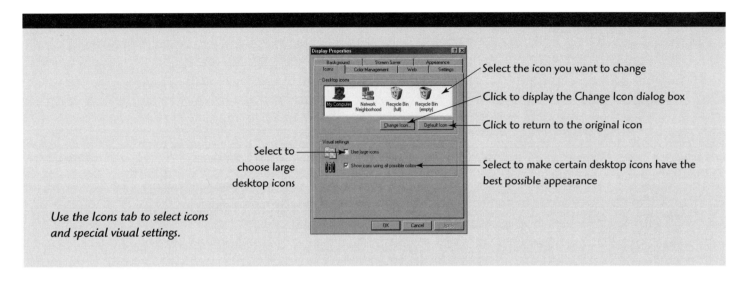

Select the icon you want to change

Click to display the Change Icon dialog box

Click to return to the original icon

Select to choose large desktop icons

Select to make certain desktop icons have the best possible appearance

Use the Icons tab to select icons and special visual settings.

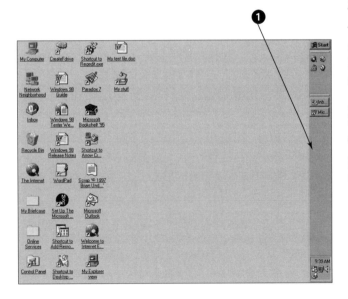

CUSTOMIZING YOUR TASKBAR

The Windows 98 Taskbar is pretty useful without any changes, but why let that stop you from playing with it a little? There's no harm in having a little fun, especially when you might end up with a more useful Taskbar.

Exercise 12: Moving the Taskbar

Your Taskbar doesn't have to be at the bottom of your screen. If you prefer, you can move the Taskbar to the top or to either side of your screen.

Follow these steps move the Taskbar:

1. Click and hold on an empty area of the Taskbar and drag it to the right edge of the screen. As you drag the Taskbar, you see a gray line indicating where the Taskbar will appear when you release the mouse button. The figure on the left shows how the Taskbar appears when moved to the right edge of the screen.

2. Drag the Taskbar to the top of the screen, then to the left edge, and finally back to the bottom of the screen.

No matter where you place your Taskbar, I refer to it as being at the bottom of your screen. If you've left it somewhere else, keep that in mind as you follow along in the exercises.

Exercise 13: Hiding the Taskbar

There are times when you need all of the screen space you can get, and the Taskbar just seems to get in the way. In those cases, you can hide the Taskbar—just be sure to remember where you hid it!
Follow these steps to hide the Taskbar:

1. Right-click an empty place on the Taskbar and choose Properties.

2. Select the Auto hide checkbox.

3. Click Apply to make the Taskbar disappear.

4. To view the Taskbar, move the mouse pointer just below the bottom edge of the screen. The Taskbar remains visible until you move the mouse pointer up above the Taskbar.

5. Deselect Auto hide by clicking in the checkbox.

6. Click OK to close the dialog box.

TIP

You can display the Taskbar and the Start menu by pressing Ctrl+Esc even when the Taskbar is hidden.

Exercise 14: Resizing the Taskbar

When you have only have a few programs running, the Taskbar has plenty of room to show a button with descriptive text for each program. This may not be the case if you have quite a few programs running together. In the figure on the right, I have ten different programs running. Windows 98 has shrunk each program's Taskbar button to such a small size that it's difficult to tell what each button represents.

To resize the Taskbar to give each program button more room, follow these steps:

1. Point to the top edge of the Taskbar. When the mouse pointer changes to a double-headed arrow, you're in the correct position.

2. Drag the top edge of the Taskbar up. You see a gray line appear above the Taskbar to indicate where the top edge of the Taskbar will be when it's resized.

3. Release the mouse button when the Taskbar is approximately triple its original height. You don't have to worry about precisely sizing the Taskbar; it automatically jumps to the correct height for the program buttons.

4. Return the Taskbar to its original size — just high enough for one row of program buttons.

If you move the Taskbar to either side of your screen, you find that resizing the Taskbar isn't quite the same because the Taskbar size doesn't change in predefined increments. If the Taskbar is on either side of the screen, you can resize the Taskbar to any size you like — up to the limit of one half the screen.

CUSTOMIZING SEND TO

In Lesson 1 you learned how to use the Send To command to copy files to a diskette quickly. There's no reason to limit this useful command to the built-in options, though. You can add other useful items to the Send To command quickly so you can have instant shortcuts available whenever you need them.

Exercise 15: Adding an item to the Send To menu

To add an item to the Send To menu, you must create a shortcut to it in the \Windows\SendTo folder. This can be a shortcut to a program or a folder, but if you create a shortcut to a program, the program should be able to correctly handle any files or documents you send to the program. That's one reason why WordPad is a good choice for adding to Send To—WordPad can open most types of files.

Here's how you can add WordPad to the Send To menu:

1. Right-click the Start button and select Explore.

2. Open the \Windows\Start Menu\Programs\Accessories folder.

3. Point to the shortcut to WordPad, hold down the right mouse button, drag the shortcut to the SendTo folder, and release the mouse button.

4. Select Create Shortcut(s) Here.

It might seem tempting to add shortcuts to all of your favorite programs in the SendTo folder so that they appear on the Send To menu, but there's really no reason to do so. Most of the time you use your favorite programs to open one type of document file, such as a spreadsheet or a word processor file. When you install programs on your PC, the installation programs tell Windows 98 which types of document files they can open. That's why Windows Explorer shows you a document is a Word document, an Excel Spreadsheet, or an Access database. Because Windows 98 already knows which program to use to open those types of files, there's no reason to clutter your Send To menu with shortcuts to the programs.

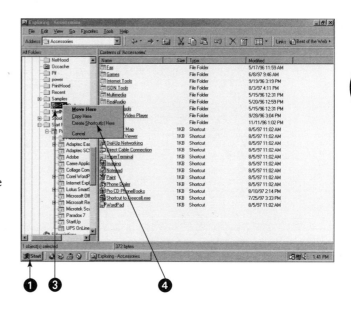

CUSTOMIZING THE MOUSE

Are you comfortable with your mouse? Do you ever get frustrated when you try to open something and Windows 98 doesn't do anything? Do you ever lose track of where the mouse pointer is on your screen? Would you rather swap the two buttons? If so, this is the right place to find the answers.

Exercise 16: Adjusting your double-click and pointer speed

Learning to double-click correctly is probably one of the hardest things for a new mouse user to master. Either you don't get the two clicks quite fast enough, or you accidentally double-click when you just meant to single-click. In this exercise you adjust the double-click setting for your mouse and end that frustration forever. Here's how:

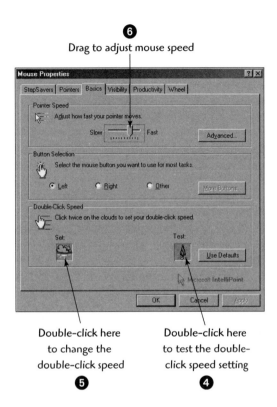

6

Drag to adjust mouse speed

Double-click here
to change the
double-click speed

5

Double-click here
to test the double-
click speed setting

4

1. Click the Start button.

2. Select Settings ➢ Control Panel.

3. Double-click Mouse to display the Mouse Properties dialog box. Your Mouse Properties dialog box may differ from the one shown in the figure on the left depending on the type of mouse you have. If so, you may need to look on more than one tab to find all the settings. You use this dialog box to perform all of your mouse customizing.

4. Double-click in the Test area to see whether your double-clicking is fast enough. If the umbrella pops up, Windows 98 recognized your double-click.

5. Double-click the Set box to change the double-click speed.

6. Drag the Pointer Speed selector to the left end of the setting and click Apply. Test this setting by moving the mouse around. Notice that you must move the mouse quite some distance to move the mouse pointer.

7. Drag the Pointer speed selector to the right end of the setting and click Apply. Move the mouse around to test this setting. Now the mouse pointer moves faster than the mouse. Choose a setting that feels comfortable.

If you set the speed too fast, Windows 98 doesn't recognize double-clicks. If you set the speed too slow, Windows 98 assumes that mouse clicks as much as a second apart are a double-click.

Exercise 17: Creating a lefty mouse

In the middle of the Mouse Properties dialog box, shown in the previous figure, you find three radio buttons. You can select Left for normal mouse operations, Right to swap the functions of the mouse buttons, or Other if you have a three button mouse and want to use the middle button.. If you're left-handed, placing the mouse at the left side of the keyboard may feel more natural. Swapping the functions of the mouse buttons enables you to comfortably use your left index finger to click the buttons. If you do swap the mouse buttons, you need to remember that you've done so as you complete the rest of the lessons: Use the correct button based on your mouse setting—when the text says `right-click`, you have to remember this means left-click on your PC.

Exercise 18: Adding trails

In this exercise you see how you can get used to the mouse by giving you a better idea where your mouse is pointing. This setting is quite useful on some low-contrast laptop PC screens, too.

    Follow these steps to add a trail:

1. If the Mouse Properties dialog box is no longer on-screen, display the dialog box.

2. Click the Visibility tab.

3. Click the Display pointer trails checkbox and then move the mouse around to see the effect of this setting.

4. Click Settings to display the Settings for Trails dialog box. Try moving the slider to various points between Short and Long to see which setting you prefer.

5. Click OK to close the Settings for Trails dialog box.

6. When you are satisfied with your settings, click OK to close the Mouse Properties dialog box.

    You may want to test your mouse settings and fine-tune your adjustments to make your mouse function the way you like. If you share a PC with other users, make certain all users enter their own names when they start Windows 98. Because Windows 98 keeps track of the settings for each user name entered, all users can have their own custom settings.

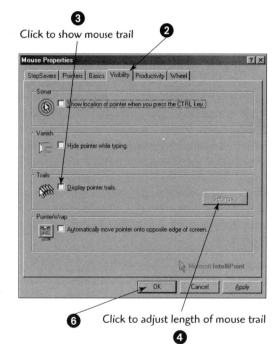

❸ Click to show mouse trail

❷

❻ ❹ Click to adjust length of mouse trail

Exercise 19: Configuring for single clicking

If you've ever wondered why you have to double-click items on your desktop but single-click items on the Internet, you don't have to wonder any longer. In Windows 98 you can configure your PC so that a single mouse click selects and activates objects. In this exercise you learn how to adjust how your desktop responds to mouse clicks.

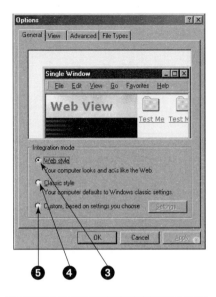

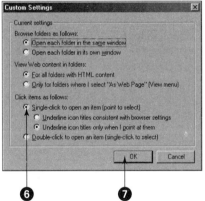

Here's how to select the mouse click style you prefer:

1. Double-click My Computer.

2. Select View ➤ Folder Options to display the Options dialog box.

3. To enable single-click selection and activation of desktop items, click the Web style radio button.

4. To use double-clicking to activate desktop items, click the Classic style radio button.

5. To use a combination of the old and new styles, click the Custom radio button and then click Settings to display the Custom Settings dialog box.

6. Choose Single-click to open an item or Double-click to open an item, depending on whether you prefer to use single- or double-clicks.

7. Click OK to close the dialog box, and click OK again to confirm your changes.

If you choose the Custom setting and later decide to return to either Web style or Classic style, make certain your choices in the Web Integration Settings dialog box match the style radio button you choose in the Options dialog box. Otherwise you may find that the mouse does not always work quite as you expect.

CUSTOMIZING YOUR KEYBOARD

You can also change the way your keyboard responds to your keystrokes. If you're a slow typist, you may find keys repeating because the delay before keys repeat is too short or the repeat rate is too high. If you're a fast typist, you may want to set a shorter delay or a faster repeat rate so that your keyboard doesn't feel so sluggish. Either way, there's help available. You can also change the rate the cursor blinks.

Exercise 20: Adjusting keyboard settings

Here's how to customize your keyboard to match your typing style:

1. Click the Start button.

2. Select Settings ➤ Control Panel.

3. Double-click Keyboard to display the Keyboard Properties dialog box. All the settings you adjust in this lesson are on the Speed tab, which is displayed automatically when you open the dialog box.

4. Drag the Repeat delay slider to the left, click the test area, and hold down a key. Notice the length of time before the key repeats.

5. Drag the Repeat delay slider to the right and test the length of time before the key repeats. Choose a setting that seems right for your typing style.

6. Drag the Repeat rate slider left and right to test the different settings. Here, too, you should select a setting that feels comfortable.

7. Drag the Cursor blink rate slider left or right to find a setting you like.

8. Click OK to save your settings and close the Keyboard Properties dialog box.

You may need to test your new keyboard settings in several of your favorite programs to determine the most comfortable combination. What works well in your spreadsheet may not be the best for your word processor, but because you can change your settings anytime, you can find out what's right for you with a little experimentation.

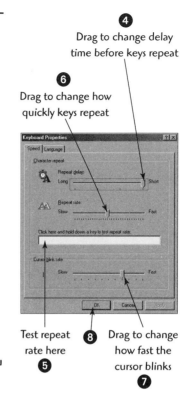

④ Drag to change delay time before keys repeat

⑥ Drag to change how quickly keys repeat

Test repeat rate here ⑤

⑧ Drag to change how fast the cursor blinks ⑦

USING THE TASKBAR CLOCK

That little time display in the lower-right corner of your Windows 98 desktop is actually your connection to your PC's internal clock and calendar. The correct date and time are quite important because every time you save a new file or modify an existing one, Windows 98 records the exact date and time as part of the file information. You can then use this information to locate the newest versions of files, find files you worked with on a specific date, or even determine how much time has passed since you last backed up your files.

Exercise 21: Adjusting the system clock

You can make several adjustments to the system clock. Not only can you correct the time, but you can also set the date, your time zone, and even whether you want automatic adjustments for daylight savings time.

Follow these steps to adjust your PC's clock:

1. Double-click the time display at the right edge of the Taskbar to display the Date/Time Properties dialog box.

2. To select a different month, click the down arrow to the right of the month list box and choose the correct month.

3. To select a different year, click the up or down arrows at the right side of the year box.

4. Click a date in the calendar display to change the date.

5. To adjust the time, click the digital time display to select the portion of the time you want to change—to change the hour, click the hour portion of the time. Use the up or down arrow to the right of the time display to make the adjustment.

6. Click the Time Zone tab to display the time zone options shown in the figure on the left.

7. To change the time zone, choose the correct time zone from the list box.

8. If you are in a location that uses daylight savings time, make certain the Automatically adjust clock for daylight savings time checkbox is selected. Windows 98 then changes your PC's clock for you when you go on or off daylight savings time.

9. Click OK to confirm your changes and close the Date/Time Properties dialog box.

❸ Use these arrows to adjust the year

❷ Select the month here

❻

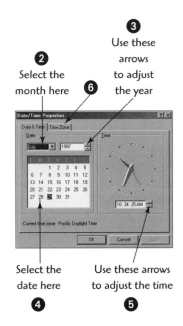

Select the date here ❹

Use these arrows to adjust the time ❺

❼

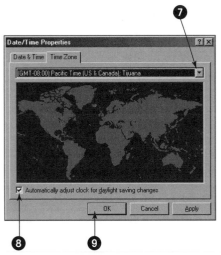

❽ ❾

NOTE

Be careful when setting your calendar so that you don't choose a date in the future. If you have any trial versions of software installed, choosing a future date could disable that software. Setting the date back to the correct date probably doesn't reenable the software, either.

USING THE NEW WINDOWS 98 UTILITIES

Windows 98 includes several new utilities you'll find quite useful. These utilities can help you maintain your computer and ensure that it is running as efficiently as possible. The following exercises cover three of the new utilities.

Exercise 22: Using the System Information Utility

The System Information Utility provides a wealth of interesting information about your PC. Much of this information can be quite valuable for troubleshooting purposes. You probably won't have much need for this troubleshooting information, but if your system experiences problems, then you'll be able to provide the technical support person with information that may help him or her solve the problem more quickly.

Follow these steps to view system information:

1. Click the Start button.

2. Select Programs ➢ Accessories ➢ System Tools ➢ Microsoft System Information Utility.

3. Select the information category you want to examine. In the figure on the right, the Printing category information is displayed.

4. Click the Print button to create a printed record of the selected category.

5. Click the Close button to close the System Information Utility.

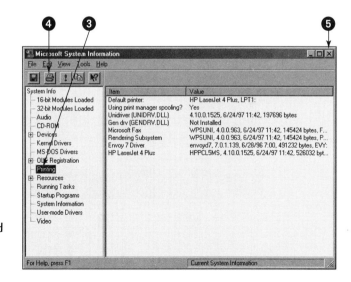

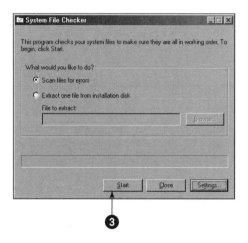

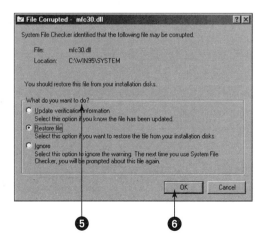

You may find the System Information Utility especially useful if you add or change hardware or system driver files. You can print a copy of the information about a category both before and after you make any changes. Then if something doesn't work correctly after the upgrade, you can examine the two printed reports to see what was changed.

Exercise 23: Using the System File Checker

The System File Checker checks important Windows 98 system files to make certain they haven't been damaged or improperly overwritten. Files can be damaged if your system crashes. In addition, poorly written software installation programs can replace important system files with out-of-date versions that may cause your computer to malfunction.

Follow these steps to verify that your system files are okay:

1. Click the Start button.

2. Select Programs ➢ Accessories ➢ System Tools ➢ System File Checker to open the System File Checker.

3. Click Start to begin checking for errors.

4. If System File Checker finds system files that have changed, you see a dialog box similar to the one shown in the figure on the left.

5. Choose Update verification information if you know the file has been updated, Restore file if you want to revert to the original Windows 98 file, or Ignore if you're not certain but want to try the changed file.

6. Click OK to continue.

7. Select Close to close the System File Checker.

If Microsoft supplies a *Service Pack*—an update for Windows 98 —be sure to run System File Checker before you apply the update. That way you'll be able to correct any problems before you run the update.

Exercise 24: Using the Windows Tune Up Wizard

Your PC probably isn't running quite as fast as it could. The Windows Tune Up Wizard is intended to help you get the most out of your system by making your favorite programs run faster, making certain your hard disk doesn't contain errors, and making certain that disk space isn't being wasted on unnecessary files.

Follow these steps to run the Windows Tune Up Wizard:

1. Click the Start button.

2. Select Programs ➢ Accessories ➢ System Tools ➢ Windows Tune Up Wizard to open the Windows Tune Up Wizard dialog box.

3. Click Next and select Do not optimize.

4. Click Next to begin and see the scheduled tasks.

5. To view the schedule for a task, select the task in the list of scheduled tasks.

6. To change a task schedule, click the Reschedule button to display the Reschedule dialog box. You may want to reschedule any tasks scheduled for times when you normally use your PC.

7. After you have adjusted the schedule, click OK to close the Reschedule dialog box.

8. Click Next to continue. The Windows Tune Up Wizard then confirms the schedule.

9. Click Finish to close the Windows Tune Up Wizard dialog box.

Make certain you don't turn off your PC during the time scheduled for Windows Tune Up Wizard tasks. You can turn off your monitor to save energy, but your system must be running for the tasks to complete.

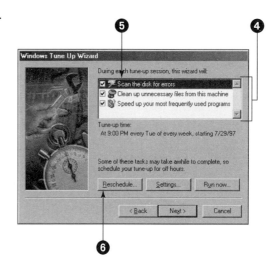

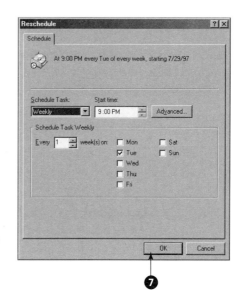

SKILLS CHALLENGE: CUSTOMIZING WINDOWS 98

It's time to see if you remember what you've learned in Lesson 2. This is a quick run through the exercises without giving you every step along the way. Here goes:

1. Find your current display resolution setting.

2. Determine how many colors your monitor can display at the current settings.

3. Change the desktop background color to gray.

 How do you change to the High Contrast White (Extra Large) color scheme?

4. Change the font used to display icon titles to Large Fonts.

 How do you increase the size of the on-screen text to five times normal so that a vision-impaired user can read the Windows 98 screen?

5. Change the desktop pattern to Buttons.

6. Check to see how your wallpaper looks when tiled, and then set it back to centered.

 How do you make a picture into wallpaper that covers your entire desktop?

7. Preview your screen saver.

8. Change the screen saver delay time to 10 minutes.

 What can you do to protect your privacy when you step away from your desk?

9. Determine the font name and size for text displayed in the inactive title bar.

 How can you hide the title bar text?

10. Move the Taskbar to the top of the screen.

11. Hide the Taskbar.

 How do you find out where someone hid the Taskbar?

12. Restore the Taskbar, move it to the bottom of the screen, and increase the Taskbar height so that two rows of program buttons can be displayed.

13. Determine whether your mouse is set to right- or left-handed.

 How do you make it easier for someone with limited physical abilities to double-click the mouse?

 What do you do to make the mouse pointer easier to find for someone who's never used a mouse before?

14. Increase the cursor blink rate by one notch.

 What two settings can you use to make the keyboard easier to use for someone just learning to type?

15. Determine whether your clock is set to automatically adjust for daylight savings time.

WRAP UP

In this lesson you've learned how you can customize the appearance of Windows 98 that so it's fun to use. You've also seen how you can protect your privacy so people aren't snooping around your computer when you walk away from your desk.

You may want to consider how you can apply what you've learned in Lesson 2 to help other people use a PC. What changes would help a young learner or a visually impaired user, for example?

Problem	Solution
I can't increase my resolution setting above 640 × 480 pixels.	Your display adapter is set as a standard VGA adapter. You need to check your owner's manual to see if you really have a different adapter that can use higher settings. If your display adapter can use higher settings, click the Change Display Type button on the Display Properties dialog box Settings tab, choose Change, and then select the correct adapter type.
I can't set my display to more than 16 colors.	This problem is caused by having your display adapter set as standard VGA. See the previous problem to determine if you can overcome this problem.
When I try to set up a screen saver, I can't find any screen savers listed in the Screen Saver list box.	You need to install the screen savers using your Windows 98 disks or CD-ROM. Click the Start button, select Settings ➤ Control Panel, and double-click Add/Remove Programs. Click the Windows Setup tab, select Accessories, and click Details. Select Screen Savers and then click OK. Click Apply and follow the prompts to install the screen savers.

In the next lesson you learn more about working with files in Windows 98. Because your files contain your work, it's pretty important to know where your files are, and how you can protect yourself from the disaster of losing your work.

Working with Files

45 MINUTES

GOALS

You've already worked with some files in Lessons 1 and 2; you simply can't get around using files when you use your PC. This lesson takes you several steps farther down the path toward really understanding the Windows 98 file management system by covering the following topics:

- Managing your files and folders

- Working with long filenames

- Changing the view

- Starting programs by opening documents

- Scheduling events

GET READY

You can't do any real work on your PC without working with files. Everything you store on your computer—your databases, your letters, your spreadsheets—is stored in files. If you lose your files, your data goes with them. If you're like most people, your data files are worth more to you than the entire cost of your computer. Just think for a minute about all of the work you have tied up in your data files and you see what I mean. That's why this lesson is so important—your files are a valuable asset you can't afford to lose.

In this lesson you use a number of files, but to keep the lesson easy to follow, these files are already on your PC or included on the *Presenting Windows 98 One Step at a Time* CD-ROM in the Exercise folder. You also create some small files as you go through the exercises. If you've completed Lessons 1 and 2, you should be ready to start this lesson without any additional items.

When you have completed the exercises in this lesson, you will have learned how to do the following: find lost files; create new folders; move, copy, delete, and sort files and folders; work with long filenames; change the width of panes and columns in Windows Explorer; display and hide different file types; register a new file type; and edit an existing file type.

If you're ready, it's on to Lesson 3. Make certain you're sitting at your PC and the Windows 98 desktop is on your screen.

MANAGING YOUR FILES AND FOLDERS

In this set of exercises you learn how to find, select, rename, copy, and move files. You also learn how to make the Recycle Bin work as your safety net, preventing you from losing files by accidentally deleted them.

Some of the tasks you practice in this lesson may seem familiar because you've already learned some of the relevant skills in Lesson 1. Here, though, you learn how to make Windows 98 do more of the work for you. You also learn some new techniques I didn't cover earlier because I didn't want to hit you with too much at one time.

Exercise 1: Finding your lost files

Lost files sometimes seem like lost sheep—they never seem to be where you're sure you left them. Windows 98 sometimes contributes to this phenomenon by offering to save your files either on your desktop or in the last folder you used. The problem with this is simple —the computer is doing what you're telling it to do, not what you're thinking it should do. Unfortunately, we still don't have computers that understand "do what I mean, not what I say." Until we do, you may find yourself looking for your lost files occasionally.

In Lesson 1 you learned that you can use the Find command in a number of different ways. For example, you can find files by looking for them by name or even part of the name, by the type of file, by the date the file was created or modified, or by searching for files containing specified text. As useful as these options are, you're likely to use just a few of the options over and over. You may, for example, want to find all word processing document files containing references to a specific project. Rather than reenter the same search parameters each time, why not have Windows 98 remember what you wanted last time and perform the same search again?

In this exercise you create a useful search and then tell Windows 98 to save the parameters so you can perform the same search in the future with just a few clicks. In this case, the search is for all files created in the past week that have doc as the file extension. The .doc file extension is used by both WordPad and Word to indicate word processing document files.

Here's how you can create a search and save the parameters:

1. Click the Start button.

2. Select Find ➢ Files or Folders.

3. Type the following text in the Named text box: ***.doc.**

4. Click the Date tab.

5. Select the during the previous X days radio button.

6. Click the up arrow until the number of days is 7.

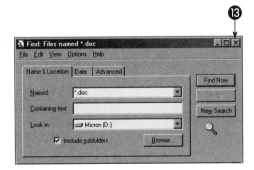

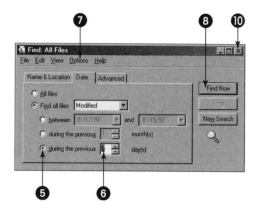

7. Select Options and make certain a check appears in front of Save Results. This command is a *toggle*—each time you select the command, it changes states from selected to deselected, or deselected to selected, as the case may be.

8. Select Find Now to start the search.

9. When Windows 98 has completed the search, select File ➢ Save Search to place an icon named `Files named @.doc.fnd` on your desktop.

10. Click the Close button to close the Find window.

11. Double-click the Files named @.doc.fnd icon to redisplay the saved search results.

12. Select Find Now to begin a new search for documents created or modified within the past week. You have to perform a new search because when you double-click the Files named @.doc.fnd icon, the results shown in the Find window are the saved results, not the results of a new search. The accompanying figure shows the results of the search on my computer. Because my document files are on drive D, I told Windows 98 to search D, not C.

13. Click the Close button to close the Find window.

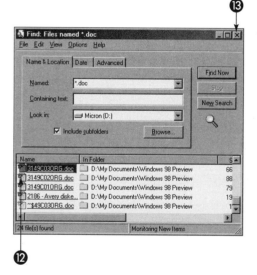

There is a potential "gotcha" you can encounter in trying to save a file search for future use. I carefully steered you around the problem, but now that you've successfully completed the exercise, I'll explain what could have gone wrong.

You must make certain that you've selected Options ➢ Save Results and clicked Find Now *before* you select File ➢ Save Search. Oh sure, Windows 98 is perfectly happy to save the Files named @.doc.fnd icon on your desktop before you've completed Steps 7 and 8, but something important is missing—the setting on the Date tab that limits the search to files created or modified in the past seven days. In fact, Windows 98 totally forgets that you wanted to place a date specification on the files you wanted to find. To see this, try the following exercise, which differs from the previous exercise in only one small detail—you don't bother to find the matching files before you save the search:

1. Click the Start button.

2. Select Find ➢ Files or Folders.

3. Type the following text in the Named text box: ***.doc.**

4. Click the Date tab.

5. Select the during the previous X days radio button.

6. Click the up arrow until the number of days is 7.

7. Select Options and make certain that a check appears in front of Save Results. Again, this command is a *toggle*—each time you select the command it changes states from selected to deselected, or deselected to selected, as the case may be.

8. Select File ➢ Save Search to place an icon named Files named @.doc (2).fnd on your desktop.

9. Click the Close button to close the Find window.

10. Double-click the Files named @.doc (2).fnd icon to redisplay the saved search.

11. Click the Date tab and you see that the All files radio button is selected rather than the during the previous seven days radio button. From this you can probably guess that Windows 98 isn't going to limit its search as you intended.

12. Click Find Now to begin a new search. This time the search finds all files with a .doc extension, not just those created or modified in the past week. The accompanying figure shows that Windows 98 found over 200 files on my computer because the search wasn't limited to files from the past week.

13. Click the Close button to close the Find window.

This exercise has shown you something few Windows 98 "experts" know—if you want to save a search that finds files modified within a specified number of days or months before today, you must actually perform the search before you save it. I don't mind if you tease your local Windows 98 expert with this one!

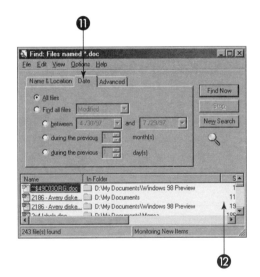

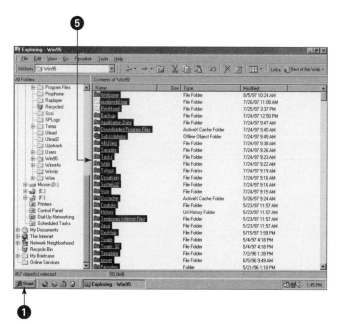

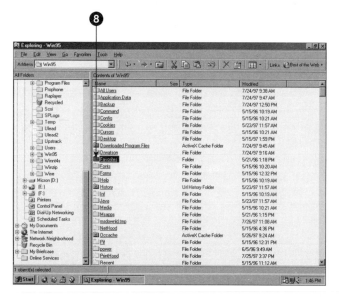

Exercise 2: Selecting files and folders

You can only work with files and folders that you've selected. That's true whether you're trying to open a document, run a program, delete old files, or copy files to a diskette. In this exercise you learn a few tricks that make navigating folders and selecting files a little easier.

To select files and folders, follow these steps:

1. Click the Start button.

2. Select Programs ➤ Windows Explorer.

3. Click the Windows folder to display its contents in the contents pane.

4. Press Tab to move the selector into the contents pane and highlight the item at the top of the listing. Remember that Windows 98 displays folders at the top of the listing, with files following the folders.

5. Press Ctrl+A to select all the files and folders in the Windows folder. Ctrl+A is a keyboard shortcut for the Edit ➤ Select All command.

6. Press End to move the selector to the last item in the Windows folder.

7. Press Home to move the selector to the first item in the Windows folder.

8. Press the letter F to move the selector to the first item in the list that begins with the letter F. This is likely to be a folder rather than a file, because Windows 98 normally has several folders under the Windows folder that begin with F.

9. Press F again to move the selector to the next item that begins with F.

10. Continue pressing F until the selector jumps back to the first item that begins with F. When there are no more folders beginning with F, the selector jumps back to the first file that begins with F.

11. Press Shift+Home to select all items between the selector and the top of the list. This shortcut allows you to quickly select a

group of items between the item you've currently selected and the top of the list.

12. Press Shift+End to select all items between the selector and the end of the list. Like Shift+Home, this shortcut allows you to quickly select a group of items.

13. Press W to select the first item that starts with W.

14. Hold down Shift while you press the down-arrow key four times. Because you're holding down Shift, Windows 98 extends the selection to include all items from the first selected to the last selected.

15. Continue to hold down Shift and click an item several rows below the last selected item. Shift also extends your selection when you use the mouse.

16. Release Shift and hold down Ctrl while you click another item several rows below the current selection. Ctrl also extends your selection, but without selecting items between the current selection and your new addition.

17. Continue to hold down Ctrl and click one of the items in the middle of the selected items. As long as you hold down Ctrl, you can click items to add them to the selection, or click selected items to remove them from the selection.

18. Release Ctrl and click one of the items in the list. This selects only the item you click and removes all other items from the selection. These same selection techniques work in the folders pane, too.

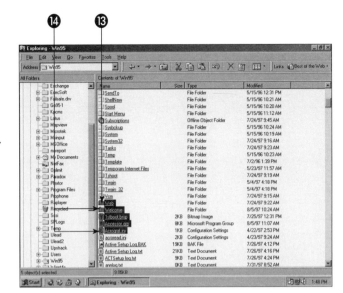

If you have enabled the Active Desktop, you need only point to files to select them. For example, to select a range of files, point to the first file, hold down Shift, and move the pointer to the last file you want to select without clicking the mouse button. Move the mouse pointer off the list of selected files to stop expanding the selection. You may want to practice this until you're comfortable with the new way your mouse works in Windows 98 — it's easy to accidentally select and open a file when you only intended to select it.

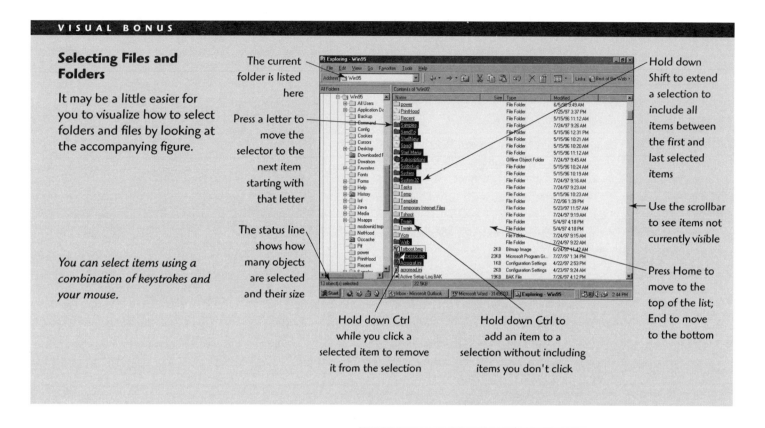

VISUAL BONUS

Selecting Files and Folders

It may be a little easier for you to visualize how to select folders and files by looking at the accompanying figure.

You can select items using a combination of keystrokes and your mouse.

The current folder is listed here

Press a letter to move the selector to the next item starting with that letter

The status line shows how many objects are selected and their size

Hold down Shift to extend a selection to include all items between the first and last selected items

Use the scrollbar to see items not currently visible

Press Home to move to the top of the list; End to move to the bottom

Hold down Ctrl while you click a selected item to remove it from the selection

Hold down Ctrl to add an item to a selection without including items you don't click

Exercise 3: Creating new folders

In Windows 98 you use folders to organize your files. You can create new folders inside existing folders, and then create new folders inside those new folders. You aren't really limited to a specific number of levels of nested folders, although the complete name of a file including all of its parent folders can't be longer than 260 characters. It's not likely that you'll ever have a problem with this limit.

Because you can nest folders within folders, it's pretty easy to use separate folders for different projects. These separate project folders are an excellent organizational tool because they make it so much easier to keep track of all the documents related to a project. You might start with a folder called My Documents and then add new folders within that folder for each different job. I always create a new folder for each book project. Each chapter of the book, all screen captures, and any auxiliary files for the book go into this folder. After I've completed a book I can simply move all the files from the folder onto diskettes to create a complete backup for a single project. Organizing your files this way makes it far less likely for you to lose a stray file that's hiding somewhere on your hard disk.

In this exercise you begin by opening the My Documents folder and then creating a new folder nested within the My Documents folder. If you don't already have a My Documents folder, creating it is one of your first tasks.

Follow these steps to create a new folder:

1. Click the Start button.

2. Select Programs ➢ Windows Explorer.

3. If the My Documents folder already exists, click it to open the folder and then skip to Step 8.

4. If you don't already have a My Documents folder, click the drive icon for drive C in the folders pane.

5. Select File ➢ New ➢ Folder to create a new folder named New Folder.

6. Type the following text to name the new folder: **My Documents.**

7. Click the My Documents folder in the folders pane to open the folder.

8. Select File ➢ New ➢ Folder to create a new folder named New Folder.

9. Type the following text to name the new folder: **Presenting Windows 98 One Step at a Time.**

10. Click the Presenting Windows 98 One Step at a Time folder in the folders pane to open the folder.

If you want to create additional new folders, make certain you start from the correct location. The exercise ended with the Presenting Windows 98 One Step at a Time folder open. If you were again to select File ➢ New ➢ Folder to create a new folder, the new folder would be nested within the Presenting Windows 98 One Step

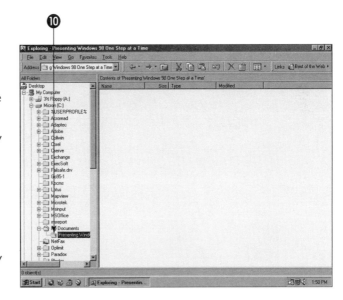

at a Time folder—which is in turn nested within the My Documents folder. To create a new folder nested within the My Documents folder but not nested within the Presenting Windows 98 One Step at a Time folder, make certain you select the My Documents folder before you create the new folder.

Exercise 4: Moving and copying files and folders

You've probably noticed that Windows 98 treats files and folders almost identically. It should come as little surprise that this similar treatment extends to moving and copying, too. Just about the only real difference you may notice is that when you move or copy a folder, any files contained in the folder are moved or copied, too.

 There's one important rule you need to remember for successful moving or copying—you can't have two folders or files with exactly the same name. You can have slight variations on the same name, such as file1.txt and file2.txt, or file1.txt and copy of file1.txt. You can use the same name for two files if they're in different folders, because the two names are actually different because the folder name is part of each file's name. The full name of file1.txt in folder1 on drive C would be C:\folder1\file1.txt while the full name of file1.txt in folder2 on drive C would be C:\folder2\file1.txt. That's why you can have a file1.txt in both folders—the two files really do have different names.

In this exercise you first copy a file from one folder to another and then move the copied file to a different folder. You also learn what happens when you try to make a copy of the file in the same folder.

Follow these steps to move and copy files and folders:

1. Click the Start button.

2. Select Programs ➢ Windows Explorer.

3. Click the plus sign to open the *Presenting Windows One Step At a Time* CD-ROM.

4. Click the Exercise folder to display the contents of the Exercise folder in the contents pane.

5. Right-click Three Horses 256 color.BMP to display the pop-up menu.

6. Select Copy to copy the Three Horses 256 color.BMP file to the Windows 98 Clipboard—an area in memory where Windows 98 temporarily holds items you've copied.

7. Right-click the My Documents folder and select Paste to copy the Three Horses 256 color.BMP file to the My Documents folder. Notice that copying the file doesn't open the My Documents folder.

8. Open the My Documents folder and verify that it now contains the Three Horses 256 color.BMP file.

9. Expand the My Documents folder in order to see the Presenting Windows 98 One Step at a Time folder.

10. Drag Three Horses 256 color.BMP to the Presenting Windows 98 One Step at a Time folder and release the mouse button, moving the file from the My Documents folder to the Presenting Windows 98 One Step at a Time folder. It doesn't matter whether you drop the file on the Presenting Windows 98 One Step at a Time folder in the folder pane or the contents pane—either one works.

11. Open the Presenting Windows 98 One Step at a Time folder and then drag Three Horses 256 color.BMP to the Presenting Windows 98 One Step at a Time folder in the folder pane. When you release the left mouse button, Windows 98 displays the error message on the right. Click OK.

12. Hold down Ctrl, drag Three Horses 256 color.BMP to the Presenting Windows 98 One Step at a Time folder, and release the mouse button to create a copy of Three Horses 256 color.BMP in the Presenting Windows 98 One Step at a Time folder. Release Ctrl after the copy is complete.

By holding down Ctrl, you told Windows 98 to make a copy of the file rather than move the file. Because the original file already existed in the folder, Windows 98 added `Copy of` to the file name. If you copy the Three Horses 256 color.BMP file to a different folder that doesn't already contain the Three Horses 256 color.BMP file, Windows 98 doesn't add `Copy of` to the filename.

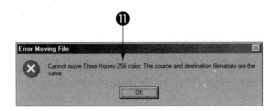

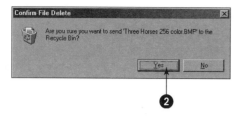

②

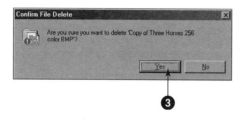

③

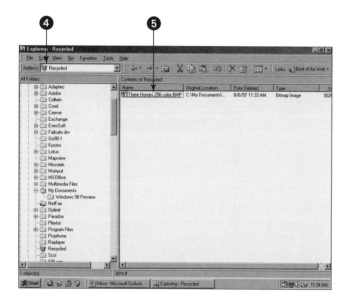

④   ⑤

Exercise 5: Deleting files and folders

Your hard disk soon fills up if you keep making extra copies of files you don't need. Rather than let that happen, in this exercise you learn how to use the Recycle Bin effectively. The copies of Three Horses 256 color.BMP you created in the last exercise seem like good candidates for recycling, don't they?

Follow these steps to use and control the Recycle Bin:

1. If you closed Windows Explorer after the last exercise, reopen it and display the contents of the Presenting Windows 98 One Step at a Time folder.

2. Right-click Three Horses 256 color.BMP and select Delete. Windows 98 displays the Confirm File Delete message. Click Yes to send the file to the Recycle Bin.

   Items you delete from a diskette don't go to the Recycle Bin — they're permanently deleted.

3. Right-click Copy of Three Horses 256 color.BMP, hold down Shift, and select Delete. Windows 98 displays the Confirm File Delete message. Do you see the difference between this message and the previous one? By holding down Shift, you tell Windows 98 to skip the Recycle Bin. Click Yes to delete the file.

4. Open the Recycled (or Recycle Bin) folder. When you do, notice that the icon for this folder looks like a miniature version of the waste basket icon on your desktop. You can work with the Recycle Bin either by double-clicking the Recycle Bin icon on your desktop or by opening the Recycled folder in Windows Explorer.

5. Right-click Three Horses 256 color.BMP and select Restore to move the file back to its original location in the Presenting Windows 98 One Step at a Time folder. Because you deleted Copy of Three Horses 256 color.BMP without sending it to the Recycle Bin, you can't restore the Copy of Three Horses 256 color.BMP file. If Copy of Three Horses 256 color.BMP had been an important file you accidentally deleted, you'd be out of luck because you bypassed the Recycle Bin.

6. Right-click the Recycled folder in the folders pane and select Empty Recycle Bin (you can't select this if the Recycle Bin is already empty).

7. Click Yes to confirm that you want to empty the Recycle Bin and permanently delete the files. Remember, though, that once you delete the files from the Recycle Bin, you can't restore them— there's no Recycle Bin for the Recycle Bin!

If you don't empty the Recycle Bin yourself, the Recycle Bin will eventually reach its capacity. When the Recycle Bin is full, the oldest files in the Recycle Bin are deleted to make room for newer files. Depending on the size of your Recycle Bin and the files you delete, it may take weeks or months before old files disappear from the Recycle Bin. But if your Recycle Bin is quite small and you delete large files, you may lose the chance to restore accidentally deleted files much sooner than you expect.

Unfortunately, simply making the Recycle Bin larger isn't always the best choice, either. Space you allocate to the Recycle Bin is lost to other uses. If you're running short on disk space, you may want to adjust the Recycle Bin size downward to free up additional room on your hard drive.

Follow these steps to adjust the Recycle Bin size up or down:

1. Right-click the Recycle Bin icon on your desktop or the Recycled folder in Windows Explorer.

2. Select Properties to display the Recycle Bin Properties (or the Recycled Properties) dialog box. If the Recycled Properties dialog box is displayed, click the Global tab. The accompanying figure shows the Recycle Bin Properties dialog box for my system, which has two hard drives. If your PC has a different number of hard drives, or if you clicked the Recycled folder in Windows Explorer, the other dialog box tabs are a little different than shown in the figure.

3. Drag the slider to the left to reduce the maximum size of the Recycle Bin or to the right to increase the size. Because the size is shown as a percentage of the disk size, a setting of 10% allocates about 120MB of space on a 1.2GB drive.

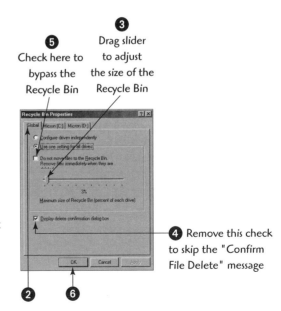

5 Check here to bypass the Recycle Bin

3 Drag slider to adjust the size of the Recycle Bin

4 Remove this check to skip the "Confirm File Delete" message

4. Deselect the Display delete confirmation dialog box by clicking the checkbox. This prevents Windows 98 from always asking if you really want to delete files.

5. Make certain the Do not move files to the Recycle Bin checkbox is not selected. If this checkbox is selected, you can't recover files you accidentally delete.

6. Click OK to close the dialog box.

If you have more than one hard drive, you can configure the Recycle Bin settings differently for each drive. It's probably just as well to use the same settings for all drives—unless you really feel the need to tinker!

WORKING WITH LONG FILENAMES

What are long filenames? That seems like a strange question, doesn't it? Long filenames aren't the names of long files, they're a wonderful improvement introduced to the PC with the introduction of Windows 95.

Before Windows 95, PC users struggled with a really tough limitation on how they could name their files. You could use from one to eight characters for a filename, and up to three characters for an extension. In Windows 98 you can use up to 255 characters in a filename. Now that you can use truly descriptive names for your files, confusion over which file is which should be a thing of the past. (But if you use any old applications that weren't designed for Windows 98, or if you need to access your Windows 98 files in DOS, you may be in for a surprise if you don't know that Windows 98 has two names for every file. See Exercise 7 for more information.)

 Although Windows 98 allows up to 255 characters in a filename, there's another limit that generally prevents filenames from being that long. The complete name of a file, including the drive letter and any folder names, is limited to 260 characters, as described in Exercise 3 earlier in this chapter. Still, you'd have to try pretty hard to create filenames that were too long for Windows 98.

If the old, short-style filenames could only include eight characters in the name and three characters in the extension, then any filename with more than 8.3 characters must be a long filename, right? As a matter of fact, yes, but there are other factors that can make even the old 8.3 style names into long filenames, too.

Any filename that includes special characters, such as spaces or commas, is a long filename regardless of the length of the name. Any filename that contains both upper- and lowercase letters is also considered a long filename. Both TEST 1.TXT and Test.txt are long filenames, but TEST1.TXT is not.

There's really only one time when you need to be concerned about long filenames. Windows 98 can store only 512 names in the root directory (C:\) on your hard drive—unless you are using the FAT32 file system (see Lesson 4 for more information on FAT32). But it takes two or more of those 512 entries to store each long filename, depending on the length of the name. This effectively cuts you down to a maximum of 256 entries in the root, and maybe even fewer. There is no limit to the number of files and folders you can store in a folder so you can use long filenames as often as you want, provided you store your files in folders rather than in the root directory.

 Although Windows 98 has no problem with long filenames, you may be restricted to using shorter names if you're on a network with computers that aren't using Windows 98 and are restricted to using the 8.3 file-naming convention. Your network administrator can tell you whether there are any restrictions on naming files on your network.

Exercise 6: Naming files and folders

You can use almost any character in a filename. In fact, the only characters on your keyboard you can't use are these:

\ / : * ? " < > |

Each of these prohibited characters has a special meaning at the command line, which is why you can't use them in filenames—doing so would confuse Windows 98.

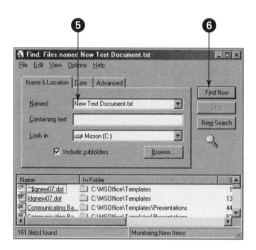

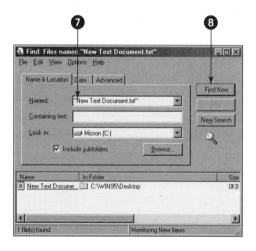

There's one other character you can use (but may want to avoid) — the space character you create by pressing the Spacebar. Windows 98 allows you to include spaces in filenames, but those spaces can cause confusion. In this exercise you learn how to work around the problem.

Follow these steps to name a file:

1. Right-click a blank space on the desktop.

2. Select New ➤ Text Document to create New Text Document.txt on your desktop.

3. Click the Start button.

4. Select Find ➤ Files or Folders.

5. Type this text in the Named text box: **New Text Document.txt.**

6. Click Find Now to search for your new file. Your results probably aren't identical to the accompanying figure, but you are likely to find quite a few files instead of the one file you just created.

7. Now type this text in the Named text box: **"New Text Document.txt".**

   Make certain you include the quotation marks.

8. Again click Find Now, and your results probably look more like the accompanying figure.

9. Right-click a blank space on the desktop and select New ➤ Text Document to create another text document.

10. Type the following text to rename the new file: **New_Text_Document.txt**

    Make certain you don't include any spaces in the name, but use the underscore (_) to connect the words in the name.

11. Now type this text in the Named text box of the Find dialog box: **New_Text_Document.txt.**

12. Click Find Now again.

If you include spaces in a filename, you must always remember to enclose the name in quotes when you use the filename in a command such as the Find command. When you use an underscore in place of a space in a filename, Windows 98 knows that the filename is one name, rather than a series of names separated by spaces. It's your choice whether you substitute an underscore (or some other character) for a space in a filename—both are acceptable to Windows 98.

Exercise 7: Working with long filenames in MS-DOS

You may never have to use the MS-DOS prompt, especially if you only use programs designed for Windows 98. If you do use the MS-DOS prompt, you soon find that Windows 98 creates a rather funny-looking short name to go along with the long filename.

Follow these steps to view both sets of names for the items on your desktop:

1. Click the Start button.

2. Select Programs ➢ MS-DOS Prompt.

3. Type the following text to change the folder and press Enter: **cd desktop.**

4. Type the following text and press Enter: **dir.**

Your screen should look something like the accompanying figure. You can leave the MS-DOS Prompt window open for now.

Windows 98 creates the short filenames by using the first six characters of the filename, converting them to uppercase, dropping any spaces, and then adding a tilde (~) and a sequential number. If more than nine files result in names similar enough that the first six characters are the same, Windows 98 uses the first five characters and keeps incrementing the numbers at the ends of the names.

The short name is shown in the first column

The long file name is shown in the last column

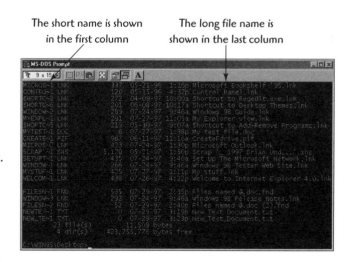

CHANGING THE VIEW

Windows Explorer has quite a few different ways of showing you your files. You want to learn how to control the view and use Windows Explorer to its fullest.

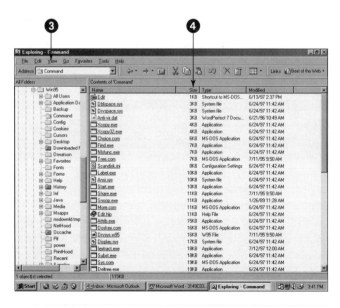

You don't have to accept the default Windows Explorer view of your files and folders. Sometimes a different view may be handier. You might want to see the files sorted in a different order, see more or less information, or maybe not even see certain types of files. You can choose the options that work best for you.

Exercise 8: Sorting files and folders

Have you ever tried to find something but weren't quite sure where to look? When you're looking for files on your PC, the problem can be even worse because you may not know the name of the file you're trying to find. Sorting the Windows Explorer file list may help you locate the file.

Follow these steps to change the Windows Explorer sort order:

1. Right-click the Start button and select Explore. If necessary, click the Views button and select Details.

2. Open the Command folder. By default, Windows Explorer sorts the file list alphabetically by name.

TIP

Regardless of the sort order you select, Windows Explorer adds new files to the end of the file listing unless you refresh the view. The quickest way to refresh the view is to press F5.

3. Select View ➢ Arrange Icons ➢ by Type to sort the file listing according to the file type as shown in the accompanying figure. This view is useful if you know what kind of file you're seeking but aren't sure of the name. Notice that Windows Explorer sorts the listing first by file type and then by name within each type.

4. Select View ➢ Arrange Icons ➢ by Size to sort the file listing according to the size of the files, as shown in the accompanying figure. This view is pretty handy when you're doing house cleaning on your hard disk. Scroll down to the bottom of the list to see which files are using the most space.

5. Select View ➤ Arrange Icons ➤ by Date to view the file listing sorted by their last creation or modification date. You can use this view to find files you've created most recently at the top of the listing, and files you haven't used for a long time at the bottom of the listing.

6. Select View ➤ Arrange Icons ➤ by Name to once again view the file listing sorted by filename. You can leave the Windows Explorer window open because you use it again in the following exercises.

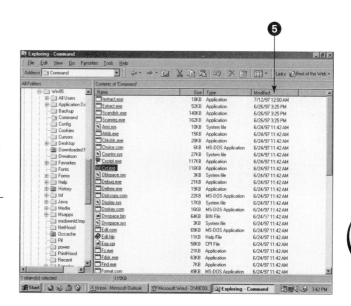

There's another way to sort the files in Windows Explorer even faster than selecting options from the View menu. In Windows 98 you can click the column title (Name, Size, Type, or Modified) to sort the files in ascending order by the selected column. Click the column title again to sort the view in descending order.

No matter which sort option you choose, the next time you start Windows Explorer, the view is once again by filename. Windows Explorer also reverts to the filename sort as you change to another folder.

Exercise 9: Changing the detail level

I'm the kind of person who likes to have as much information as possible, so I prefer the full-detail view in the Windows Explorer file listing. You may find all this information distracting, or you may just prefer to see icons instead of the file information. If you skip the file details, more files can be shown in the same space, and you don't have to use the scrollbars as often.

Follow these steps to change the level of details shown in the Windows Explorer window:

1. Click the down arrow to the right of the Views button, and choose Large Icons to change the file view to large icons as shown in the accompanying figure. This view uses file icons similar in size to those you see on your desktop.

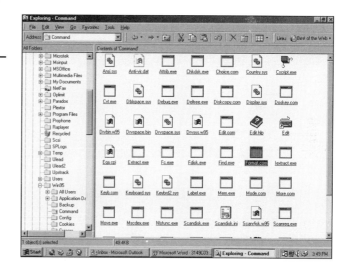

2. Click the down arrow to the right of the Views button and choose Small Icons to change the view to the smaller file icons you normally see in Windows Explorer. In this view the file icons are arranged across the top of the contents pane.

3. Click the down arrow to the right of the Views button and choose List to change the view once again. The list view uses the same small file icons as the small icon view, but it displays the files in columns rather than in rows.

4. Finally, click the down arrow to the right of the Views button and choose Details to return the listing to the full-detail view.

You can also use the View ➤ Large Icons, View ➤ Small Icons, View ➤ List, or View ➤ Details commands to change the level of detail, but I think clicking a button is easier and faster than using a menu command.

Exercise 10: Changing the width of panes and columns

You may be pleasantly surprised to discover that you aren't stuck with the sometimes crowded way Windows Explorer displays file listings. If you have deeply nested folders, for example, the folder pane may be too narrow to show all the folders. If your file names are quite long, the names may be cut off in the contents pane.

Follow these steps to adjust the width of panes and columns:

1. Make certain you have the Windows Explorer Details view showing on your screen, as shown in the accompanying figure.

2. Move the mouse pointer onto the separator between the folders pane and the contents pane. When the mouse pointer changes to a double-headed arrow, hold down the left mouse button and drag the separator left or right to adjust the width of the panes. The vertical gray line shows where the separator will appear when you release the button.

3. Drag the vertical bar between the Name and Size columns of the content pane left or right to adjust the width of the Name column. The vertical bar is at the top of the contents pane. You can adjust each column by dragging the bar at the right edge of the column.

❷ Drag right or left to change the width of the panes

❸ Drag to change the width of the columns

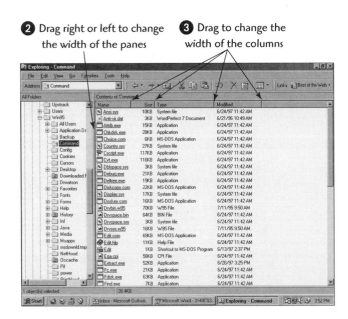

Double-click the vertical bar between columns in the contents pane to automatically size the column to fit the widest entry. For example, double-click the vertical bar between the Name and Size columns to resize the Name column to display the longest filename completely.

The best compromise is first to adjust the column widths just a little wider than necessary to view all the information in the columns and then adjust the width of the contents pane so all the file details are just visible. This makes the folders pane wide enough so you're able to see most nested folders without using the horizontal scrollbar at the bottom of the folders pane.

Exercise 11: Displaying or hiding different file types

The Windows Explorer file display can be a little overwhelming with all the different types of files it shows. Worse yet, many of the files you can see in Windows Explorer are needed by Windows 98; if you move or delete the wrong files, you may not be able to start Windows 98.

Follow these steps to protect yourself from the hazard of deleting important files accidentally and, at the same time, clean up your display:

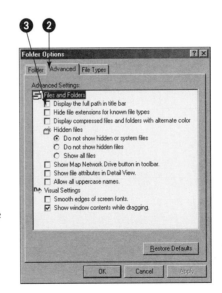

1. In the Windows Explorer, select View ➢ Folder Options to display the Folder Options dialog box shown in the accompanying figure.

2. Click the Advanced tab to display the dialog box shown in the accompanying figure.

3. Select Display the full path in the title bar if you want to see the complete path name to the selected folder rather than just the name of the folder. You may find this option especially useful if you're on a network and sometimes forget whether you've opened a local folder or one on the network.

4. Select the Hide file extensions for known file types if you don't want to see the three character file extensions. This only changes the filename display for file types that Windows 98 knows, such as text files and applications. If Windows 98 can't determine the file type from the extension, Windows Explorer still shows the file extension.

5. Click OK to confirm your changes and close the dialog box.

If you choose to hide some types of files rather than showing all file types, the Windows Explorer status line at the bottom of the Windows Explorer window tells you if a folder contains any hidden files that aren't being displayed. Be sure to look at the status line before you delete any folders that appear empty. If the folder contains hidden files, it's usually best to leave the folder alone—otherwise you run the risk of disabling some of your programs or even Windows 98 itself.

OPEN SESAME—STARTING PROGRAMS BY OPENING DOCUMENTS

In Windows 98 you can open most documents directly without opening a program first. By learning a few tricks you can make this feature even more useful. You can, for example, tell Windows 98 which program to use to open new file types, or tell Windows 98 to use a different program than it normally would to open certain types of files.

By now you've started programs by opening documents several times. You may well wonder how Windows 98 knows which program to use to open a document. The answer is the file extension—the one to three characters that follow a period at the end of the filename. When you install programs, the programs register the types of files they can open with Windows 98. For example, Microsoft Word registers the .doc extension for its document files, while Microsoft Excel registers the .xls extension for its spreadsheet files.

Once a file extension is registered, Windows 98 knows which application program to use to open any files with that extension. You can use this to your advantage by adding new file types or adjusting existing ones to suit your needs.

Exercise 12: Registering a new file type

Why would you want to register a new file type? I can give you an example from my experience showing one reason why I registered my own file type. A magazine publisher I sometimes write for wants authors to use their initials as the file extension on the document files they submit. In my case this means I use .bju as the file extension. But because Windows 98 doesn't have an application registered to open files with a .bju extension, I can't tell my word processor to automatically start and open my .bju files when I double-click those files. The solution is to register .bju files as a new file type, which is what you do in the following exercise.

Follow these steps to register a new file type:

1. Open Windows Explorer.

2. Select View ➢ Folder Options to display the Folder Options dialog box.

3. Click the File Types tab. This tab shows each of the registered file types and their associated applications.

4. Select New Type to display the Add New File Type dialog box. You use this dialog box to begin adding the new type.

5. Type the following text in the Description of type text box: **Magazine Article.**

6. Type the following text in the Associated extension text box: **bju.**

Your screen should now look like the figure on the right.

7. Click New to display the New Action dialog box.

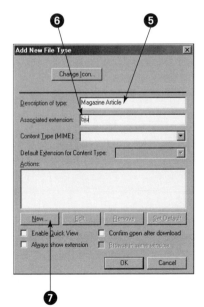

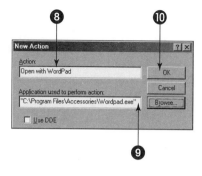

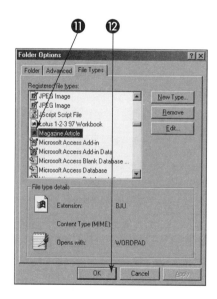

8. Type the following text in the Action text box: **Open with WordPad.**

9. Type the following text in the Application used to perform action text box: **"C:\Program Files\Accessories\Wordpad.exe".**

Your screen should now look like the figure on the left.

10. Click OK to close the New Action dialog box.

11. Click Close to close the Add New File Type dialog box. The Folder Options dialog box should now display your new registered file type.

12. Click OK to close the Folder Options dialog box.

Now that you've added the Magazine Article file type with the .bju file extension, all you need to do is double-click on any files with a .bju extension to open them in WordPad. (To see for yourself, open TheFox.bju, which is located in the Exercise folder on the CD-ROM that accompanies this book. Double-click to launch the file.) Of course, you probably want to use your own initials for the file extension. You can also create other file types that open with different applications. Just specify the correct application program in the New Action dialog box. If you don't know the correct command line necessary to start the program, use the Browse button to search for the program.

Exercise 13: Editing an existing file type

You may occasionally need to change the action associated with a registered file type. You might, for example, upgrade to a new word processor and want to use the new program to edit files with the .bju extension. Or perhaps you want the option to open the .bju files with either WordPad or your new word processor.

Follow these steps to edit an existing file type:

1. Open Windows Explorer.

2. Select View ➢ Folder Options.

3. Click the File Types tab.

4. Choose the file type you want to edit, in this case, Magazine Article.

5. Click Edit to display the Edit File Type dialog box.

6. To change the existing action, click Edit, correct the entry in the Application used to perform action text box, and then click OK.

7. To add an additional action, click New and fill in the Action text box and the Application used to perform action text box. Click OK (or Cancel if you didn't add an additional action).

8. Click OK twice more to close the dialog boxes.

If you have more than one action associated with a file type, you can select the action you prefer from the pop-up menu when you right-click the file in Windows Explorer.

USING THE TASK SCHEDULER

The Task Scheduler program helps you keep your Windows 98 system in good shape by performing some of the routine maintenance chores you may not perform as often as you should. Two examples of these chores are defragmenting your hard disk and checking your hard disk for errors. Both of these tasks are important in keeping your files safe and your system performance at an acceptable level, but both are also tasks people tend to forget about. In the following exercise you learn how to use the Task Scheduler to schedule these types of tasks.

Exercise 14: Viewing the Task Scheduler schedule

When you install the Windows 98 beta, certain events are automatically added to the Task Scheduler schedule. Depending on your personal schedule, you may want to adjust events on the Task Scheduler schedule to better suit your needs. In this exercise you learn how to view and adjust events that appear on the Task Scheduler schedule.

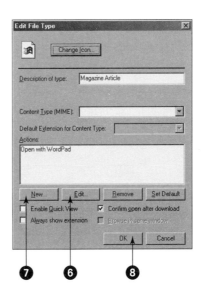

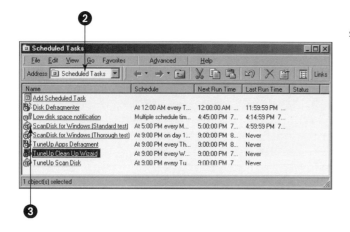

To view and adjust the Task Scheduler schedule, follow these steps:

1. Click the Start button.

2. Select Programs ➤ Accessories ➤ System Tools ➤ Scheduled Tasks to open the Task Scheduler's Scheduled Tasks folder. If you have items scheduled, you can also double-click the Task Scheduler icon on the Taskbar to open the Task Scheduler.

3. Double-click ScanDisk for Windows (Standard test) to display the Properties dialog box for this event, as shown in the accompanying figure.

4. Click the Schedule tab. This tab box provides the most important scheduling options for an event.

5. To change the time when the selected program is run, select one of the options in the Schedule Task list box. It's not a good idea to select Once, because the event will only run one time rather than at scheduled intervals. Likewise, the At System Startup option is generally a poor choice, too, because this would run events every time you started your PC rather than when you weren't using your system.

6. Type the time you want the event to begin in the Start time box.

7. Click the Settings tab.

8. Make certain the Only start the scheduled task if computer is idle for checkbox is selected. This ensures that the event won't disrupt your work if you happen to be using your PC when an event is scheduled to run.

9. Click OK to close the Change Schedule dialog box.

It's important to remember that the Task Scheduler can run scheduled events only if your PC is running. Modern PCs take very little power, especially if you turn off your monitor or use the screen saver options to power down your monitor automatically. If you prefer not to leave your PC running, you can schedule events for times when your system is on, such as during lunch.

NOTE *The Task Scheduler can cause problems for you if you use your PC for certain types of tasks, such as recording a CD-ROM. If you have a CD-R drive in your PC and intend to record a CD-ROM, open the Task Scheduler window and select Advanced ➤ Stop Using Task Scheduler, and then click Yes to remove the Task Scheduler before you attempt to record the CD-ROM. You can restart Task Scheduler by selecting Scheduled Task from the Programs ➤ Accessories ➤ System Tools menu.*

SKILLS CHALLENGE: MASTERING YOUR FILES

Here's a chance for you to practice what you've learned in this lesson.

1. Find all the text files with a .txt file extension on your hard drive.

 What is the one step you must always remember to do before saving a find files search if you want Windows 98 to remember any date specification you entered?

2. Select the first text file that has a filename that starts with M.

 What is the fastest way to find the first item that starts with W in the Windows Explorer contents pane?

3. Select all files between the currently selected file and the end of the list.

 How can you remove one item from a selection?

4. Move the newest text file to the desktop.

5. Delete the text file you just moved to the desktop.

6. Restore the text file you just deleted.

Problem	Solution
There are no buttons to click in my Windows Explorer window.	Select View ➢ Toolbar to display the buttons.
I can't find a folder called Windows.	Right-click the Start button and select Explore to open the Start Menu folder. Your Windows 98 folder is in the next column of dotted lines to the left of the column containing the Start Menu folder. The Windows folder is above the Start Menu folder.

7. View the Desktop folder, but change the sort order to show the files by date.

8. Add an action that opens a file with a .tmp extension using WordPad.

 How can you add an option to open the Text Document file type with WordPad in addition to keeping the default action?

WRAP UP

You've learned quite a bit about managing your files in this lesson. Not only did you learn how to find, copy, and move files and folders, but you also practiced with long filenames and saw how you can change the Windows Explorer view. You also learned how to teach Windows 98 a little about yourself, allowing you to use your own file extensions.

In the next lesson you play around with disks and see how to prepare disks for use. You also see how you can use disk compression to make more room for your files, how you can make your computer run a little faster, and how to back up your files.

Working with Disks

45 MINUTES

GOALS

Almost everything you do on your PC requires working with your disk drives. You can't save a file, load a program, or view a document without using your disks. Even though you've worked with disks a little in some of the earlier lessons, this lesson takes you beyond the basics to show you how to use your disks more effectively so you can store more information and get better performance at the same time. In this lesson you learn about the following topics:

- Formatting a floppy disk

- Copying a file to a disk

- Copying a disk

- Compressing files

- Improving disk performance

GET READY

To complete this lesson, you need at least two blank diskettes. It doesn't matter if the diskettes are empty, but any files on the diskettes will be destroyed. Don't use diskettes that contain any files you may need.

This lesson also uses several Windows 98 disk tools that may or may not already be installed on your PC: DriveSpace, Defrag, and ScanDisk. These tools are included in the Windows 98 beta and must be installed before you can complete this lesson. You can wait until you reach the point in the exercises where a tool is needed before worrying about whether each tool is installed. If a tool is missing, you can select the Add/Remove Programs icon in Control Panel and use the Disk Tools option on the Windows Setup tab to add any missing tools.

When you complete the exercises, you will have learned how to do the following: format a diskette, copy files to a diskette, copy a diskette, compress a drive and adjust the size of the free space on the compressed drive, convert your disks to the new FAT32 format, defragment your disks, use ScanDisk, and back up and restore your files.

 Working with disks can be hazardous to the health of your programs and data files. In this lesson you practice using some tools that can cause you to lose data or destroy your programs if you don't follow the directions carefully. To lessen the danger, the exercises use diskettes whenever possible. Please be careful not to substitute different drive letters for the ones shown in the exercises!

PREPARING TO USE YOUR DISKS

Disks are one of the few mechanical parts of your PC. Because disks are a mechanical component, they need a little preparation before they're ready to use. In the following exercises you learn the basics you need to know to use your disks.

Exercise 1: Formatting a diskette

If you've ever watched young children learning to print, you know that they need some help to get the job done. You may do quite well writing on blank paper, but young children need those lines on the paper if they are to have any hope of creating characters anyone else can understand. In many ways, your PC is similar to a young child— without some extra help your PC simply can't write anything useful on a disk.

The extra help your PC needs to be able to write on a disk is called *formatting*—the process of creating the electronic marks that allow your disk drives to write in the right places on a disk. When you format a disk, any existing information on the disk is wiped out. That's why you should never format a disk that contains data or program files you may need—you can't get the data or programs back after you format the disk!

TIP *You can often buy preformatted diskettes for about the same price as unformatted diskettes and save the time and trouble of formatting the diskettes yourself. If you buy preformatted diskettes, make certain they are formatted in IBM PC format.*

Here's how you can format a diskette:

1. Place a blank diskette in drive A. If you need to reuse a diskette you've already used, be certain you choose one that does not contain any important files—use Windows Explorer to verify this before you continue! Be sure to close Windows Explorer before you continue to Step 2.

2. Click the My Computer icon on your desktop to display the My Computer window, which should be similar to the window shown in the accompanying figure. Your My Computer window may not show as many objects as this figure, but it includes an icon for each of your disk drives, the Control Panel, and Printers.

⑤
Select formatted
capacity here

⑥ Select type of format

⑦ Enter a name
for the disk here

⑧ Select to skip
the disk label

⑨ Select to see
a summary report

⑩ Select to make
a boot disk

⑪

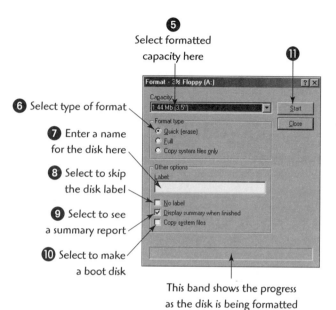

This band shows the progress
as the disk is being formatted

3. Right-click the icon for drive A. On my computer, drive A is listed as 3 1/2 Floppy (A:), which is probably the way it is shown on your computer, too. If your PC is a bit older, it's possible that your drive A is shown as 5 1/4 Floppy (A:).

4. Select Format from the pop-up menu that appears to display the Format dialog box shown in the accompanying figure. The Capacity list box may show a different size depending on the diskette you placed in drive A.

5. Verify that the correct diskette capacity shows in the Capacity list box. The most common sizes are 1.44MB or 720K for 3 1/2-inch diskettes, and 1.2MB or 360K for 5 1/4-inch diskettes. While 3 1/2-inch disk drives can automatically sense whether the diskette can be formatted at the greater 1.44MB capacity, 5 1/4-inch drives cannot automatically determine the diskette's capacity. Generally, you want to use the highest capacity supported by your drive.

6. Select the type of format to perform:

Full format takes the longest but has the advantage of checking the entire disk surface for any errors. If the diskette is unformatted, you can only select Full format. Always use Full format if you seem to be having problems with your diskettes. Select Full format for this exercise.

TIP

Choose Full format to verify whether a diskette has any errors before saving data you can't afford to lose. If formatting uncovers errors on the diskette, throw the diskette away rather than trust the diskette not to fail further.

Quick format simply erases any files that may already be on the disk by marking the entire diskette as available; it also doesn't check for errors. Quick format doesn't use any areas already marked as damaged, but it also doesn't find any new errors that may have appeared. Quick format is considerably faster than Full format.

Copy system files adds only the files necessary to create a *boot disk*—a disk you can use to start Windows 98—to a diskette that's already formatted. You seldom use this option.

7. Type the following text in the Label text box to name the diskette: **w98preview**. You can use up to 11 characters to name a disk, and Windows 98 automatically changes the label to all uppercase letters.

8. Make certain the No label checkbox is not selected. If you select this option, Windows 98 ignores any name you type in the Label text box.

9. Make certain the Display summary when finished checkbox is selected so you can see the summary report after the diskette has been formatted. This report shows the final formatted capacity of the diskette, and it tells you whether any errors were found. It's a good idea to discard diskettes that contain errors, because you can't be certain more errors won't occur later.

10. Select the Copy system files checkbox only if you want to make a boot disk. Boot disks have less room available for your files because part of the space is used up by the system files.

11. Click Start to begin formatting the diskette. The progress band at the bottom of the dialog box shows how far along the format is at any time during the format. When the format is complete, the Format Results dialog box shows you a summary of the format process.

12. Click Close to return to the Format dialog box. Click Close to return to the My Computer window, and click the Close button to close My Computer.

Although a full format is a little safer because the diskette is checked for errors, quick formats are useful, too. A quick format is the fastest way to erase any files and folders on a diskette, especially if the diskette contains a large number of files and folders.

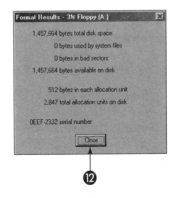

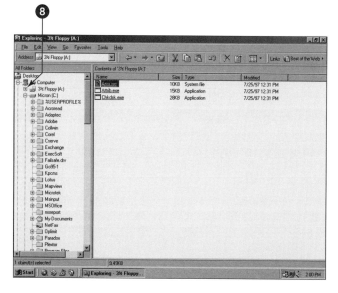

Exercise 2: Copying files to a diskette

Now that your diskette has been formatted, it's ready to use. There are several different methods you can use to copy files to diskettes, and in this exercise you try a few of them.

Follow these steps to copy files to a diskette:

1. Make certain your newly formatted diskette is in drive A.

2. Right-click the Start button and select Explore.

3. Choose the Command folder by clicking it to open the folder and display its contents in the contents pane.

4. Right-click Ansi.sys and select Send To ➢ 3 1/2 Floppy (A) (if your A drive is a 5¹/₄-inch drive, select 5 1/4 Floppy (A)) to copy the file to drive A.

5. Right-click Attrib.exe and select Copy.

6. Right-click drive A in the folders pane and select Paste to copy Attrib.exe to drive A.

7. Point to Chkdsk.exe in the contents pane, hold down the left mouse button, and drag the file to drive A. When the mouse pointer changes from a shortcut arrow to a plus sign, release the mouse button to copy the file.

8. Click the icon for drive A in the folders pane to display the contents of drive A. The three files you just copied should appear in the contents pane.

Each of the three methods of copying a file works quite well, and you can choose the method that seems the most comfortable. You aren't limited to copying a single file at a time, either. You may notice, however, that the drag-and-drop method can be a little tricky, especially if you're copying a number of files at the same time. It can be difficult to drop the files in the correct location. If you make a mistake, choose Edit ➢ Undo Copy immediately—you can only undo the copy if you do so before you copy or move any more files.

Exercise 3: Copying a diskette

Even though the 3 1/2-inch diskettes, which are most commonly used in PCs today, are much more rugged than the older 5 1/4-inch diskettes, it's still possible to damage or lose a diskette. Needless to say, the one diskette you do manage to destroy will be the one containing your only copy of some important file. Backup copies of your important diskettes provide some of the best insurance against disaster, especially when you can quickly and easily make those copies.

NOTE *Some diskettes you cannot easily copy. The diskettes Microsoft uses to distribute software, for example, are specially formatted to prevent you from copying all except disk 1. This special format, DMF—Distribution Media Format—can only be copied using special tools that are not part of Windows 98. A shareware program called Winimage is designed to copy DMF formatted diskettes, but the program can be tricky to use and may not work on all PCs.*

When you copy diskettes, you'll probably have to use the same disk drive to read the original disk, or *source* disk, and write to the disk, or *destination* disk. It's extremely important to make certain you insert the correct diskette when you change disks. If you don't watch carefully, you can lose the files you're trying to copy.

TIP *You can only copy a diskette to another diskette of the same size.*

Here's how to copy a diskette:

1. Turn over the source diskette so you can see the little plastic *write-protect* slider. Move the slider toward the edge of the diskette so you can see through the hole. This prevents your PC from writing anything on this diskette until you move the slider back to cover the hole. (If you're copying a 5 1/4-inch diskette, place a piece of dark tape over the notch in the side of the diskette to write-protect the diskette.)

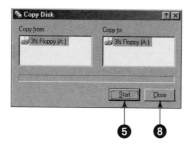

2. Place the source diskette in drive A.

3. Open Windows Explorer if it is not already open.

4. Right-click drive A and select Copy Disk from the pop-up menu to display the Copy Disk dialog box. Unless you have two identical diskette drives, the Copy from and Copy to drives are the same. If you have two diskette drives, make certain the correct drive is selected.

5. Click Start to begin the copy.

6. When the source diskette has been completely read, Windows 98 displays the Copy Disk message. When you see this message, remove your source diskette from drive A and insert the destination diskette.

7. Click OK to continue.

8. After the copy is complete, click Close to return to Windows Explorer.

9. Remove the diskette copy from drive A. Be sure to mark the diskette label so you know what is on the diskette.

Don't forget that you moved the slider to write protect the source diskette. If you need to place additional files on the source diskette or change any of the files already on the source diskette, you need to move the slider back to the closed position to allow writing on the diskette.

MAKING MORE ROOM AT THE INN

It seems like there's never enough room for everything. That huge hard disk that came inside your PC can look pretty small after you start loading your favorite programs, can't it? Fortunately, Windows 98 includes DriveSpace, a tool that can help create more free space on your disks by compressing your files into less space. If you've ever ridden a subway train at rush hour, you probably already know about how compression can fit more people into less space—everyone just gets packed a bit tighter together so there's room for more people in each car.

TIP

Windows 98 DriveSpace disk compression isn't compatible with other operating systems such as Windows NT, OS/2, or UNIX. If your PC sometimes has to run another operating system in addition to Windows 98, then don't use DriveSpace to compress your hard disks—the other operating system won't be able to access the hard drive. You can follow along with the DriveSpace exercises even if you don't want to use DriveSpace on your hard disk because the exercises use diskettes rather than your hard drive.

TIP

Windows 98 beta introduces a new disk format called FAT32 that more efficiently uses the available space on disk drives larger than 512MB. Unfortunately, FAT32 and DriveSpace are not compatible—you can choose to use either FAT32 or DriveSpace, but you can't choose both. How do you decide whether to use FAT32 or DriveSpace? The answer isn't always easy to determine, but here are some guidelines you can use:

- If your hard disk is larger than 2GB, and you want to use the entire disk as a single drive, your only choice is FAT32. No other format enables you to have more than 2GB on one drive letter.

- If your hard disk is smaller than 512MB, FAT32 offers no advantage. DriveSpace is the only way to increase the efficiency of disk space usage on drives under 512MB.

- If you store many compressed files, such as ZIP files, on your hard drive, then use FAT32 because DriveSpace cannot compress files that are already compressed.

- If you need to dual boot your system so you can run another operating system, don't use DriveSpace or FAT32—neither one is currently compatible with other operating systems. There are indications that Windows NT 5 may support FAT32, but there's no guarantee until Windows NT 5 is actually released.

- Both DriveSpace and FAT32 can cause slight performance losses, although you probably won't notice the difference.

See Exercise 8 for more information on FAT32.

4

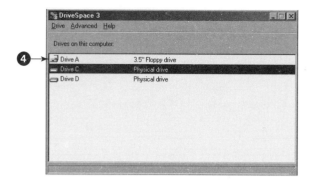

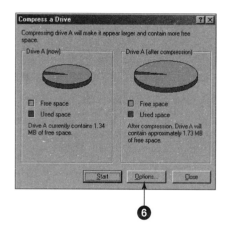

Exercise 4: Compressing a drive with DriveSpace

In this exercise you use DriveSpace to compress a diskette, resulting in more free space for storing additional files. After you compress the diskette, you can only use the diskette on a PC running Windows 95 or Windows 98 beta and that has DriveSpace loaded. You can use the same diskette you used as the destination diskette in the last exercise.

Follow these steps to compress a disk using DriveSpace:

1. Place the diskette you want to compress in drive A.

2. Click the Start button.

3. Select Programs ➢ Accessories ➢ System Tools ➢ DriveSpace to display the DriveSpace dialog box. This dialog box shows each disk drive on your system, so you may have slightly different options than in the figure in the upper left.

4. Choose the icon for drive A to select the drive.

5. Select Drive ➢ Compress to display the Compress a Drive dialog box. This dialog box shows the current status of the drive and an estimate of how much room will be available after the drive is compressed.

6. Click Options to display the Compression Options dialog box. Normally you want to accept the default settings, but you can change the drive letter of the host drive or the amount of free space left on the host drive, if necessary. (Windows 98 creates a *host* drive for each compressed drive—this is the drive letter used to access the physical rather than the compressed drive. But you don't really need to worry about host drives.)

7. Click OK to continue. You may see a caution message, but because you're only compressing a diskette and not a hard drive, you can click OK to continue.

If you want to compress a large hard disk that contains many files, plan to start the process at a time when you can let DriveSpace work by itself, such as during lunch or at night when you don't need to use your system.

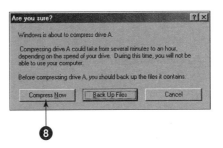

8. Compressing a disk can take a long time, so Windows 98 warns you with a message similar to the one shown in the accompanying figure. It's much faster to compress disks that don't already contain many files. Click Compress Now to continue.

9. After DriveSpace has compressed the drive, the Compress a Drive dialog box reappears and shows more accurate information than the earlier estimate. In the accompanying figure, DriveSpace reports that the diskette now has almost twice the free space it had before it was compressed. Click Close to return to the DriveSpace dialog box.

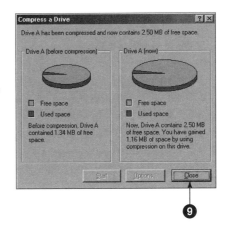

The DriveSpace dialog box includes a new drive, the host drive for drive A. You don't need to worry about the host drive, though, because all your files are on drive A, the compressed drive.

The free space that DriveSpace reports as available on a compressed drive can be a little confusing. While it's true you can store more files on a compressed drive, different types of files compress differently. As a result, you may not be able to store quite as much on a compressed disk as it would appear by looking at the available free space. The bottom line is that the only way you know for sure how much you can add to a disk is to try copying the files to the compressed drive—if you don't get an out of disk space message, you're in luck!

Exercise 5: Adjusting the size of the free space on a compressed drive

DriveSpace creates additional space on a disk by storing the files in a special file called a *compressed volume file,* or CVF. The files stored in the CVF are compressed and are accessible only after DriveSpace is loaded into memory. This means that Windows 98 has to be able to read some system files — notably the DriveSpace program files — before it can read the compressed files. These important system files must be stored as normal files, not compressed files, which means they must be stored on an uncompressed drive. That's the point of having a host drive for a compressed drive. The host drive contains both the compressed volume file and any system files needed to access DriveSpace volumes. Any space reserved for system files on the host drive reduces the available free space on the compressed drive.

The system files needed to start your PC and read compressed disks take up much more room than is available on a diskette and are normally stored on your hard disk. When you compress a diskette, you usually use all the available space for the CVF, because there's generally no reason to leave part of the diskette uncompressed (the files necessary to read a compressed disk generally already reside on your hard disk). However, because you're compressing a diskette rather than your hard disk for these exercises, you need to adjust the free space on your compressed diskette. If you later compress your hard disk, you can use the same methods to adjust the free space on it, too.

There are actually two different ways to adjust the apparent free space on a compressed disk. The first, which I just mentioned, changes the allocation of the space on the host drive so the CVF uses more or less of the physical space. The second method doesn't actually change the amount of space that is available, but it does change the estimate of the extent to which files can be compressed when they're stored on the compressed drive. Because some files can be compressed more than others, changing the estimated compression ratio is more an art than a science, but it's an option you get to practice in this exercise.

Follow these steps to adjust the free space on a compressed disk:

1. Place the compressed diskette in drive A.

2. Click the Start button.

3. Select Programs ➤ Accessories ➤ System Tools ➤ DriveSpace to display the DriveSpace dialog box.

4. Choose the icon for drive A.

5. Select Drive ➤ Adjust Free Space to display the Adjust Free Space dialog box shown in the accompanying figure.

6. You can enter an exact value in either the compressed drive or the host drive free space text box, or you can drag the slider right or left to adjust the ratio between the compressed and uncompressed space. In this case, drag the slider to the right until the host drive shows 0.30MB free space. Notice that as you increase the free space on the host drive, the free space on the compressed drive decreases.

7. Click OK to tell DriveSpace to change the ratio of free space. You have to wait a few minutes while DriveSpace completes the adjustment.

8. When DriveSpace finishes the adjustment, you see a message that lets you know the operation is complete. Click OK to return to the DriveSpace dialog box.

9. Select Advanced ➤ Change Ratio to display the Compression Ratio dialog box. In this case the dialog box shows that the files currently on the diskette are actually compressed at a 3.0 to 1 ratio.

10. Drag the slider to the far right side of the scale to make the estimated compression ratio 64.0 to 1. Although it's highly unlikely for you to see an actual compression ratio this high, DriveSpace doesn't care if you want to fool yourself into thinking there's more free space available than is reasonable.

11. Click OK to adjust the estimated compression ratio. When DriveSpace completes the adjustment, you see a message similar to the message shown in the figure on the left. Click OK to return to the DriveSpace dialog box.

12. Double-click the drive A icon to display the Compression Properties dialog box. Because you changed the estimated compression ratio to 64.0 to 1, DriveSpace now reports that the diskette has 62.0MB of free space.

6 You can enter exact values here

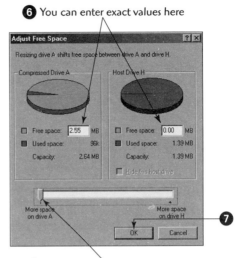

6 Drag slider to adjust free space

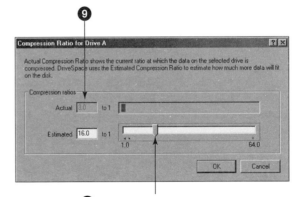

10 Drag the slider to change the
Estimated Compression Ratio

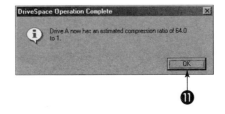

13. Click OK to close the Compression Properties dialog box, and then click the Close button to close the DriveSpace dialog box.

As you can probably imagine, the DriveSpace report of 62MB of free space on the compressed diskette bears little relationship to reality. If you start copying files to the diskette, you'll run out of disk space long before you come close to adding 62MB of files. It's much safer to assume that DriveSpace was correct in estimating that the actual compression ratio would be close to 3 to 1.

Windows 98 automatically recognizes when a diskette or a hard disk has been compressed with DriveSpace, and it loads the appropriate software to read the compressed files. If none of your hard disks are compressed and you have finished removing the compression from a compressed diskette, Windows 98 gives you the option of deleting DriveSpace from memory. It's a good idea to allow Windows 98 to remove DriveSpace when it isn't needed to free up memory so your programs can run faster. Windows 98 reloads DriveSpace if it's needed at a later time.

Exercise 6: Adjusting compression properties

When you compress a disk for the first time, the level of compression DriveSpace uses is a compromise between performance and the amount of space saved. DriveSpace can, however, squeeze out more room by compressing files even tighter.

DriveSpace has three levels of compression. In addition to the standard compression, DriveSpace can perform HiPack compression and UltraPack compression. *HiPack* compression generally reduces files to a smaller size than standard compression, and *UltraPack* compression can make files even smaller.

In this exercise you learn how to adjust the DriveSpace settings to control whether DriveSpace uses standard or HiPack compression during normal operations. In the next exercise you learn how to apply UltraPack compression using the Compression Agent.

To specify the type of compression DriveSpace uses to store your files, follow these steps:

1. Click the Start button.

2. Select Programs ➢ Accessories ➢ System Tools ➢ DriveSpace.

3. Select the drive and then click Advanced ➢ Settings to display the Disk Compression Settings dialog box.

4. To compress your files to the smallest size, select the HiPack compression radio button. The remaining compression method options are generally not good choices unless you have a very slow system.

5. Make certain the Automatically mount new compressed drives checkbox is selected so that Windows 98 automatically recognizes compressed diskettes.

6. Click OK to close the Disk Compression Settings dialog box.

7. Click the Close button to close the DriveSpace window.

HiPack compression is generally much more efficient than standard compression and may give you as much as 15 to 20 percent more free disk space than if you use standard compression. You can use the DriveSpace Disk Compression Settings dialog box to switch between the two types of compression and determine whether your system experiences any performance degradation when you choose HiPack rather than standard compression.

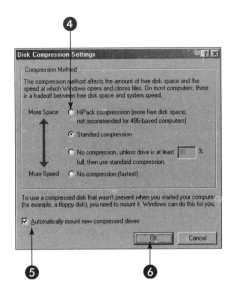

Exercise 7: Using the Compression Agent

The Compression Agent is a special DriveSpace utility that can compress your files even more than DriveSpace alone. The Compression Agent can compress files you don't use often using the UltraPack compression format. Although DriveSpace can't compress files using the UltraPack compression format, it has no problem reading files compressed using the UltraPack compression format.

TIP

Because you can add the Compression Agent as a scheduled task, you can have the best of both worlds in disk compression. You can achieve highest performance by telling DriveSpace not to compress your files when you save them to your hard disk, but you can still have the largest amount of free disk space by having the Compression Agent compress your files to their smallest possible size.

4

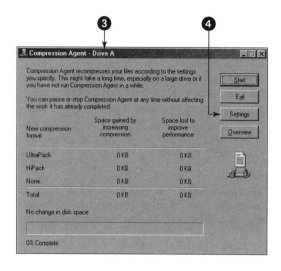

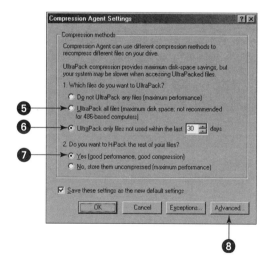

The Compression Agent only runs if you have a DriveSpace compressed disk. You can use a DriveSpace compressed diskette or use the Compression Agent to compress the files on a compressed hard disk. In this exercise the figures show the results of using the Compression Agent on a compressed diskette—you may want to use a compressed diskette until you're comfortable using DriveSpace and the Compression Agent.

To use the Compression Agent to compress files, follow these steps:

1. Click the Start button.

2. Select Programs ➢ Accessories ➢ System Tools ➢ Compression Agent.

3. If necessary, choose the compressed disk you want to use for this exercise. The accompanying figure shows the Compression Agent window when compressed drive A is chosen.

4. Select Settings to display the Compression Agent Settings dialog box.

5. For maximum free disk space, make certain the UltraPack all files radio button is selected. When you choose this option, the Compression Agent uses the highest level of compression on all files. Because DriveSpace cannot save files using UltraPack compression, any new or modified files are saved using the DriveSpace compression settings.

6. As a compromise between performance and disk space, you may want to select UltraPack only files not used within the last *X* days. This compresses the files you use the least using UltraPack compression format.

7. If you selected UltraPack only files not used within the last *X* days, make certain the Yes radio button is selected so that any remaining files are compressed using the HiPack compression format.

8. Click the Advanced button to display the Advanced Settings dialog box.

9. To prevent the Compression Agent from reducing the amount of free disk space below an acceptable level, use the up and down arrows to set the amount of free disk space in the spin box. You may also want to select the Leave all UltraPacked files in UltraPack format checkbox. Because DriveSpace automatically converts UltraPacked files to another format if the files are modified, you probably don't want the Compression Agent to change any of these files.

10. Click OK to return to the Compression Agent window.

11. Click Start to begin changing the compression formats. When the Compression Agent finishes, you see a screen similar to the screen shown in the accompanying figure. In this case, changing from standard compression to UltraPack compression increased the free disk space by 98K.

12. Click Exit to close the Compression Agent window.

If you schedule the Compression Agent as a scheduled event after you've selected your desired Compression Agent settings, you probably won't run the Compression Agent manually again. You can run Compression Agent any time you want to adjust the compression settings—by default, any changes you make are stored as the settings that Compression Agent uses until you make further changes. Of course, you wouldn't want to make Compression Agent a scheduled event if the only disk you've compressed is a diskette—you'd have to leave the same diskette in the drive all the time.

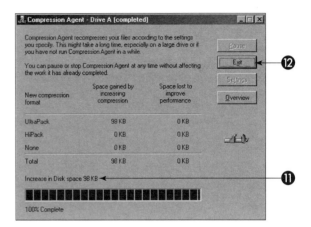

Exercise 8: Using FAT32

Since the introduction of the original IBM PC, a *File Allocation Table*, or FAT, has mostly been used to track and control the allocation of space on disk drives (Windows NT and IBM's unpopular OS/2 both offer additional options, but the majority of PCs use a FAT). When Microsoft originally created MS-DOS, hard disks were rare, and those which did exist were generally limited to 5 to 10MB. Early versions of MS-DOS included support only for hard disks up to 32MB, while later versions allowed for larger sizes by increasing the minimum amount of space allocated to each file. Unfortunately, these larger allocation units tended to waste a lot of disk space because even the smallest file needed a complete allocation unit. A one byte file could take 32KB of disk space!

Still, until the introduction of FAT32, the maximum size of a drive was limited to 2GB. As PCs become more powerful and users play around with multimedia, combining video and sound, 2GB starts looking smaller every day. FAT32 overcomes this limitation by replacing the old File Allocation Table structure with a new method of allocating disk space. With FAT32, disk space allocation is much more efficient, the 2GB limit on the size of disks is removed, and you can store many more files in the same amount of space because the allocation units are so much smaller. In fact, a one byte file on a FAT32 disk would take 4KB of space—one eighth the space needed under the old FAT system.

NOTE *If your PC has the Windows 98 beta installed, or if it was built during 1997 and came installed with Windows 95, there's a chance FAT32 may already be installed on your system. To check, open My Computer, right-click on the icon for drive C, and select Properties. You'll see an item on the General tab marked "File system." If this says FAT32 rather than FAT, then the drive is already formatted in FAT32 format.*

You can convert your hard disks to FAT32 using the FAT32 Converter tool that comes with the Windows 98 beta. However, keep in mind the following limitations:

- The FAT32 Converter is a one-way tool. You can convert to FAT32, but you cannot reverse the process without destroying all the data on your hard drive.

- You cannot convert a compressed disk to FAT32. DriveSpace and FAT32 are not compatible, so you can choose one but not both.

- If you convert a disk to FAT32, you will not be able to load any other operating system, such as Windows NT.

- FAT32 is intended for drives over 512MB and offers no benefit for smaller drives.

To use the FAT32 Converter to convert your hard drive to FAT32, follow these steps:

1. Click the Start button.

2. Select Programs ➢ Accessories ➢ System Tools ➢ FAT32 Converter to display the FAT32 Converter Wizard.

3. Click Next to continue. You'll see a warning similar to the figure at the bottom right.

4. Click Next to continue. A dialog box appears saying that the FAT32 Converter must reboot your system. Before you continue, close all other programs and save your work.

5. Click Next to continue. You won't be able to use your system until the conversion is completed.

After you've completed the conversion to FAT32, you won't really notice much difference in the way your system operates. You may notice additional free space on your hard disk, but all file-related operations should operate normally.

IMPROVING DISK PERFORMANCE

You may not realize it, but one of the best ways to speed up your computer is to improve the performance of your disk drives. Your disk drives are mechanical components and are much slower than the electronic components that make up most of your system. Even a small improvement in the performance of your disk drives can make a big difference in the overall performance of your whole PC.

Because disk performance can make such a difference, Windows 98 includes the tools you need to correct any problems that may be slowing down your disk drives. In the following exercises you learn how you can make your computer perform a little better by using these tools.

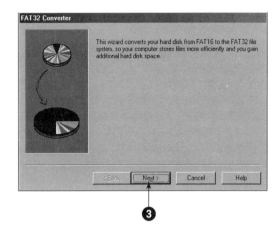

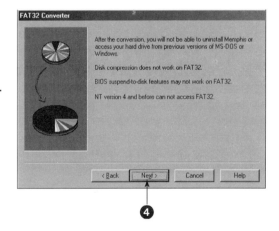

Exercise 9: Improving performance by defragmenting your disks

The more you use your PC, the more your files become *fragmented* — stored in several noncontiguous pieces on your disks. To understand why this happens, imagine that you and a group of your friends want to go to your favorite bookstore to look for the latest books from IDG Books Worldwide. There are too many of you to fit in one car, so you drive off together in six different cars. If you go early in the morning so that you arrive just when the mall opens, you might be able to park your cars together in adjacent parking spots. But if you go later in the afternoon when quite a few people have already gone shopping, you'll probably end up parking at various points around the parking garage because you can't find six spots together.

When you save files on your disks, Windows 98 encounters a similar situation to the parking garage — there's room for the first files you save to be placed in contiguous blocks, but as you delete and save more files, there may not be room to store all the pieces of some files in adjacent blocks. Sure, the small files that need only a single block are okay, but larger files have to be broken up into several pieces — fragmented — in order to find room for them to park on your hard drive.

It takes longer to store and to read fragmented files. Rather than reading or writing a complete file in one motion, your disk drive has to jump around to locate all the pieces of a fragmented file. As fragmentation becomes worse, any disk operations may seem to take forever. If it seems like it takes longer to open programs or to save documents than it used to, disk fragmentation may well be the culprit.

TIP

Anything that writes to your disk drives can cause Windows 98 to start the disk defragmentation process all over again. Ultimately you save yourself a lot of time and frustration if you make certain no other programs are running while you defragment your disk drives.

Defragmenting a large hard disk can take quite a bit of time. In this exercise you practice by defragmenting a diskette, which takes less time.

Follow these steps to defragment a diskette:

1. Double-click the My Computer icon on your desktop.

2. Insert a diskette into drive A. This diskette should be one you've used so that it contains some files. If necessary, copy some files to the diskette — it doesn't matter which files are on the diskette.

3. Right-click the drive A icon and select Properties from the pop-up menu to display the Properties dialog box.

4. Click the Tools tab to see the available disk tools.

5. Click Defragment Now and wait while Windows 98 checks the fragmentation status of the disk. In the accompanying figure, Windows 98 has determined that the disk performance will be improved by defragmenting the disk.

6. Click Start to begin defragmenting the diskette. While you're defragmenting a diskette, the dialog box shows the progress of the defragmentation process. The progress is usually slow but steady. When you defragment a hard disk, you may notice that Windows 98 starts the process over from the beginning one or more times. This is your clue that some other program you're running is interfering with the defragmentation, and you should exit from the other program unless you really like to waste a lot of time.

7. When you see the message telling you the defragmentation is complete, click Yes.

Don't be fooled by the relatively short amount of time it takes to defragment a diskette. It can take quite a bit of time to defragment a large hard disk, especially one that is quite full. Still, if you schedule defragmentation for times when you don't need to use your PC, you improve the performance enough to make up for the time required to defragment your disks.

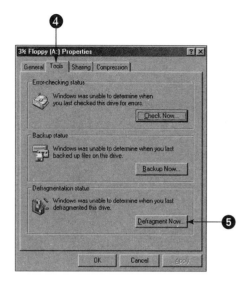

Exercise 10: Using ScanDisk to check for damage

I almost hate to tell you this, but your PC and your files may be damaged. I don't want to scare you, but you may have problems right now and not know about them. Parts of files may be lost, your hard disk may be defective, or pieces of old files may be eating up space without serving any useful purpose. It doesn't sound too good, does it? Fortunately for you, the Windows 98 beta has just the tool to find and correct most of these types of problems. ScanDisk, the subject of this exercise, comes to your rescue.

ScanDisk serves as a replacement for CHKDSK, a disk repair tool found in earlier versions of MS-DOS. CHKDSK still exists in the Windows 98 beta, but ScanDisk does a much better job of finding and correcting errors.

Disk errors fall into two general categories: physical errors and file errors. Physical errors are problems with the surface of the disk that make particular areas on the disk unreliable for storing data. File errors are problems stemming from errors in allocating disk space, making it possible for two files to try to use the same space, part of a file to be lost, or space not being released when a file is deleted.

Always use the Shut Down option on the Start menu before you turn off your PC. Skipping this step is the surest way to cause file errors.

For this exercise you can use the same diskette you used in the last exercise. Here, too, the procedure is the same whether you work with a diskette or a hard disk, but the exercise goes much faster if you practice on a diskette.

To use ScanDisk, follow these steps:

1. Make certain the Tools tab of the 3 1/2 Floppy (A:) Properties dialog box is on-screen. If you closed the dialog box after the last exercise, double-click the My Computer icon, right-click the drive A icon, select Properties from the pop-up menu, and click the Tools tab.

2. Click Check Now to display the ScanDisk dialog box. Because ScanDisk can take a long time to perform its tests, you can choose more than one drive to test.

3. Click Advanced to display the ScanDisk Advanced Options dialog box. You may want to make several changes to the default settings.

4. Select the Only if errors found radio button so ScanDisk only shows you a report if there were errors on the disk. This setting allows ScanDisk to continue on to the next selected disk without stopping.

5. Select the Replace log radio button if it is not selected to make ScanDisk create a text file (Scandisk.log) in the root folder. You can use this file to determine which errors were corrected.

6. Select the Make copies radio button if it is not selected so ScanDisk makes copies of any files that appear to be sharing the same disk space. If ScanDisk finds *cross-linked* files, you can examine Scandisk.log to see which files were cross-linked. One of each pair of cross-linked files is probably okay, while the other is likely to be unusable.

7. Select the Free radio button to free up the space occupied by *lost file fragments* — left-over pieces of files taking up space, even though the file was supposed to be deleted.

8. Make certain the Invalid file names and Invalid dates and times checkboxes are selected. You want to make certain ScanDisk finds and corrects all possible errors.

9. Make certain the Check host drive first checkbox is selected. If you have any disks compressed with DriveSpace, ScanDisk checks both the compressed and the host drive for errors.

10. Click OK to return to the ScanDisk dialog box.

11. Select the Thorough radio button to tell ScanDisk to look for physical errors on the disk surface as well as file system errors. The test takes much longer when ScanDisk examines the disk for physical errors, but the extra time may prevent your PC from writing data to a place on a disk that it can't read later.

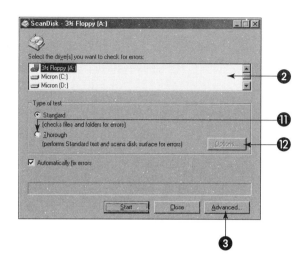

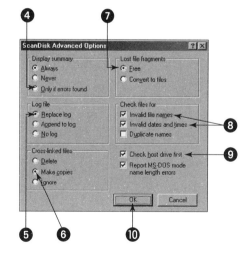

12. Click Options to display the Surface Scan Options dialog box.

13. Make certain the System and data areas radio button is selected so that ScanDisk examines the entire surface of the disk for errors. You don't want to take a chance that either area has a bad spot that isn't detected.

14. Do not select the Do not perform write-testing checkbox. If you select this option, ScanDisk only reads the data and does not write to the disk. It's better to find out now whether any spots are failing on your disks than to wait until your system unsuccessfully tries to write data later.

15. Do not select the Do not repair bad sectors in hidden and system files checkbox unless you're using old copy-protected software. A long time ago certain software manufacturers used a bizarre method of copy protection that required certain hidden or system files to be located at a specific place on a disk. You're better off allowing ScanDisk to correct any errors than worrying about whether this may cause a problem.

16. Click OK to continue.

17. Make certain the Automatically fix errors checkbox is selected. Otherwise, as the testing proceeds, you may see error messages similar to the messages shown in the accompanying figure, and you have to respond to each error as it is found.

18. Click Start to begin the disk scan, and then sit back and wait. When you use ScanDisk to test a large hard disk, be prepared to wait a long time.

19. If any errors were found (or if you selected the Always display summary radio button), ScanDisk may show you a report. Click Close when you're finished examining the report.

20. Click Close to close the ScanDisk dialog box.

If you're lucky, ScanDisk won't find any errors on your disks. If it does find errors, you should consider yourself lucky, too, because ScanDisk probably found the errors before they became a problem for you or your data.

TIP *If ScanDisk finds bad sectors on a diskette, copy the files to another diskette as soon as possible and then discard the diskette containing the bad sectors. This type of error on a diskette can easily get worse, and* continued use of a diskette with bad sectors can damage your disk drive.

SKILLS CHALLENGE: MASTERING YOUR DISK DRIVES

Now you can practice some of what you've learned in this chapter to see how much you remember.

1. Format a diskette.

 What format option can you use to make certain a diskette doesn't contain any bad sectors?

 What can you do to prevent a diskette from being formatted and destroying any data it contains?

2. Copy a file to drive A.

 How can you copy a file on your desktop to a diskette without using Windows Explorer?

3. Compress drive A using DriveSpace.

4. Change the estimated compression ratio of the diskette to 3.0 to 1.

5. Change the free space on drive A's host drive to 1MB.

 How can you specify an exact amount of free space rather than a percentage?

6. Check to see whether drive A needs to be defragmented.

7. Check for errors on Drive A.

Problem	Solution
I see an error message telling me the disk is write-protected when I try to format a diskette.	If the diskette is a 3 1/2-inch diskette (the most common size), turn the diskette over and look for a small plastic slider. The slider must be slid toward the center of the diskette to cover the opening. If the diskette is a 5 1/4-inch diskette, make certain the notch along the side of the diskette isn't covered with a piece of tape.
DriveSpace doesn't appear on the Windows 98 menu.	You need to install DriveSpace using the Add/Remove Programs icon in the Control Panel. Click the Windows Setup tab, choose Disk Tools ➤ Details, and make certain DriveSpace is checked (you don't see the DriveSpace option after DriveSpace is installed). Click Apply to install DriveSpace.

 What setting checks for file-system errors without doing a surface scan?

 How can you specify that you want to check all of your disk drives for errors in one operation?

 What setting is necessary to keep ScanDisk from stopping and showing a summary report if there are no errors?

WRAP UP

You can't work with your PC without using your disk drives. In these exercises you learned a number of important things about using your disks, from preparing your diskettes for use, to making more room, to improving performance, and finally doing backups of your data. You learned that backing up and restoring your data is a lot easier than most PC users realize.

The next lesson shows you how to make your PC come alive with sound and video. You can have fun playing with some of the advanced capabilities built into today's PCs.

Lights, Action, Multimedia!

GOALS

Nothing adds to the fun of using your PC as much as the multimedia capabilities built into virtually all modern systems. Although most PCs have sound and video capabilities built in, making those capabilities work properly can be difficult. This lesson helps you learn how to use the multimedia features in your PC and how to make your PC a more lively companion. This lesson covers the following topics:

- Using your PC's sound capabilities

- Viewing video on your PC

- Using the Imaging utility

- Configuring multimedia for performance

GET READY

To complete this lesson you need a multimedia PC—one with a sound card, speakers, a CD-ROM drive, and a VGA- or higher-level monitor. You also need the *Presenting Windows 98 One Step at a Time* CD-ROM, because some of the exercises use multimedia samples included on the CD-ROM. To record sounds with the Sound Recorder, you need a microphone attached to your PC's sound card. If you don't have a microphone, you can still try out most of the features of Sound Recorder. You also need a regular audio CD to complete Exercise 6, "Using the CD Player." The TV Viewer requires a special video board to display TV programs on your PC screen, but you can download and view the TV listings on any PC as long as you have an Internet connection.

If you don't have the beta version of Windows 98, you can find many of the extras on the Internet at http://www.microsoft.com/ msdownload/.

You may notice a few small differences between some of the dialog boxes pictured in this lesson and what appears on your screen. Audio and video board manufacturers sometimes add their own unique features, or in some cases may even replace the standard Windows 98 dialog boxes with their own variations. Even if this is the case on your system, you should be able to complete the lesson by looking for options similar to those shown in the figures.

The *Presenting Windows 98 One Step at a Time* CD-ROM contains a sound file that you will use in some of the exercises in this lesson. You may want to copy this file from the CD-ROM to your hard disk to make it more convenient to use the sound—for example, to attach the sound to events.

If you want to copy the sound files to your hard disk before you begin the exercises, follow these steps:

1. Insert the CD-ROM that accompanies this book into your CD-ROM drive.

2. Start Windows Explorer and open the \Windows\Media folder.

3. Select Tools ➢ Find ➢ Files or Folders.

4. Type this text in the Named text box: ***.wav.**

5. Click the down arrow at the right side of the Look in list box, and then select the icon for your CD-ROM drive (this is probably D, depending on how many hard disks you have installed).

6. Click Find Now to begin the search.

7. When the search is complete, press Ctrl+A to select the sound files in the Exercise folder.

8. Point to the selected files in the Find dialog box, hold down the left mouse button, and drag the files to the \Windows\Media folder in Windows Explorer.

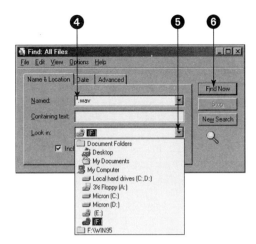

LET'S MAKE SOME NOISE!

Almost everyone likes to have a computer that makes some noise. Whether it's something simple like playing a sound when you start Windows 98 or a bit more complex like playing audio CDs while you work, Windows 98 can make a lot of noise.

TIP *Although almost everyone likes their computer to make sounds, not everyone appreciates the sounds made by someone else's PC. If you share an office with other people, keep the volume down or wear earphones to keep your PC from becoming a nuisance.*

Exercise 1: Playing sounds

Windows 98 includes a program called Media Player that you can use to play several different types of multimedia files. Windows 98 sound files are one of the types of multimedia files Media Player plays quite well. Windows 98 sound files are also called *wave* files—a reference to their .wav file extension. This type of sound file is simply a digital recording of sounds. Wave files can include everything from sound effects to voice recordings to musical performances.

Drag slider to change
position in a multimedia file

Scroll
Backward

Scroll
Forward

Eject

Stop

Play

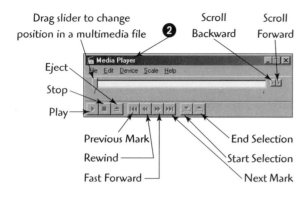

Previous Mark

Rewind

Fast Forward

End Selection

Start Selection

Next Mark

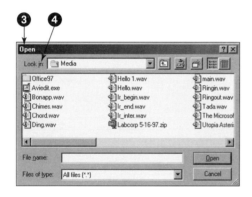

To use Media Player to play sound files, follow these steps:

1. Click the Start button.

2. Select Programs ➣ Accessories ➣ Multimedia ➣ Media Player. The figure at the left shows the Media Player and identifies the various controls you can use to control the playing of multimedia files.

3. Select File ➣ Open.

4. Make certain the Media folder is shown in the Look in text box. This is the folder in which Windows 98 normally looks for multimedia files, and it should be the folder in which you store any multimedia files so they're easy to locate.

5. Double-click Main.wav to open the sound file. This file is the sample sound file from the *Presenting Windows 98 One Step at a Time* CD-ROM.

6. Click the Play button to play the file.

7. Click the Play button again to replay the file. Because you didn't stop the playback before the end, Media Player plays the file from the beginning.

8. Hold down the Rewind button until the slider is about in the middle of the scale, and then click the Play button. This time Media Player plays the file from the point at which you left the slider.

9. Drag the slider to the 0:10 mark on the scale and click the Play button. You can also use the Scroll Forward and Scroll Backward buttons to move to different points in the file.

With so many sound files available, you can spend a lot of time sampling each of them. One method you can use to speed up the process is to have both Media Player and Windows Explorer open at the same time, and drag sound files from the Media folder onto Media Player. As you drop each file onto Media Player, the file automatically plays, saving you quite a few steps as you look for your favorites.

You can find additional sound files in many places. Many of the CD-ROMs of popular office suites contain short sound files. You can probably find additional sound files on many other CD-ROMs, too. Just use the Find ➢ Files or Folders command and look for files with a .wav extension.

Exercise 2: Placing an audio clip in a document

Windows 98 documents don't have to be boring. You can easily spice them up with audio clips. You might, for example, want to include an audio "hello" in a note you're sending to someone. In this exercise you learn how to clip out part of an audio file and place the clip in a document. You can select any part of an audio file — you don't have to include the entire file unless you want to.

To place an audio clip in a document, follow these steps:

1. If you don't still have Main.wav open in Media Player, reopen the file.

2. Place the slider at the beginning of the file and click the Start Selection button.

3. Move the slider to the right until the time indicator shows 00:10 (min:sec) — 10 seconds into the sound file.

4. Click the End Selection button to select the first 10 seconds of the recording. Media Player highlights your selection.

5. Select Edit ➢ Copy Object to copy the selected portion of the sound file to the Clipboard.

6. Click the Start button.

7. Select Programs ➢ Accessories ➢ WordPad to open a new WordPad document.

8. Select Edit ➢ Paste to place the audio clip in the WordPad document.

9. Double-click the Main.wav icon in the document to play the audio clip. Because you selected the first 10 seconds rather than the whole file, only the first part of the file plays.

A document file with only a "Main" audio clip probably isn't too useful, so you'd probably want to add additional text if you were really going to send the document to someone. For now, though,

This section of the sound file is selected

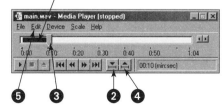

Double-click to play the audio clip

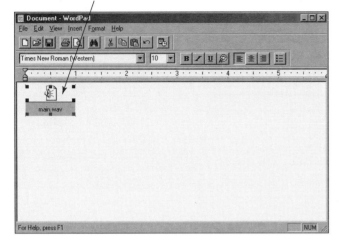

you can either save the document and close WordPad or leave the document open for later when you add a video clip to the document.

TIP

Because you can't easily rename an audio clip you've inserted into a document file, rename the sound file in Windows Explorer before you open it in Media Player. You might, for example, make a copy of Main.wav and call it Music.wav before you open it in Media Player and clip out the greeting for your document.

Exercise 3: Using the volume control

You probably wouldn't put up with a radio or a television that lacked a volume control, so you probably want to be able to control the sound level in Windows 98, too. Windows 98 actually has a sophisticated volume control with different settings for different types of sounds. You can choose different levels for audio CDs and wave files, for example. Windows 98 also has a simple volume control that you can use to adjust the overall sound level or quickly mute all sounds.

Follow these steps to access the Windows 98 volume controls and adjust your sound levels:

1. Click the speaker icon on the Taskbar to display the simple volume control. You can move the slider up or down to control the overall volume level. When you use this volume control, all sound sources are adjusted together. You can select the Mute checkbox to mute the speakers.

2. Click a blank space on your desktop to remove the simple volume control from your screen.

3. Double-click the speaker icon to display the full volume control. The simple volume control is also shown so you can compare the two.

4. Play a sound file in Media Player while you drag the Wave Volume slider up and down to hear the effect on the volume.

5. Drag the Wave Balance slider left and right as you play a sound file. This slider affects the balance between the right and left speakers.

6. Select the Wave Mute checkbox to silence the sound file. Be sure to deselect this checkbox before you close the volume control so you can once again hear wave sounds.

7. Click Advanced to display the Advanced Controls dialog box. This dialog box has sliders to adjust the bass and treble response, and it may include additional controls such as a loudness control if your sound card supports additional controls.

8. Click the Close button to close the Advanced Controls dialog box.

9. Click the Close button to close the Volume Control dialog box.

Different sound sources tend to play at different sound levels. By accessing the full volume control you can fine-tune the volume to your liking.

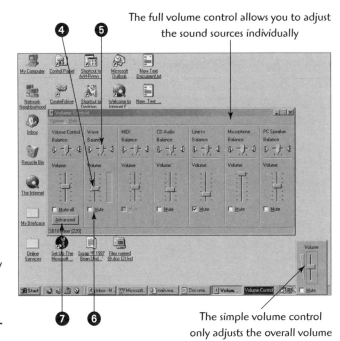

The full volume control allows you to adjust the sound sources individually

The simple volume control only adjusts the overall volume

Exercise 4: Using the Sound Recorder

Another of the Windows 98 multimedia accessories is the Sound Recorder. This handy little accessory enables you to record and modify sound files. If you have a microphone attached to your PC, Sound Recorder can create wave files of you singing or talking. Even if you don't have a microphone, you can use Sound Recorder to create a wave file from any sounds that pass through your sound card. You can also apply several different types of modifications to existing sounds.

In this exercise you sample some of the capabilities of the Sound Recorder. You start by recording a short sound file using your microphone—if you don't have a microphone attached to your PC, make a copy of Main.wav to use to practice modifying sound files.

To record and modify a sound file using Sound Recorder, follow these steps:

1. Click the Start button.

2. Select Programs ➢ Accessories ➢ Multimedia ➢ Sound Recorder.

Position indicator
Waveform window
Length of file
indicator

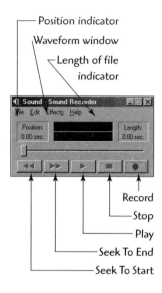

Record
Stop
Play
Seek To End
Seek To Start

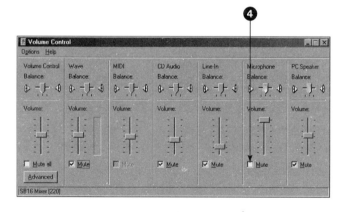

3. Double-click the speaker icon on the Taskbar to display the full volume control.

4. Make certain the Microphone Mute checkbox is not selected. If you have any other sounds coming from your speakers, select the Mute checkbox for those other sound sources; otherwise, they will be recorded along with your voice.

5. Position your microphone so you can speak into it, click the Record button, and say **Hello, I'm learning a lot about Windows 98**, and then click the Stop button. If you make a mistake, select File ➢ New ➢ No to erase the recording so you can start over.

6. Select File ➢ Save to display the Save As dialog box.

7. Change the Save in location to the \Windows\Media folder.

8. Type the following text in the File name text box: **Hello 1.**

9. Click Save to save the file and return to Sound Recorder. If you don't have a microphone, you can select File ➢ Open and open your copy of Main.wav.

10. Click the Play button to play back your recording.

11. Drag the slider to a point about a quarter of the way into the file. You can use the position indicator and the length of file indicator to determine the current position of the slider. Notice, too, how the waveform window shows a thicker line at some points. This thicker line shows where the file contains sounds.

12. Click the Play button to see where the file starts playing. You should be able to find the point where you finished saying hello and went on to the rest of the message.

13. Select Effects ➢ Increase Volume (by 25%) and then click the Play button again. Notice that the line in the waveform window increases in thickness as you increase the volume.

14. Select Effects ➢ Increase Speed (by 100%) and then click the Play button.

15. Select Effects ➢ Decrease Speed to return your recorded voice to normal.

16. Select Effects ➤ Add Echo and click Play. Your recording should sound like you were in a large room with a lot of echos.

17. Select Effects ➤ Reverse and click Play. You just learned the secret to putting hidden, backward-playing messages on recordings!

18. Select File ➤ Revert ➤ Yes to return the file to its original state.

19. Click the Close button to close Sound Recorder.

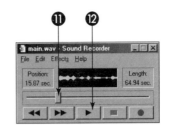

You can have a lot of fun playing with Sound Recorder. You can even record your own messages to use as sounds to attach to Windows 98 events, which is the subject of the next exercise.

Exercise 5: Adding sounds to Windows 98 events

Your PC can make a lot of noise. Almost any *event*—such as starting Windows 98, opening a menu, closing a program—can be assigned a sound. Assigning sounds to every possible event would probably be overkill in most cases, but you have to determine what's best for you. You may want to consider adding sounds to certain important events, such as error messages or new mail, and leaving most other events silent.

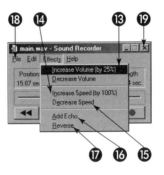

TIP

You can record short descriptions of Windows 98 events using Sound Recorder and then assign the resulting sound files to those events to assist a visually impaired or a young user in using Windows 98.

To assign sounds to Windows 98 events, follow these steps:

1. Click the Start button.

2. Select Settings ➤ Control Panel.

3. Double-click the Sounds icon to display the Sounds Properties dialog box.

4. To hear the sound already assigned to an event, look for an event that has a speaker icon to the left of the event name, and click the event to choose it.

5. Click the Play button to hear the sound.

5

Use the scrollbar to view
additional events

④ A speaker icon
indicates a sound is
assigned to this event

Click here to stop

⑤ Click here to play
the sound

⑦ The name of the
sound file assigned to
this event is shown here

Click here to find sound
files to assign to events

Select named sound
schemes here

⑫   Click here for information
on the sound file   ⑨

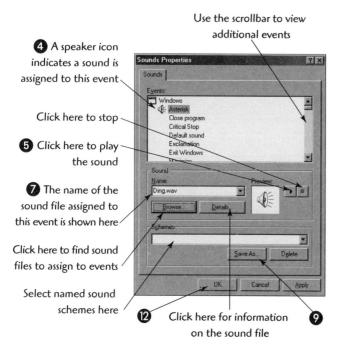

6. Choose an event that does not have an assigned sound. In this case, choose Open Program to play a sound when you open a program.

7. Click the down arrow at the right side on the Name list box, and select Hello 1.wav to assign the Hello 1.wav sound file to the Open Program event.

8. Click the Play button to hear the sound.

9. When you have assigned sounds to several events, select Save As to display the Save Scheme As dialog box.

10. Type the following text: **My sound scheme.**

11. Click OK to save your sound scheme. You can then choose your named scheme or another scheme using the Schemes list box.

12. Click OK to close the Sounds Properties dialog box.

Although you can assign any sounds you like to Windows 98 events, it's better to assign relatively short sounds to most events. Otherwise, your PC makes so much noise that the sounds are distracting rather than helpful.

Exercise 6: Using the CD Player

Most of the time your CD-ROM drive sits there unused. Oh sure, you use it when you install programs or when you run programs from a CD-ROM, but that's probably a small fraction of the time you use your PC. There's no reason you can't use the CD-ROM drive at other times to play audio CDs and have some pleasant music while you work. Mozart would certainly have approved of the idea!

Windows 98 includes a CD Player to play audio CDs in your CD-ROM drive. There's actually little difference between audio CDs and CD-ROMs. Both use the same type of disc, and a disc can even hold both audio and data tracks.

The Windows 98 CD Player even has some tricks your normal audio CD player probably lacks. You can set up play lists for your favorite audio CDs, and CD Player even remembers audio CDs between sessions.

Follow these steps to use CD Player:

1. Place an audio CD in your CD-ROM drive. CD Player should start automatically.

2. If CD Player doesn't start automatically, click the Start button, and then select Programs ➤ Accessories ➤ Multimedia ➤ CD Player. The accompanying figure shows CD Player while it is playing a Mozart CD (after the play list has been manually entered). You may need to select View ➤ Toolbar if the toolbar doesn't appear.

3. You may need to click the Play button to begin playing the CD. Generally, CD Player begins playing the first CD automatically unless you started CD Player before you inserted an audio CD. Subsequent audio CDs don't start playing automatically.

4. Click the Edit Play List button to display the CD Player: Disc Settings dialog box. In this case the information for an audio CD has already been entered, so you can see how a CD Player play list functions.

5. Type the name of the artist in the Artist text box; in this case **Wolfgang Amadeus Mozart.**

6. Type the CD title in the Title text box; in this case **Eine Kleine Nachtmusik.**

7. Type the name of track one in the Track 01 text box and click Set Name; in this case: **Allegro.**

8. Continue typing in the track names until all of the track names have been entered. CD Player remembers the artist, title, and track names and correctly displays them the next time you play this CD.

9. To prevent a track from playing, choose the track in the Play List box and click Remove.

10. To change the order in which tracks are played, first click Clear All. Then choose a track in the Available Tracks list box and click Add. Continue until you've chosen all the tracks you wish to play.

11. Click OK to return to the CD Player.

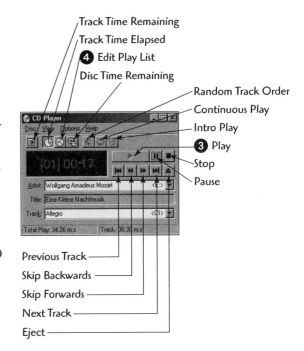

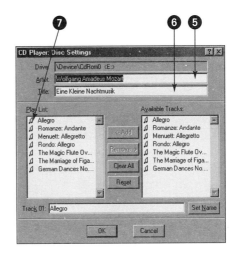

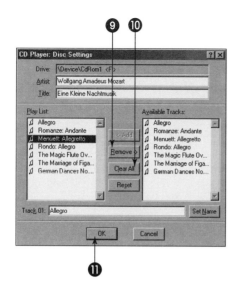

12. Select the type of time display you prefer by clicking the Track Time Elapsed, Track Time Remaining, or Disk Time Remaining buttons.

13. Click the Random Track Order button if you prefer to have the tracks play randomly.

14. To play the same CD over again until you click the Stop button, click the Continuous Play button.

15. To preview the first ten seconds of each track, click the Intro Play button. You can change the length of the preview by selecting Options ➢ Preferences ➢ Intro play length.

16. To stop playing and eject a CD, click the Eject button.

The remaining CD Player controls work very much like the controls on a standard audio CD player, except that you use your mouse to click the buttons on CD Player. If you enjoy music while you work, you'll find CD Player pretty handy—especially if you take the time to enter play lists for your favorite audio CDs.

LET'S HAVE SOME ACTION!

Windows 98 multimedia isn't only about sound. You can also play video pieces on your screen. Your Windows 98 CD-ROM has some excellent examples that can show you just how impressive multimedia can be. In the following exercises you see how to use those examples.

NOTE

Playing video clips takes a great deal of computing power. Although you can get by with less, you really should have at least a 120 MHz Pentium system with 16MB of RAM and a quad-speed CD-ROM drive to play most video clips without problems. Slower systems can usually play video clips, but they may display jerky motion in the video or contain gaps in the audio track.

Exercise 7: Playing the fun stuff

Windows 98 video files use a format called *Audio Visual Interleave,* or AVI. In this type of file, the audio and video portions are both included — interleaved — in the same file. The Media Player recognizes files with an .avi extension as AVI files. The *Presenting Windows 98 One Step at a Time* CD-ROM contains a sample AVI file called gulls.avi, which can be found in the Exercise folder.

To play the sample video from the *Presenting Windows 98 One Step at a Time* CD-ROM, follow these steps:

1. Insert the *Presenting Windows 98 One Step at a Time* CD-ROM into your CD-ROM drive.

2. Click the Start button, and then select Programs ➢ Accessories ➢ Multimedia ➢ Media Player.

3. Select Device ➢ Video for Windows to display the Open dialog box.

4. Choose your CD-ROM drive (probably drive D) in the Look in list box, and then choose the Exercise folder.

5. Double-click gulls.avi to open the video file. If you manually started Media Player, click the Play button to view the video.

6. You can click the Pause button to stop the video at any point, and then click Play to resume.

7. Drag the slider left or right to move to different frames in the video.

8. Click the Close button to close Media Player. Depending on how you started the video clip, you may need to click the video window Close button first.

9. Right-click gulls.avi in the folder displaying the AVI files, and select Properties from the pop-up menu to view information on the video clip. The information shown tells you the length of the clip as well as the audio and video formats — remember that AVI means that the file contains both audio and video tracks.

10. Click OK to close the Properties dialog box.

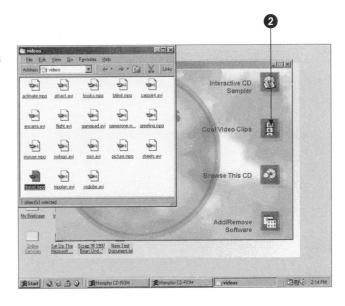

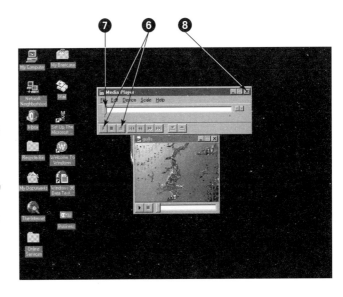

Although you can easily create your own sound files, creating your own video files is generally beyond the capabilities of most PC users. You need a special video capture board and a video source, such as a video camera, to create digital movies. Unfortunately, this type of equipment is still quite rare and expensive.

Exercise 8: Placing a video clip in a document

Video clips tend to be quite large. These large sizes mean that placing a video clip in a document, while possible, isn't always the most practical idea. Still, there may be times when you want to include a video clip in a document—perhaps to add a little excitement to an on-screen presentation. Just remember that a document containing a video clip probably won't be a good candidate for saving on diskettes!

Follow these steps to place a video clip in a document:

1. Click the Start button.

2. Select Programs ➤ Accessories ➤ Multimedia ➤ Media Player.

3. Select Device ➤ Video for Windows.

4. Click the down arrow at the right edge of the Look in list box and choose the drive letter for your CD-ROM drive.

5. Select the Exercise folder.

6. Double-click gulls.avi to open the AVI file.

7. Select Edit ➤ Copy Object to place the AVI file on the Clipboard.

8. Click the Start button.

9. Select Programs ➤ Accessories ➤ WordPad.

10. In WordPad, select Edit ➤ Paste to place the video clip into the document.

11. Double-click the video clip in WordPad to play the video clip.

12. Select File ➤ Save.

13. Type the following text to name the file: **A video clip.**

14. Click Save.

15. Click the Close button to close WordPad.

16. Click the Media Player Close button.

You don't have to include an entire video file in a document. You can also use the Start Selection and End Selection buttons to clip out a portion of the video file. If you do want to use a portion of a video file, you may also find the Scale ➤ Frames command helpful in locating the exact frames to copy. When you use this command, Media Player shows the frame numbers on the scale rather than the elapsed time.

NOTE *Whenever you include audio or video clips in a document, you must always be aware of the copyright issues. While you probably won't have too much to worry about if you include a small audio or video clip in a personal note to a friend, you need the permission of the copyright owner before you use a clip in a business presentation.*

Exercise 9: Using the TV Viewer

Windows 98 includes a new multimedia component called the TV Viewer. If you have a special video adapter compatible with the TV Viewer, then you can watch TV programming on your computer. Of course, you also need a special high speed Internet connection, a digital cable television connection, or a digital satellite TV connection to see live programming. If you do have all the right pieces, you'll be able to receive high definition digital TV, get gigabytes of data daily, and see enhanced TV shows that enable you to interact with the show using your computer.

Even if you don't have special video adapters and expensive data connections, you'll find you can still use some TV Viewer features. You can download TV program listings for your local viewing

5

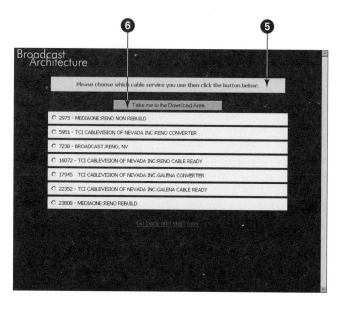

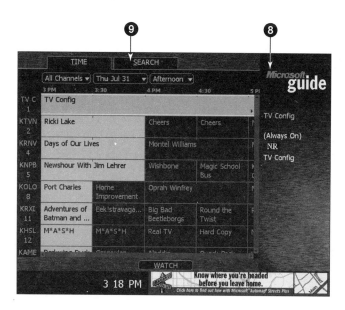

area and even have TV Viewer remind you when your favorite programs will be broadcast.

The TV Viewer is an optional component that you must install before you can use it. To install TV Viewer, double-click the Add/Remove Programs icon in Control Panel. Click the Windows Setup tab, choose TV Viewer, and then click Apply.

To try out TV Viewer, follow these steps:

1. Click the Start button.

2. Select Programs ➢ TV Viewer.

3. Click Download my local TV listings to continue. Next you must enter your postal code as directed by the dialog box that appears.

4. After you've entered your postal code, click the Submit button.

5. Now you must select which set of program listings to download. You'll probably have a different set of selections, but you should choose the set that most closely matches your viewing habits.

6. When you've made your selection, click the Take me to the Download Area button.

7. Click Download to begin downloading your local listings.

8. When the download is complete, press F10 and select Guide to view the program guide. Programs are listed in a grid that shows the schedule for your local channels as well as a number of special TV Viewer channels.

9. Click the Search tab to display a list of categories. In the accompanying figure the educational category has been selected.

10. To view the schedule for your favorite show, choose the show in the listing and click Other Times to find any additional times during the coming week when the show can be seen.

11. If you want to be reminded just before a program airs, select the program in the listing and click Remind to display the Remind dialog box.

12. Choose the reminder options you prefer and click OK to return to the program guide. You can continue to look through the program guide for additional programs. As you select programs in the listings, notice that the Remind and Other Times buttons sometimes disappear and the Watch button appears. This indicates a program you may be able to watch on your computer screen. Unless you have a special video adapter, however, you won't be able to view any of the selections.

13. Press F10 and select Guide to return to the programming guide.

14. To close TV Viewer, press F6 and then click the Close button.

Because few PCs currently include the necessary hardware to enable viewing programs on screen, TV Viewer is primarily a program guide for now. It's clear, however, that Microsoft would like TV Viewer to be much more in the near future.

Exercise 10: Using Imaging

If TV Viewer seems to be a little ahead of its time, the Imaging tool will seem much more down to earth and useful. This utility enables you to scan images (if you have a Twain-compliant scanner), view faxes, and annotate images. You can, for example, view a fax you've received, add annotations to show your comments about a part of the fax, and then forward the fax to someone else for review.

Most modern scanners are Twain-compliant. This is simply a standard that allows different brands of scanners to work with Windows programs so that you can scan directly into many applications. You don't need a scanner to use Imaging, but if you have a scanner, you can easily create and send faxes from almost any printed document.

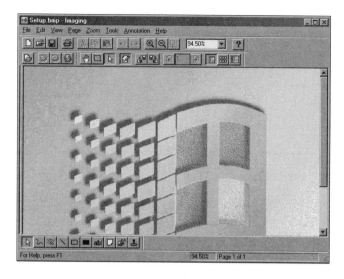

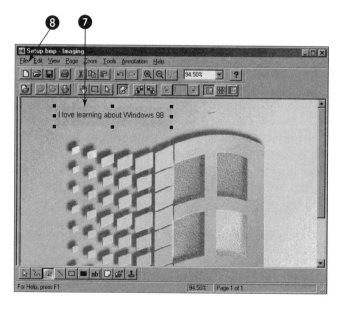

To try Imaging, follow these steps:

1. Click the Start button.

2. Select Programs ➢ Accessories ➢ Imaging.

3. Select File ➢ Open and choose your \Windows folder in the Look in list box.

4. Double-click Setup.bmp to open the Setup image file. If you can't find this image file, choose a different one. The accompanying figure shows Setup.bmp opened in Imaging.

5. Click the Text tool button and drag a text box across the top of the image.

6. Type the following text: **I love learning about Windows 98**.

7. Click the Highlighter tool button and drag the highlighter over the text you just added to make the text stand out.

8. Select File ➢ Save As.

9. Type the following text in the File name text box: **My Setup**

10. Click Save to save the image.

11. Click the Close button to close Imaging.

If you want, you can use the new image as desktop wallpaper. If the original image had been a fax that someone sent you, you could add your comments to the fax before sending it back or forwarding it to another person. After you save a modified image, any annotations you add become a permanent part of the image. If you need a copy of the original, unmodified image, be sure to use a new name when you save your modified copy.

CONFIGURING MULTIMEDIA FOR PERFORMANCE

You can't get around the fact that multimedia uses a lot of your computer's power. To get the best performance from multimedia applications, you have to make certain your multimedia settings are adjusted correctly. Windows 98 gathers all the multimedia settings in one place, the Multimedia Properties dialog box, which you access through the Control Panel.

Exercise 11: Adjusting your multimedia settings

You probably use some multimedia settings pretty often, such as the various volume-level settings. On other settings, such as the quality of sound recordings, you are likely either to use the default settings or adjust them once and use the same settings most of the time. Still others, such as the *MIDI* — Musical Instrument Digital Interface — settings, are of little interest to anyone except those who use their PC to compose music. In this exercise you see how to adjust some of the more common multimedia settings.

To adjust the primary multimedia settings, follow these steps:

1. Click the Start button.

2. Select Settings ➢ Control Panel.

3. Double-click the Multimedia icon to display the Multimedia Properties dialog box.

4. Make certain the Show volume control on the taskbar checkbox is selected. If the speaker icon ever disappears from the Taskbar, selecting this checkbox brings the icon back.

5. To change the quality level of any recordings, choose CD Quality, Radio Quality, or Telephone Quality from the Preferred quality list box. CD quality recordings use approximately 172K per second of recording time, radio quality recordings use approximately 22K per second, and telephone quality recordings use about 11K per second. The differences arise from the *sampling rate*, the number of data bits, and whether the recording is stereo or mono. You may want to record the same message at different quality levels to see how much recording quality you really need.

6. Click the Customize button to display the Customize dialog box. You can use this dialog box to choose the exact audio compression format and type of recording you need.

7. Click the down arrow at the right edge of the Format list box to see which audio compression formats are supported by your PC.

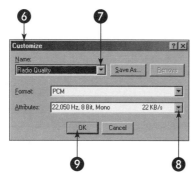

It's generally best to use a format such as PCM that is supported by most PCs, although you can use one of the other formats if it is supported on your system as well as any other system that plays your sound files. The different formats differ in the amount of compression as well as the quality of the recording.

8. Click the down arrow at the right edge of the Attributes list box to see which recording parameters are compatible with the chosen audio compression format. Higher sampling rates and more data bits usually result in higher-quality recordings, but they use more disk space.

9. Click OK to return to the Multimedia Properties dialog box.

10. Click the Video tab to display the video playback window settings.

11. Choose a size for the video playback window in the Window list box. For the best performance and highest quality image, choose Original size. Any other setting (including Full screen) results in a poorer quality image and may make the video playback jerky.

12. Click the MIDI tab to view the MIDI settings. MIDI files, which share the extension of mid, are a type of music file that plays through your sound card or through an external digital musical instrument. Unless you're a musician, you probably won't have any reason to change any of the MIDI settings.

13. Click the CD Music tab to view the audio CD headphone settings. If you use headphones connected directly to your CD player, you can use this tab to adjust the volume.

14. Click the Advanced tab to view all of the multimedia devices installed in your system. Depending on what is installed, some devices may have optional settings, but unless you know for certain that you should change a setting, it's best to leave them alone. Incorrect settings can make your multimedia features stop working.

15. Click the Close button to close the Multimedia Properties dialog box, and then close the Control Panel.

Adjusting Multimedia Settings

All of the primary multimedia settings are available on one of the five tabs of the Multimedia Properties dialog box shown in these figures.

Use the Audio tab to change sound settings.

Choose sound card

Select to show speaker icon on Taskbar

Drag slider to adjust playback volume

Move slider to adjust recording volume

Choose sound card microphone input

Choose CD quality, Radio Quality, or Telephone Quality for recording

Click to select custom recording quality

Select only if you use programs that require a specific sound card

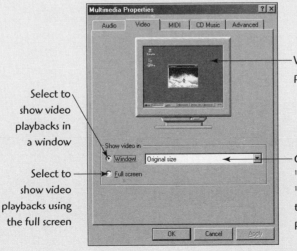

Use the Video tab to change the appearance of video playback.

Select to show video playbacks in a window

Select to show video playbacks using the full screen

View relative size of video playback window here

Choose Original size, Double original size, $1/16$ of screen size, $1/4$ of screen size, $1/2$ of screen size, or Maximized to change the relative size of the video playback window

5

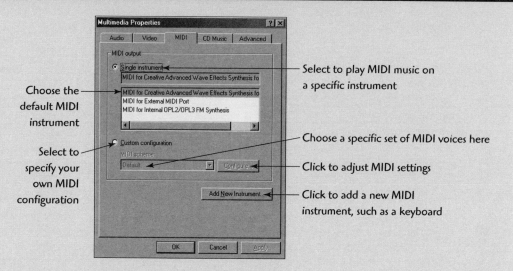

Choose the default MIDI instrument

Select to specify your own MIDI configuration

Select to play MIDI music on a specific instrument

Choose a specific set of MIDI voices here

Click to adjust MIDI settings

Click to add a new MIDI instrument, such as a keyboard

Use the MIDI tab to change sound synthesizer settings.

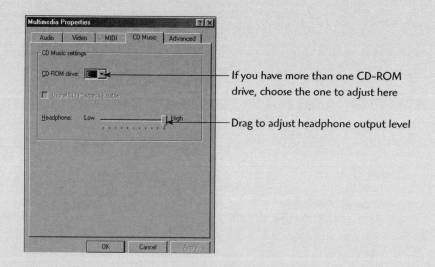

If you have more than one CD-ROM drive, choose the one to adjust here

Drag to adjust headphone output level

Use the CD Music tab to change how audio CDs are played.

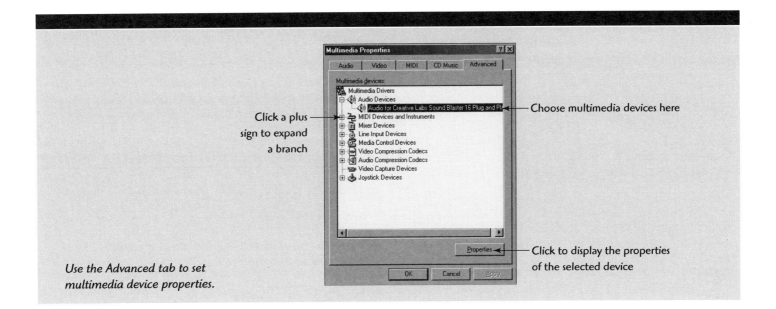

Click a plus sign to expand a branch

Choose multimedia devices here

Click to display the properties of the selected device

Use the Advanced tab to set multimedia device properties.

If you make any changes on either the MIDI or Advanced tabs of the Multimedia Properties dialog box, it's always a good idea to note which settings you changed, how they were set before your changes, and the new settings you selected. Include the date and time as well as a brief description of why you changed the settings. This type of record helps you return to the previous settings if you later discover that something is no longer working as you expect.

SKILLS CHALLENGE: MAKING MULTIMEDIA WORK!

Now it's time to try some of the skills you've learned in this lesson.

1. Play the Microsoft Sound wave file.

 How can you tell the length of a sound file without playing the file?

 What artist created the Microsoft Sound?

2. Add the first three seconds of the Microsoft Sound to a document.

3. Mute the playing of wave sounds.

 How can you quickly mute all sounds from your PC?

4. Reenable the playing of wave sounds.

5. Record a message counting from 1 to 10.

6. Add an echo to your recording.

 How can you create the effect of having an echo occur before the sound?

 How can you remove all changes from a sound recording?

7. Enter a play list for an audio CD.

How can you play the songs on an audio CD in reverse order of the way they appear on the CD?

 How can you make the same set of songs play several times in a row?

8. Find the current setting for audio recordings.

 How much disk space does the lowest quality PCM format audio recording require for each second of recording?

WRAP UP

Multimedia is a lot of fun. In this lesson you learned how to play both audio and video files as well as how to record your own audio files. You also learned how you can use clips from audio or video files in your documents and how you can adjust your multimedia settings to make your PC perform a bit better.

The next lesson gets back down to business and shows you how to install and uninstall programs on your Windows 98 system. It also shows you how to make those old DOS applications work a little better under Windows 98.

Problem	Solution
When I double-click a sound file, I see the Open With dialog box.	You need to install the Media Player from the Windows 98 beta. Double-click the Add/Remove Programs icon in the Control Panel, click the Windows Setup tab, select Multimedia ➢ Details, and click Media Player. Click OK and then Apply to add Media Player to your hard disk.
My volume control doesn't show the same set of controls shown in the figures.	You can choose which controls are displayed using the Options ➢ Properties command in the volume control menu.
I don't see the speaker icon on my Taskbar.	Select the Multimedia icon in Control Panel, and make certain the Show volume control on the taskbar checkbox is selected on the Audio tab.

5

Installing and Uninstalling Programs

GOALS

Your PC probably came with a number of programs already installed. There's no reason, however, for you to use what's already there and miss out on newer, more capable programs as they become available. Windows 98 makes installing programs easier than it used to be, but there are still quite a few considerations in making the process go smoothly. Removing old programs is another task that is easier in Windows 98, but you still need to watch out for a number of potential pitfalls. This lesson guides you along the path and shows you how to keep the problems associated with installing and removing programs to a minimum. This lesson covers the following topics:

45 MINUTES

- Installing Windows applications

- Removing Windows applications

- Adding additional Windows components

- Using MS-DOS applications

GET READY

To complete this lesson you need the CD-ROM that accompanies this book. You work with the shareware program, ThumbsPlus, and two sample programs: InstallSample.exe and Wolf.com, all of which are in the Exercise folder. You also need the Windows 98 beta to install some of the optional components of Windows 98. You may find a printer handy but not absolutely necessary; you can view information on-screen if you can't produce a printout.

INSTALLING WINDOWS APPLICATIONS

In the early days of personal computing, installing a program was pretty easy. If you had enough disk space, you just installed the program and ran it. Of course, each program you installed had to support every piece of your PC or you'd be out of luck. If the program's manufacturer didn't know about your type of printer or monitor, there was a pretty good chance you wouldn't be able to use the program, or at least not to its fullest extent. As bad as that sounds, things got even worse if you wanted to upgrade to a new piece of hardware. Unless the software manufacturer was willing to add support for new hardware, you were probably stuck with your old equipment as long as you wanted to keep using your existing software. You couldn't, for example, upgrade to a new laser printer, a fancy color printer, a higher resolution monitor, or even a faster modem because your old software didn't support any of those new items.

Although most people look at Windows — whether Windows 98 or the older Windows versions — and think the graphical user interface is the biggest change between Windows and MS-DOS, there are many other changes possibly more important under the surface. One of the biggest changes is the difference in the way Windows programs and MS-DOS programs deal with the various components of your system. While MS-DOS programs need to provide direct support for each component, Windows programs only need to know how to communicate with Windows itself. Windows then communicates with the individual components. Your Windows program doesn't have to know anything about your new color

holographic-data-sculpting output device, as long as the
manufacturer of the device provides drivers so that Windows knows
how to work with the device.

What does this have to do with installing Windows programs?
Quite a bit, actually. Because Windows programs don't need to know
as much about your PC and its hardware components as MS-DOS
programs had to, Windows programs share many software
components. This sharing means that some of the pieces a Windows
program needs may already be on your system and in use by several
other programs. Of course, this also means that removing a program
you no longer need may be a bit more complicated, too; any shared
components may still be needed by another program.

But even leaving aside the issue of removing programs for now,
consider what happens when you install a program that uses shared
components. Suppose you want to install program B, which uses a
shared component XX.dll. You already have program A installed, and
it uses XX.dll, too. If both programs use the same version of XX.dll,
there's no problem. But what if there's a newer version of XX.dll, and
it happens to be the one installed along with program A? You
wouldn't want program B to install the older version and perhaps
make program A not function correctly anymore. Well-designed
installation programs are supposed to watch for these types of
conflicts, but knowing about the potential problems can help you
resolve any problems that do pop up.

Exercise 1: Adding new Windows 98 programs

There are two primary types of Windows programs you may want to
install and use on your PC—those designed for Windows 98 and
those designed for Windows 3.x. Microsoft created an entire series of
guidelines for software manufacturers to follow when creating
programs for Windows 98. Some of the most important of these
relate to how software is installed. Briefly, when you install new
programs on your PC, you should be concerned with whether the
program recognizes when newer versions of shared components are
already installed, and whether the program includes a method for
uninstalling the program.

NOTE *The Presenting Windows 98 One Step at a Time CD-ROM contains a shareware program that is used in this exercise. Shareware is a method of software distribution that enables you to try out the software before you buy it. If you decide you like the software and want to continue using it, you must register the shareware with the software author or manufacturer. In some cases, such as the ThumbsPlus software used in this exercise, you receive additional features or functions when you register the software.*

In this exercise you practice installing a program designed for Windows 98 — ThumbsPlus. This is a shareware program you can use to browse, convert, organize, view, edit, and catalog graphic files. The installation program you use to install ThumbsPlus has some special features. When you install ThumbsPlus, you can choose to place the shared Windows 98 components used by ThumbsPlus in either the ThumbsPlus folder or in the \Windows\System folder. In addition, ThumbsPlus does not automatically assume you always want to use it to view every graphics file. While you may not fully appreciate these features right now, the longer you use your PC, the gladder you'll be that some considerate programmers give you the installation options you have with ThumbsPlus.

To install ThumbsPlus, follow these steps:

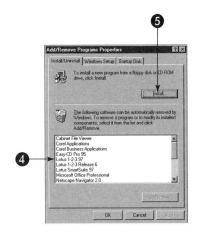

1. Place the *Presenting Windows 98 One Step at a Time* CD-ROM into your CD-ROM drive.

2. Click the Start button.

3. Select Settings ➢ Control Panel.

4. Double-click the Add/Remove Programs icon to display the Add/Remove Programs Properties dialog box. The list box in the lower portion of this dialog box shows the Windows 98 programs installed on your system, but it probably won't have the same set of programs shown in the figure.

5. Click the Install button to display the Install Program From Floppy Disk or CD-ROM dialog box.

6. Click Next to continue. Windows 98 then looks for an installation program on a diskette or in the root folder of the CD-ROM. When you install programs that come on their own CD-ROMs, the installation program is usually called something like Setup.exe or Install.exe and is located in the root folder.

7. Because ThumbsPlus is not in the root directory of the CD-ROM, click Browse to display the Browse dialog box.

8. Click the down arrow at the right edge of the Look in list box, and then choose the Exercise folder.

9. Choose Thmpls32.exe as shown in the accompanying figure. Because you're installing a new program, the Files of type list box displays only program files.

10. Click Open to continue.

11. Click Finish to begin installing ThumbsPlus. Notice that the installation program covers up your desktop. Some installation programs also hide the Taskbar.

12. Click Next to continue. Generally, you have the option of choosing a destination folder for the program installation. You can click the Browse button to choose a different folder or click Next to continue.

13. You can choose to place ThumbsPlus in its own nested menu under the Programs selection on the Start menu, or you can choose to place ThumbsPlus in another menu. Make certain the Add a ThumbsPlus icon on the desktop, too checkbox is selected if you want to have a ThumbsPlus icon on your desktop. Click Next to continue.

14. At this point the ThumbsPlus installation program gives you an option you won't see in most installation programs. You can choose to install the shared Windows 98 components in the \Windows\System folder or in the ThumbsPlus program folder. If you choose to install these files in the \Windows\System folder, they are shared by other Windows 98 programs. Installing these files in the ThumbsPlus program folder uses a bit more disk space, but it is easier to uninstall the ThumbsPlus program—you

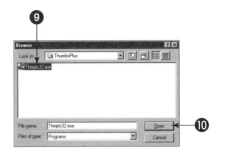

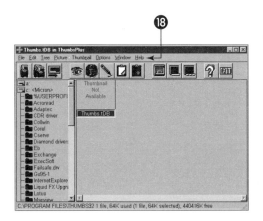

won't have to worry whether any other programs are using the files. Click Next to continue.

15. After you've made all the installation decisions, you're ready to actually install the program. Click Next to continue, or Back if you want to change any of your selections.

16. After the installation program finishes installing ThumbsPlus, the Installation Completed message is displayed.

Make certain the Show me the release notes checkbox is checked so you can see any special information about the program. Not all installation programs include release notes or README files, but when you're given the option to view this type of information, it's always a good idea to view it. Click Finish to exit the installation program.

17. Click the Close button to close the ThumbsPlus Release Notes screen.

18. Check your success by double-clicking the ThumbsPlus icon on your desktop. When the credits screen appears, click the thumb icon in the upper-left corner to view the program. You can learn how to use ThumbsPlus by selecting Help ➢ Contents.

Installing Windows 98 programs using the Add/Remove Programs icon in Control Panel is pretty easy and straightforward. Not all programs give you as much control over the installation process as ThumbsPlus does. If a program is designed for Windows 98, however, it should at least allow you to choose where to install the program, to choose where the program appears in the menu, and to uninstall the program without too much trouble.

Exercise 2: Using old Windows applications in Windows 98

Although programs specifically designed for Windows 95 or Windows 98 generally offer additional features compared to older programs, most programs designed for Windows 3.x can still be run in Windows 98. Quite often, though, these older programs lack many of the modern conveniences such as an uninstall option. If you really need to use an older Windows program—perhaps because a Windows 98 version isn't available—you can probably install the program in

Windows 98. You should take a few precautions to protect yourself, however, in case you have problems or later decide you don't want the old program cluttering your hard disk anymore.

In this exercise you learn how to create a log of the changes made to your system when you install a program. This log won't include everything that an installation changes, but it shows you which files were added or changed by the installation. The log is especially helpful if, after you install an older program, you later discover that some of your existing programs no longer work. Generally, this type of problem can be traced to the replacement of one of the shared files with an older version lacking in some of the enhancements present in the newer version.

Rather than actually installing an old program, you simulate installing a program by adding a file to your \Windows\System folder — the folder where most installation problems can be found.

To practice adding a file to your Windows system folder, follow these steps:

1. Click the Start button.

2. Select Programs ➤ MS-DOS Prompt to display the MS-DOS Prompt window. You can use this window to enter the commands to create your before and after logs.

3. Type the following command and then press Enter: **DIR \Windows\System /on > Filesbefore.txt.**

This command creates a text file named Filesbefore.txt that contains a sorted listing of the files in the \Windows\System folder before you install the program. If you're lucky you won't need to search through this file — it lists hundreds of files!

4. To simulate installing a program that places files in the \Windows\System folder, type the following command and press Enter: **COPY Filesbefore.txt \Windows\System\ Filesbefore.txt.**

If you were actually installing a program, you would use the Add/Remove Programs icon to install the program as you did in Exercise 1 and follow through the installation program steps until the program installation was complete.

6

5. Type the following command and then press Enter: **DIR \Windows\System /on > Filesafter.txt.**

This creates a text file named Filesafter.txt that contains a sorted listing of the files in the \Windows\System folder after you install the program.

6. Type the following command and then press Enter: **FC /L /LB99 /N Filesbefore.txt Filesafter.txt > Filechanges.txt.**

This creates a text file named Filechanges.txt showing you exactly the changes that occurred when you installed the new program.

7. To print a copy of the changes, type the following command and press Enter: **COPY Filechanges.txt PRN.**

You should write the date, time, and the name of the program you just installed on the printout for future reference.

8. To view a copy of the changes on-screen, type the following command and press Enter: **TYPE Filechanges.txt.**

The accompanying screen shows how the before and after differences show up in Filechanges.txt. An extra file, filesbefore.txt, appeared in the 115th line, and the directory listing showed 616 files instead of 615 files.

9. Type the following command and press Enter to close the MS-DOS prompt window: **EXIT.**

You won't find every change an installation program makes to your system using this method, but you can get a good idea of any major changes that were made. Be sure to continue to Step 5 immediately after you finish installing the program; otherwise, you won't know for certain that the installation program made the changes you logged. Also, keep in mind that you must start the entire procedure from the beginning each time you add new software for this method to be useful.

Okay, so you have a printed log of the changes made by an installation program—so what? What good is the printout? If one or more of your programs don't work properly after you install another program, the chances are pretty good that the problem is one of the files that were changed in the \Windows\System folder. Your printout not only shows any new files, but also any files that have a different size or date. If you call a software technical support line for assistance, the fact that you know what changes were made saves a lot of time getting to the bottom of the problem. Tell the technical support person that you installed some additional software, and inform them of the changes you logged. I'm sure he or she will find a solution many times faster with this important information.

REMOVING WINDOWS APPLICATIONS

Removing a program should be easy. When you no longer use an old program and want to free up some disk space, you can just delete the program's folder, right? Actually, no. Removing Windows programs is seldom that easy. Because of the way Windows programs share components and the way Windows 98 stores important configuration information, removing old programs can be quite complicated.

Windows 98 uses a special database called the *Registry* to keep track of important information. When you install a program, change your screen saver settings, swap your mouse buttons, or make any other change important for Windows 98 to remember, the information is stored in the Registry. When you uninstall a program, you have to use the correct method so Windows 98 can properly update the Registry and adjust the way Windows 98 works when the old program is gone.

Exercise 3: Removing a Windows 98 program

In this exercise you see how easy it is to remove a program designed for Windows 98 and installed using the Add/Remove Programs icon. You uninstall ThumbsPlus, which you installed from the CD-ROM earlier. Don't worry—you can always go back and reinstall ThumbsPlus after you've completed this exercise.

To uninstall a Windows 98 program, follow these steps:

1. Click the Start button.

2. Select Settings ➢ Control Panel.

3. Double-click the Add/Remove Programs icon.

6

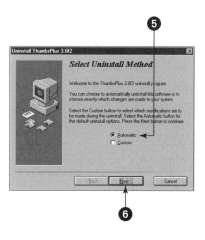

⑤

⑥

⑦

4. Choose ThumbsPlus from the list of programs that can be removed. When you select a program from this list, the Add/Remove button becomes active.

5. Click the Add/Remove button to continue. Each program's uninstall screens differ, so if you uninstall other programs, you have to watch the prompts carefully to make certain you know what is happening. In this case make certain the Automatic radio button is selected.

6. Select Next to continue.

7. Click Finish to uninstall the program. After the program has been removed, you may see a series of screens similar to the accompanying figure.

8. In this case the shared files were installed in the ThumbsPlus program folder rather than the \Windows\System folder, so it's highly unlikely any other programs are actually using these copies. You should be safe in deleting all of the shared files by clicking Yes for each one. If the shared files were installed in the \Windows\System folder, however, you may want to make note of each one in turn and decline to delete them. Later, you can move them to the Recycle Bin, and if everything still works, delete them from the Recycle Bin after several days.

You probably want to reinstall ThumbsPlus now that you know how easy it is to install and uninstall a program designed for Windows 98. Other programs have different install and uninstall routines than the ones used to install and uninstall ThumbsPlus, of course. Some programs, especially the large, multiapplication office suites, have complex sets of options that allow you to customize the operation to suit your exact needs. Regardless of the number of options you need to select, always make certain you read and understand the prompts before you continue from one screen to the next.

Exercise 4: Taking out the garbage

Not all uninstall operations go quite a smoothly as the one you practiced in the last exercise. You may encounter a number of problems that leave behind garbage—files and folders that serve no useful purpose—to clutter up your hard drive. That's when you need to do some cleanup work if you don't want to continue wasting space on the leftovers from programs you no longer use.

The Exercise folder on the *Presenting Windows 98 One Step at a Time* CD-ROM contains a sample installation program for this exercise. This sample installation program installs a small program file onto your hard disk but does not include an uninstall program, which is what you'd probably encounter if you were to install old Windows programs that aren't designed for Windows 98. As a result, you have to uninstall the sample program as part of the exercise.
To more closely simulate the problems you may encounter in uninstalling programs that don't include an uninstall program, the installation program places another file on your hard disk, too.

To practice uninstalling programs that lack uninstall programs, follow these steps:

1. Place the CD-ROM that accompanies this book into your CD-ROM drive.

2. Click the Start button.

3. Select Programs ➢ MS-DOS Prompt.

4. Type the following command and then press Enter: **DIR \Windows\System /on > Filesbefore.txt**.

5. Click the Start button.

6. Select Programs ➢ Windows Explorer.

7. Choose the Exercise folder on the CD-ROM.

8. Double-click InstallSample.exe to begin the program installation.

9. Click OK to display the Select Destination Directory dialog box. This dialog box informs you that the sample program will be placed in the C:\Program Files\SampleProgram folder. It doesn't tell you the whole story, however, so you need to do a little detective work to clean up when you uninstall the sample program.

10. Click OK to complete the installation.

11. Go back to the MS-DOS Prompt window, and type the following command and then press Enter: **DIR \Windows\System /on > Filesafter.txt.**

12. Type the following command and then press Enter: **FC /L /LB99 /N Filesbefore.txt Filesafter.txt > PRN.**

In this instance the report shows that no changes were made to the \Windows\System folder, so you don't have to worry about that folder's contents when you uninstall the sample program

13. Type the following command and press Enter to close the MS-DOS prompt window: **EXIT.**

14. Open the C:\Program Files\SampleProgram folder to see what was installed. In this case the program is named Wolfie.com, a program created for this exercise that simply opens and immediately closes an MS-DOS prompt window when double-clicked. In addition to Wolfie.com, the folder also contains a file named Install.log. Like many old Windows programs, the installation program created another file located in another directory. Before programs were designed for Windows 98, many Windows programs stored their settings in a file with an .ini extension, so our example does so too.

15. Click the Start button.

16. Select Settings ➢ Control Panel.

17. Double-click the Add/Remove Programs icon and look for Wolfie in the list of programs Windows 98 can automatically uninstall. Because our sample program wasn't designed for Windows 98, it won't be in the list, and you have to uninstall the program yourself. But first you want to find the .ini file. In most cases the .ini file has the same name as the program file, so the file you want to find is probably called Wolfie.ini. Click the Close button to close the dialog box.

18. Click the Start button.

19. Select Find ➢ Files or Folders.

20. Type the following text in the Named text box: **Wolfie.***

21. Click Find Now to locate the files. In this case, Windows 98 finds two files, Wolfie.com in the C:\Program Files\SampleProgram folder, and Wolfie.ini in the C:\Windows folder. Now you know where the extra file was installed—your \Windows folder.

22. Right-click Wolfie.ini and select Delete from the pop-up menu. Depending on your Recycle Bin settings, you may also have to click Yes to delete the file.

23. Click the Close button to close the Find dialog box.

24. Return to the Windows Explorer window, choose the SampleProgram folder, and click the Delete button. If the Delete Confirmation dialog box appears, click Yes. If you see a message telling you that Wolfie.com is a program and you might not be able to edit some files if it is deleted, click Yes to delete the file.

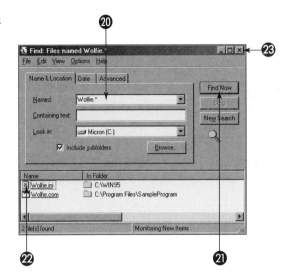

Successfully removing old Windows programs not designed for Windows 98 takes quite a bit more effort than uninstalling Windows 98 programs. Although this exercise showed you some of the pitfalls, there were other issues that simply could not be reliably addressed. If the installation program had made changes to the \Windows\System folder, for example, you would have no way to know for certain that it was safe to remove any files that were added to that folder. You're probably safe removing any extra files added to the \Windows\System folder when you immediately uninstall programs as you did in this exercise. However, you can't be certain that the files are safe to remove if you have added any additional programs between installing the sample program and uninstalling it.

TIP

Your computer retailer has programs available designed specifically to aid you in uninstalling programs. While these programs are often more capable than the Windows 98 Add/Remove Programs component, you should keep in mind that these uninstaller programs work best if you use them before you install programs you may want to uninstall. That's because the uninstaller program needs to keep track of any changes made to your system.

6

ADDING ADDITIONAL WINDOWS COMPONENTS

You might be surprised to learn that all of the Windows 98 beta probably isn't installed on your PC. There are a number of optional components you may want to try out. In the following exercises you learn how to find and install the additional pieces of the Windows 98 beta.

Exercise 5: Installing extra Windows components

You install the optional Windows 98 components by selecting them from the various groups on the Windows Setup tab of the Add/Remove Programs Properties dialog box. Table 6-1 lists the optional components you find in each of the component groups. A few of these options, notably the disk compression tools, disappear from the component group after you've installed the option, because these options cannot be removed once installed.

TABLE 6-1 OPTIONAL WINDOWS COMPONENTS

Group	Option	Description
Accessibility Options	Accessibility Options	Features to assist disabled users
Accessories	Briefcase	Used to synchronize files on two computers
Accessories	Calculator	An on-screen calculator
Accessories	Character Map	Used to insert characters and symbols into documents
Accessories	Clipboard Viewer	Displays contents of the Clipboard
Accessories	Desktop Management	Helps manage system services
Accessories	Desktop Wallpaper	Bitmap images you can use on your desktop
Accessories	Document Templates	Assists with creating new documents
Accessories	Games	Windows 98 games

Group	Option	Description
Accessories	Imaging	Graphics viewer and Twain scanner support
Accessories	Mouse Pointers	Different mouse pointers you can select
Accessories	Net Watcher	Allows you to see who is accessing your PC on a network
Accessories	Online User's Guide	Additional help files
Accessories	Paint	A drawing program
Accessories	Quick View	Enables you to view documents even if you don't have the original program
Accessories	Screen Savers	Enable you to disguise your screen
Accessories	System Monitor	A tool for checking system performance
Accessories	System Resource Meter	A tool for checking system resources
Accessories	Windows Scripting Host	Task automation tool
Accessories	Windows 98 Tour	A basic Windows 98 tutorial
Accessories	WinPopup	Enables you to send messages on a network
Accessories	WordPad	A simple word processor
Communications	Dial-Up Networking	Allows you to use a modem
Communications	Direct Cable Connectionusing	Allows you to connect a serial or parallel cable
Communications	HyperTerminal	A program for communicating with other computers
Communications	Phone Dialer	Dials your phone through your modem

continued

TABLE 6-1 *(continued)*

Group	Option	Description
Communications	Virtual Private Networking	Enables you to connect to your network privately via the Internet
Disk Tools	Backup	Backs up files
Disk Tools	Defrag	Defragments your disks for better performance
Disk Tools	Disk compression tools	Compresses files to create additional disk space
Disk Tools	Disk Space Cleanup Applet	Removes unneeded files from your hard disk
Disk Tools	FAT32 Converter	Converts hard disks to FAT32 file system
Microsoft Fax	None	Enables you to send and receive faxes
Multilanguage Support	Baltic	Estonian, Latvian, and Lithuanian languages
Multilanguage Support	Central European	Albanian, Czech, language support Croatian, Hungarian, Polish, Romanian, Slovak, and Slovenian languages
Multilanguage Support	Cyrillic language support	Bulgarian, Belarusian, Russian, Serbian, and Ukrainian languages
Multilanguage Support	Greek language support	Greek language
Multilanguage Support	Turkish language support	Turkish language
Multimedia	Audio Compression	Enables you to record and play compressed audio files
Multimedia	CD Player	Enables you to play audio CDs

Group	Option	Description
Multimedia	DVD Player	Enables you to play DVD movies
Multimedia	Media Player	Enables you to play audio and video files
Multimedia	Multimedia Sound Schemes	Additional sounds
Multimedia	Sample Sounds	Additional sounds
Multimedia	Sound Recorder	Enables you to record and play sounds
Multimedia	Video Compression	Enables you to record and play compressed video files
Multimedia	Volume Control	Enables you to adjust sound levels
Online Services	AOL	America Online
Online Services	AT&T WorldNet Service	AT&T WorldNet
Online Services	CompuServe	CompuServe
Online Services	Prodigy Internet	Prodigy Internet
Online Services	The Microsoft Network	The Microsoft Network
TV Viewer	Broadcast Data Services	Announcement Listener, Webcast, TV Enhancements
TV Viewer	TV Viewer	TV Viewer, Program Guide
Windows Messaging	Internet Mail	Enables you to send and receive e-mail via the Internet
Windows Messaging	Microsoft Mail Services	Enables you to use Microsoft Mail Post Offices (not usually necessary)
Windows Messaging	Windows Messaging	Enables you to send and receive e-mail

6

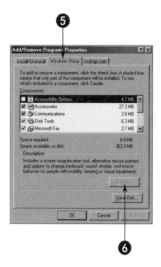

Some of these optional components are probably already installed on your PC. For this exercise you install the Multimedia Sound Scheme, a component you probably haven't installed previously.

To install optional Windows 98 components, follow these steps:

1. Place the Windows 98 beta in your CD-ROM drive.

2. Click the Start button.

3. Select Settings ➢ Control Panel.

4. Double-click the Add/Remove Programs icon.

5. Click the Windows Setup tab to display the Components list box. You can tell which items are already installed by looking at the checkboxes. An empty checkbox means the component is not installed. A white checkbox with a check means the component is completely installed. A gray checkbox with a check means the component is partially installed.

6. Select the Multimedia component and then click Details to view the individual multimedia components you can choose. If the Details button in this dialog box is grayed out, no further options for the selected item. If the Details button is not grayed out, you can make further selections by again clicking the Details button.

7. Select the Multimedia Sound Schemes checkbox.

8. Click OK to return to the Add/Remove Programs Properties dialog box. If you wish to add additional components, select them now.

9. Click Apply to copy the added components from the Windows 98 beta.

10. Click the Close button to close the Add/Remove Programs Properties dialog box.

You can just as easily remove most of the optional Windows 98 components. To remove a component you no longer need, click the Windows Setup tab on the Add/Remove Programs Properties dialog box and deselect the component's checkbox. When you click Apply, Windows 98 removes the component from your hard disk.

Unfortunately, Windows 98 sometimes simply marks the item as removed without actually erasing it from your hard disk—you just have to take your chances on this one.

Exercise 6: Installing other Windows 98 components

The Windows 98 beta contains a number of additional useful items. Some of these are essential tools and others are handy utilities: the Windows 98 Resource Kit and help for Macintosh users who upgrade to a PC running Windows 98.

Table 6-2 shows the more useful items on the Windows 98 beta that aren't automatically installed on your system.

TABLE 6-2 MORE USEFUL THINGS YOU FIND ON THE WINDOWS 98 BETA		
Name	**Folder**	**Description**
CFGBACK.EXE	\OTHER\MISC\ CFGBACK	Configuration Backup Utility used to make backups of your system registry
EPTS.EXE	\OTHER\MISC\EPTS	Enhanced Print Troubleshooter, a diagnostic tool used to solve printing problems
ERU.EXE	\OTHER\MISC\ERU	Emergency Recovery Utility used to provide a backup of your system configuration each time you make any significant system hardware or software changes, in case a problem occurs
LFNBK.EXE	\TOOLS\APPTOOLS\ LFNBACK	Long filename backup utility necessary for most hard disk utility programs released before Windows 98
LOGVIEW.EXE	\OTHER\MISC\ LOGVIEW	Microsoft Log Viewer used to display contents of all your log files

(continued)

TABLE 6-2 *(continued)*

Name	Folder	Description
MACUSERS.HLP	\TOOLS\RESKIT\ HELPFILE	Help file for people who upgrade to a PC from a Mac
MSD.EXE	\OTHER\MSD	Microsoft System Diagnostics used to locate system problems
MSPSRV.EXE	\TOOLS\NETTOOLS\ PRTAGENT	Microsoft Print Agent for NetWare Networks used to direct print jobs from a NetWare server to a computer running Windows 98
POLEDIT.EXE	\TOOLS\APPTOOLS\ POLEDIT	System Policy Editor used to create or edit system policies to standardize the appearance and capabilities of Windows 98
PWLEDIT.EXE	\TOOLS\APPTOOLS\ PWLEDIT	Password List Editor used to edit a user's password list file
REGSERV.EXE	\TOOLS\NETTOOLS\ REMOTREG	Microsoft Remote Registry service used to allow changing Registry entries over a network
SETUP.EXE	\DATALINK	Timex Data Link used to share data between a PC and a Timex Data Link watch
WIN98RK.HLP	\TOOLS\RESKIT\ HELPFILE	Windows 98 Resource Kit in help file format

The method you use to install any of these "extras" varies, depending on the item. For example, the Windows Resource Kit files can be copied from the \TOOLS\RESKIT\HELPFILE folder on the Windows 98 beta to the \Windows\Help folder on your hard disk. Some of the other items have setup information files Windows 98 can use to properly install the program.

In this exercise, you see how to install one of the more useful tools, the Password List Editor, using the setup information file.

To install the Password List Editor, follow these steps:

1. Place the Windows 98 beta into your CD-ROM drive if it isn't already there.

2. Click the Start button.

3. Select Settings ➢ Control Panel.

4. Double-click Add/Remove Programs.

5. Click the Windows Setup tab.

6. Click Have Disk to display the Install from Disk dialog box.

7. Click the Browse button, choose your CD-ROM drive, choose the \TOOLS\Apptools\Pwledit folder, and click OK.

8. Click OK to display the Have Disk dialog box.

9. Make certain the Password List Editor checkbox is selected, and click Install. You find the Password List Editor in the Programs ➢ Accessories ➢ System Tools list on your Start menu.

The Password List Editor enables you to remove passwords from your system. Normally Windows 98 stores any passwords you enter, so you won't have to retype the same passwords. You may want to remove passwords before allowing someone else to use your system, especially if you work with sensitive data.

You find that quite a few of the useful tools on the Windows 98 beta have setup information files so Windows 98 can easily install them on your system. If the program you'd like to install lacks a setup information file, look for a text file with the same name as the program file. Double-click the text file to see further information on setting up and using the program.

USING MS-DOS APPLICATIONS

Even though Windows 98 programs are generally easier to use than MS-DOS programs, some tasks simply can't be done in the Windows 98 graphical environment. Certain game programs, for example, won't

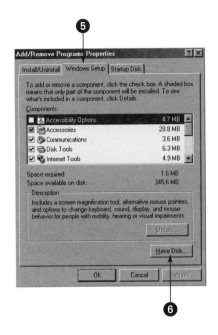

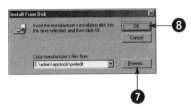

run properly in Windows. Also, you might need to use an old business program that only runs under MS-DOS. Finally, some MS-DOS commands just have no equivalent in Windows 98 itself.

Exercise 7: Using the MS-DOS command prompt

It's important to realize that Windows 98 has two distinct methods you can use to run MS-DOS commands and programs. This exercise deals with the first method, which is to run the *MS-DOS prompt* at the same time as the Windows 98 graphical environment. Using this method you can switch back and forth between MS-DOS programs and Windows 98 programs, and you can even share data via the Clipboard. Most MS-DOS programs are quite happy to run this way, and it's by far the easiest method for you to use.

The second exercise shows you how to use *MS-DOS mode*, in which your entire system is dedicated to running the MS-DOS program. Running programs in MS-DOS mode can be more work for you, and you cannot run Windows 98 while you're operating in MS-DOS mode.

To access the MS-DOS prompt and try a few commands, follow these steps:

1. Click the Start button.

2. Select Programs ➢ MS-DOS Prompt to display the MS-DOS Prompt window. If your MS-DOS prompt hides your entire Windows 98 desktop so only the MS-DOS prompt is visible, press Alt+Enter to switch the MS-DOS prompt to a window.

3. Type the following text and press Enter: **DIR *.exe > PRN.**

    This MS-DOS command prints a list of all the application programs in the current folder. This is an example of a task that is easy to accomplish using MS-DOS commands but difficult to do within Windows 98 itself. Windows 98 provides no simple way to print a file listing.

4. Click the Start button.

5. Select Programs ➢ Accessories ➢ WordPad to open a new, blank document.

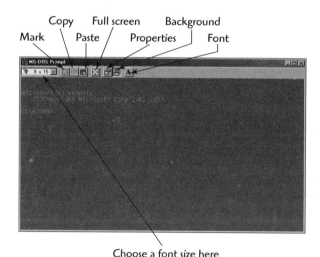

Mark   Copy   Full screen   Background
     Paste   Properties   Font

Choose a font size here

6. Click the MS-DOS Prompt button on the Taskbar to return to the MS-DOS Prompt window.

7. Type the following text and press Enter: **DIR /on /b *.bmp.**

8. Click the Mark button and then drag the mouse pointer to highlight the filenames. If you make a mistake, point to the first letter of the first file, hold down the left mouse button, and drag the mouse pointer down and to the right again until you successfully highlight all the file information.

9. Click the Copy button to copy the selected data to the Clipboard.

10. Click the WordPad button on the Taskbar.

11. Select Edit ➢ Paste to paste a copy of the data from the MS-DOS prompt into the WordPad document. This shows how easy it is to copy information from the MS-DOS prompt to a Windows 98 program. You can also copy information from a Windows 98 program to the MS-DOS prompt, but you may need to copy one line at a time when going in that direction.

12. Click anywhere within the MS-DOS Prompt window to bring the MS-DOS Prompt window to the front.

13. Click the down arrow at the right edge of the font selection list box, and select 4×6 to change the font size in the MS-DOS Prompt window to 4 pixels wide by 6 pixels high. Notice that the MS-DOS Prompt window shrinks to a much smaller size and the text becomes difficult to read.

14. Select 10×18 in the font selection list box. Notice the appearance of the type in the MS-DOS Prompt window.

15. Next, select 11×18 in the font selection list box. The 11×18 font is one of the *TrueType* fonts—scaleable fonts—so the appearance of the text is better than the 10×18 selection. Depending on your display driver, you may have choices other than 11×18—if so, choose a TrueType font in a similar size.

16. Type the following text and press Enter to display a listing of the Windows bitmap files in the current folder: **DIR *.bmp.**

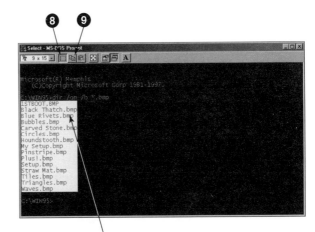

Drag the mouse pointer to highlight the information as shown here

6

The short file name
is shown here

The long file name
is shown here

⑰

⑱

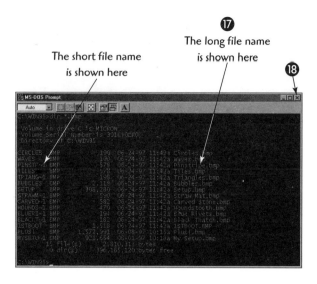

Your display should look something like the accompanying figure.

17. Compare the short filenames in the first column of the listing to the long filenames shown in the last column. When you use most MS-DOS programs (as well as older Windows programs not designed for Windows 98), you must use the short filename. In the MS-DOS Prompt window you can use either name with MS-DOS commands, but remember to enclose long filenames that include spaces within quotation marks. Entering the command **COPY Black Thatch.bmp A:** generates the error message `Too many parameters` that tells you Windows 98 didn't understand that you wanted to copy the file to a diskette. The correct command would be **COPY "Black Thatch.bmp" A:**

18. Click the Close button to close the MS-DOS Prompt window. Close WordPad, too—you can discard the changes in the document.

If you need to run MS-DOS programs, always try running them in the MS-DOS Prompt window first before you resort to using MS-DOS mode. You may need to press Alt+Enter to run the MS-DOS program full screen, but you can still switch back to your Windows 98 programs by holding down Alt while you press Tab. Each time you press Tab, another of your programs is selected. Release the Tab key when the program you want to use is selected. Press Ctrl+Esc to display the Start menu.

Exercise 8: Using MS-DOS mode

When nothing else seems to work, MS-DOS mode may be the key to allowing finicky MS-DOS programs to run on your Windows 98 PC. When you run MS-DOS mode, MS-DOS programs think they're running in plain old MS-DOS. If you have an MS-DOS program that won't even run in MS-DOS mode, it's time to think about dumping the overly-picky program and getting something designed for modern PCs.

NOTE *Depending on the specific brand and model of your CD-ROM drive, you may need to load special drivers to access your CD-ROM drive while your PC is operating in MS-DOS mode. Because each CD-ROM drive is different, you have to examine your owner's manual or call the CD-ROM drive technical support line for assistance if you absolutely must access your CD-ROM drive while in MS-DOS mode.*

In this example you use the program Wolf.com in the Exercise folder on the CD-ROM accompanying this book to simulate an MS-DOS program that requires MS-DOS mode to run. It's not possible to determine in advance if you are able to access your CD-ROM drive in MS-DOS mode, so you can begin by copying the Wolf.com file to your hard disk. Then you adjust the various settings to allow you to run Wolf.com in MS-DOS mode.

To practice setting up an application to run in MS-DOS mode, follow these steps:

1. Place the CD-ROM into your CD-ROM drive.

2. Click the Start button.

3. Select Programs ➢ Windows Explorer.

4. Choose your CD-ROM drive and open the Exercise folder.

5. Right-click Wolf.com and select Copy from the pop-up menu.

6. Right-click the \Windows folder on your C drive and select Paste from the pop-up menu.

7. Right-click Wolf.com and select Properties from the pop-up menu to display the Properties dialog box General tab. This tab shows basic information about an MS-DOS program.

8. Click the Program tab. You can make a number of setting changes on this tab, such as specifying parameters for the program in the Cmd line text box. For this exercise you won't need to make any adjustments.

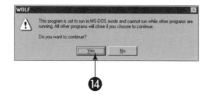

9. Click Advanced to display the Advanced Program Settings dialog box. This dialog box contains the important options you use to specify that the program must run in MS-DOS mode.

10. Select MS-DOS mode and make certain Warn before entering MS-DOS mode is also selected. Because all other applications must be shut down before you enter MS-DOS mode, it's pretty important to be warned so you don't lose unsaved data in any programs you may have open. For this example you can select the Use current MS-DOS configuration because Wolf.com doesn't require any special settings. If you select Specify a new MS-DOS configuration, you can create both a CONFIG.SYS and AUTOEXEC.BAT file just for the particular MS-DOS-mode program.

11. Click OK to continue. When you select MS-DOS mode, you cannot select any additional settings because Windows 98 won't be controlling programs you run in MS-DOS mode. The accompanying figure shows how the Font tab appears for programs that run in MS-DOS mode. The Memory, Screen, and Misc tabs show the same message because none of those settings are supported in MS-DOS mode, either.

12. Click OK to close the Properties dialog box and save your changes.

13. Make certain all other programs are closed and that you have saved any open files, and then double-click the Wolf.com program icon. Windows 98 displays a warning message.

14. Click Yes to run Wolf.com in MS-DOS mode. When the program runs, your Windows 98 desktop and Windows Explorer both disappear, your screen turns blue, and the following message is displayed: `Windows is now restarting`. If Wolf.com had been a program that actually did something, you wouldn't see the Windows is now restarting message until you exited from the program. Wolf.com simply turns the MS-DOS screen blue with yellow text and then exits.

Because MS-DOS mode shuts down Windows 98 and allows only a single program to run at a time, you should avoid using MS-DOS mode if at all possible. If you cannot find a Windows 98-compatible program, at least try to find an MS-DOS program that doesn't require everything else to shut down.

SKILLS CHALLENGE: INSTALLING AND RUNNING PROGRAMS

Now it's time to try out some of the skills you've learned in this lesson.

1. Install ThumbsPlus.

2. Install the Multimedia sound schemes.

3. Determine whether the WinPopup accessory is installed.

4. Install InstallSample.exe.

 How can you tell whether a program you installed can be uninstalled using Add/Remove Programs?

 Which folder generally holds shared program components?

5. Remove the program InstallSample.exe added to your system and all its related files.

 How can you find the configuration files used by old Windows programs?

6. Add the Help program from the old MS-DOS programs folder on your Windows 98 CD-ROM to the C:\Windows\Command folder.

 How can you find out what additional program is needed to run the MS-DOS Help program?

7. Change the properties for Wolf.com so the program runs at the MS-DOS command prompt rather than in MS-DOS mode.

 How can you run Wolf.com and then run another MS-DOS command in one MS-DOS session?

6

Problem	Solution
My MS-DOS Prompt window doesn't have buttons to click at the top of the screen.	Right-click the MS-DOS Prompt window titlebar and then click Toolbar.
There is no titlebar at the top of the MS-DOS Prompt window.	Press Alt+Enter to run the MS-DOS prompt in a window instead of full screen.
When I click the Close button on an MS-DOS window, I see a message telling me Windows 98 cannot close the program.	You need to close the MS-DOS program yourself before you can close the MS-DOS window. Look on the program's menu to find an exit command (or something similar) that closes the program.
When I run Wolf.com, Windows 98 shuts down without any warning.	Make certain the Warn before entering MS-DOS mode checkbox is selected in the Advanced Program Settings dialog box.

8. Copy a list of the names of all files in the \Windows folder with a .com extension into a WordPad document.

 How can you print a list of file names without first copying the list into WordPad?

 What do you need to include in an MS-DOS command if you want to use a long filename that includes spaces?

WRAP UP

Installing and removing programs is more work than fun, but knowing how to install and remove programs correctly saves you a lot of work and frustration in the long run. In this lesson you learned some tricks that make the whole process less of an ordeal, and you also learned how to make certain you have the information that can help solve the problems when things don't work out quite right.

This lesson also showed you that you're probably missing quite a few interesting pieces of Windows 98 and how to add those missing pieces to your PC. Along the way you discovered how to remove some of those items you never use so it's easier to find what you really want.

In the next lesson you learn how to connect to the Internet with Windows 98. You also learn about the interesting and exciting new Internet-related tools that were added to Windows 98.

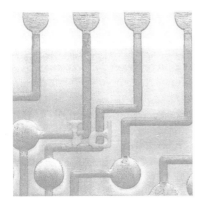

Let's Get Connected to the Internet

50 MINUTES

GOALS

Getting connected to the Internet can be a frustrating experience. Without some first-class help it's pretty easy to find yourself yelling "Why won't this work?" Once you're connected it's easy to forget about all the problems, and maybe that's why it can be so difficult to find someone who knows how to lead you through the process and help you make the connection. This lesson helps you overcome these potential problems and then shows you how to start using the Internet. You learn about the following topics:

- Getting ready to explore the Internet

- Using Internet Explorer

- Surfing the Internet

- Creating a simple Web site

- Communicating over the Internet

GET READY

The Internet probably generates more excitement and interest than any other topic in the world of computing today. It's become almost impossible to read anything about computers without seeing some reference to the Internet. If you're not already connected, you probably feel as though you're being left out—it's almost like knowing there's a big, fun party going on and you weren't invited. That's about to change as you learn how to get connected and start surfing the Internet yourself.

This lesson requires that you have access to the Internet. For most people, this means opening an account with an *Internet service provider*, or ISP; having a modem; and having access to a telephone line. There are hundreds of ISPs, from small local operations to large companies serving millions of users. An ISP is a company that provides connections to the Internet, mail servers so you can send and receive electronic mail, and news servers so you can browse news groups on the Internet. If you don't already have an account with an ISP, you need to set up an account before you're able to complete this lesson. (Refer to Exercises 1 to 4 in this lesson for help in setting up an account with an ISP.)

Make sure Dial-Up Networking is already installed on your system, or else you also need the Windows 98 beta to complete this lesson.

GETTING READY TO EXPLORE THE INTERNET

There are a number of important steps you need to complete before you're ready to begin exploring the Internet. The first step is one you have to take on your own—opening an account with an ISP. The following "mini" exercise makes certain you have the information you need to continue.

Exercise 1: Obtaining information from your ISP

The ISP should provide you with a list of technical information you need in order to connect. At the very least, this list includes the following information:

- The *dial-in phone number* — the phone number your computer must call.

- Your *user name* — may or may not be case-sensitive.

- Your *password* — may or may not be case-sensitive.

- The *IP address* — either a series of four numbers separated by periods, as in 255.12.27.67, or the instruction to obtain an IP address automatically from the server.

- The *default gateway* — similar to the IP address.

- The *DNS* addresses — similar to the IP address. There are usually two of these.

- The *mail server* — may be two names, one being the *SMTP outgoing host*, and the other being the *POP* (or *POP3*) *server host*.

- The *Usenet News Server* — is another name.

If possible, obtain all of the above information in writing before you continue. If you aren't sure you understand part of the information, check now before you go on. It's a lot easier to enter the correct information in the first place than to try to figure out what is causing problems later. If you enter any one of the pieces of information incorrectly, you probably won't be able to connect to the Internet, and you'll encounter nothing but frustration trying to correct the situation!

Exercise 2: Installing Dial-Up Networking

Dial-Up Networking is the Windows 98 component that enables you to use your modem to connect to a network. Because the Internet is just a huge collection of computers connected to networks, you need to have Dial-Up Networking installed on your PC before you can connect to the Internet through your modem.

To install Dial-Up Networking, follow these steps:

1. Click the Start button.

2. Select Settings ➢ Control Panel.

3. Double-click the Add/Remove Programs icon.

7

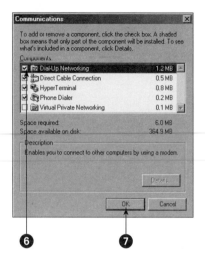

4. Click the Windows Setup tab.

5. Select Communications ➢ Details to display the Communications dialog box.

6. Make certain Dial-Up Networking is checked. The remaining four items aren't too important right now, but because they don't require much disk space, you can select them if you like.

7. Click OK to return to the Add/Remove Programs Properties dialog box.

8. If you chose to add any new components, click Apply. You may need to insert the Windows 98 beta to continue.

9. Click OK to close the dialog box. If Dial-Up Networking was not already installed, you probably need to restart your PC.

Once your system has restarted, you can continue on with the rest of the setup.

Exercise 3: Connecting to your ISP

To complete the setup, you use the information you obtained from your ISP. Sorry, you can't delay any longer—if you haven't taken the time to get all the required information, you won't be able to go any farther.

Okay, now that you're ready, you can continue. The next steps use the Internet Connection Wizard to help you enter all the necessary information for a successful connection. Because different ISPs require different settings, you need to be careful to enter the correct information for your connection.

To complete the setup, follow these steps:

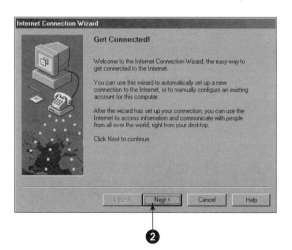

1. Double-click The Internet icon on your desktop to display the Internet Connection Wizard. If you don't see the Internet Connection Wizard, someone has already set up an Internet connection on your PC—click the Start button and select Programs ➢ Internet Explorer ➢ Connection Wizard.

2. Click Next to continue and select the Setup Options.

3. Select the I want to set up a new connection on this computer to my existing Internet account using my phone line or local area network radio button. If you don't already have an ISP, you can use the I want to choose an Internet service provider and set up a new Internet account option.

4. Click Next to continue and display the Internet Connection Wizard.

5. Make certain the Connect using my phone line radio button is selected. Even if your PC is connected to a network, it's unlikely that your network is connected directly to the Internet. If your network is connected directly to the Internet, you want to select the Connect using my Local Area Network radio button.

6. If you see the message shown in the accompanying figure, choose Create a new dial-up connection, unless you want to use one of the existing connections.

7. Click Next to continue.

8. Type the correct information to connect to your ISP in the Area code and Telephone number text boxes. The information you want to use is the dial-in phone number your ISP provided. You must include the area code even if the dial-in number is a local call.

9. If necessary, choose the correct country from the Country code list box. This code represents the dialing prefix used to initiate a long-distance call.

10. Click Next to continue and display the user name and password entries.

11. Click Next to continue and display the Advanced Settings options. For now, choose No to indicate you do not want change these settings. If you have problems connecting you can adjust these settings later.

12. Enter a name for the connection. Type the name of your ISP in the Connection name text box.

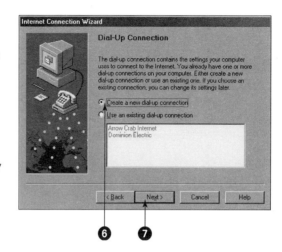

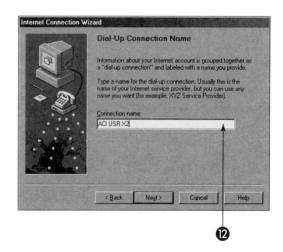

7

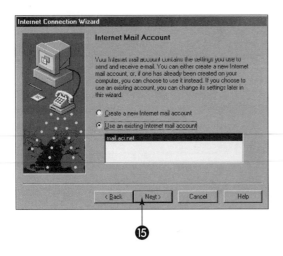

⑮

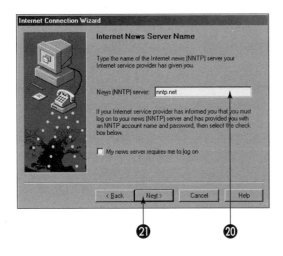

㉑   ⑳

13. Make certain the Yes radio button is selected. This allows you to send electronic mail more easily, because you won't have to set up a separate program.

14. Click Next to continue.

15. If you already have an Internet mail account, you can use the existing account. Otherwise you'll have to set up a new account to use Internet mail. Click Next to continue.

16. If you chose to use an existing account, confirm your account.

17. Click Next to continue and choose whether to set up an Internet news account.

18. If you selected Yes, make certain your name is shown correctly in the Display name text.

19. Click Next to continue and confirm your email address.

20. Click Next to continue and enter the name of the news server.

21. Click Next to continue and enter a friendly name for the news server or leave the name as it.

22. Click Next to continue and decide whether to use a directory service. Unless you've already signed up for an LDAP account, choose No.

23. You're almost done setting up your connection. Click Finish to continue.

After your Internet connection has been completely configured, you are ready to give the Internet a try. Fortunately, you probably won't have to go through the setup process again. Make certain, however, to keep all of the information about your connection in case you need to redo any of the settings in the future. You may want to see if your ISP will provide you with a printed copy of all your account information.

USING INTERNET EXPLORER

Internet Explorer is a *Web browser*—a program that enables you to view the contents of pages on the *World Wide Web*, the graphical portion of the Internet, often simply called the *Web*. Internet Explorer isn't the only Web browser you can choose, but because it's included free with the Windows 98 beta, it's pretty hard to go wrong using Internet Explorer as your Windows 98 Web browser.

In the Windows 98 beta, Internet Explorer is more than just a Web browser. Internet Explorer is also the tool you use to view the files and folders on your PC. In fact, in Windows 98 there's little difference between looking at a Web page and viewing a file on your local hard drive. Because you already know how to explore your PC, the following exercises concentrate on how to use Internet Explorer to explore the Internet.

Web browsers do more than simply display graphical information on your screen. They also play sounds, show animations, play movies, allow you to choose the sites you want to visit on the World Wide Web, keep track of where you've been, enable you to buy items online, and much more. In short, Internet Explorer is your window to the Internet. In the following exercises you get a feel for Internet Explorer and see how to make Internet Explorer work best for you.

Unless your computer is attached to a network directly connected to the Internet, most of the time you're using Internet Explorer, your computer has to be connected to the Internet through your modem. If you have a single telephone line that you use for both voice and modem calls, you won't be able to make or receive voice calls while you're using Internet Explorer. Also, if someone picks up an extension phone while you're using Internet Explorer, it's quite likely that your connection to the Internet will be disrupted. Make certain you keep these factors in mind, and free up the telephone line when you're not actively using Internet Explorer.

Exercise 4: Starting Internet Explorer

Although you use Internet Explorer for some offline tasks, such as viewing Web pages you've stored previously or looking at the files and folders on your PC, starting Internet Explorer by clicking on the desktop icon labeled The Internet also starts your connection to the Internet. Before you begin this exercise, make certain you're ready to connect to the Internet with Windows 98 on your screen, your modem turned on (if your modem is an external modem), and your telephone line available.

TIP *You may want to set your screen to a higher resolution setting, such as 800×600 or 1024×768 before you start Internet Explorer so you can see more of each Web page without so much scrolling.*

To start Internet Explorer, follow these steps:

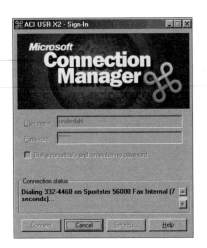

1. Double-click the icon labeled The Internet on your desktop (or the Internet icon on the Quick Launch toolbar next to the Start button). This begins the loading of Internet Explorer and displays the Connection Manager dialog box. Of course, your dialog box will show the information you entered for your connection.

2. After your account has been verified, Internet Explorer loads and displays a start page similar to the accompanying figure. Keep in mind, however, that the information shown on Web pages is constantly being updated, so your start page will certainly include a different set of articles.

4. Move your mouse around the screen and notice when the pointer changes to a hand. The hand indicates that you're pointing to a *link*—a connection to another Web page. If you click one of the links, Internet Explorer displays a different page.

5. Click the Close button to exit from Internet Explorer. Windows 98 asks if you wish to disconnect from your ISP.

6. Click Yes to close the connection and free up the phone line. You may then see a dialog box telling you that you were disconnected and asking if you want to reconnect. If so, click No.

Internet Explorer

There's a lot on the Internet Explorer screen. This Visual Bonus helps you identify the important elements that help you use Internet Explorer. Note in the accompanying figure that the Address list box was dragged to the top toolbar row so that all the toolbar buttons would be visible.

The Internet Explorer screen give you many tools for browsing the Internet.

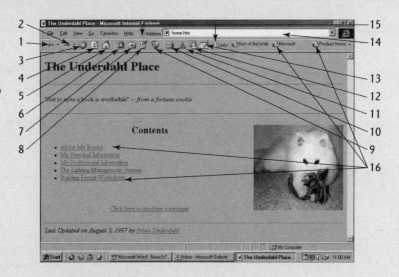

1. Click here to return to the previous page
2. Click here to go forward to a page you've already visited
3. Click here to stop loading the current page
4. Click here to reload the current page
5. Click here to return to your home page
6. Click here to search for Web pages
7. Click here to add, organize, or visit your favorite Web pages
8. Click here to see a list of the pages you've visited
9. Click here to view the available channels
10. Click here to print the current page
11. Click here to adjust the font size on the pages
12. Click here to send e-mail
13. Click here to open FrontPage Express
14. Enter or view the Web page address here
15. Drag here to change the size of the address and links sections
16. Click one of these links to visit the associated Web site

7

You should always make certain you disconnect from the Internet when you're finished browsing. If you don't, your ISP will likely automatically disconnect you after several minutes to a half an hour of inactivity.

Your first session with Internet Explorer was a short one, but you at least saw a glimpse of the Internet. Later, you learn more about surfing the Internet.

Exercise 5: Controlling your Internet Explorer view

You can make many changes to the way Internet Explorer displays the Web sites you visit. Some of these changes are simply cosmetic, some affect the speed with which pages load, and others are just for fun. In the following exercise you see examples of a number of settings you can use to change the Internet Explorer view.

To change the Internet Explorer view settings, follow these steps:

1. Double-click the The Internet icon on your desktop.

2. Click Connect.

3. Select View ➢ Internet Options and then click the Advanced tab of the Internet Options dialog box.

4. Select the Multimedia options you prefer. In most cases you want to leave the Show pictures, Play Animations, Play sounds, and Play videos checkboxes selected, but removing the checks enables you to view Web pages more quickly. Of the four checkboxes, Show pictures is likely to have the most effect because so many Web pages include graphics. If you remove the check from the Show pictures, Play Animations, or Play videos checkboxes, you can view the pictures or videos after the page has loaded by right-clicking and selecting Show picture.

5. To change the colors used for text or for the background, click the General tab and then click Colors to display the Colors dialog box. Remove the check from the Use Windows colors checkbox, and then click the rectangle to the right of Text or Background to display the color selection palette.

6. Links are generally shown underlined and in a contrasting color. You can use the Visited color palette to change the color of

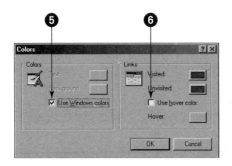

links you've already visited, and the Unvisited color palette to change the color of links you haven't visited. Select the Use hover color checkbox to make links change color as your mouse pointer is over a link. Click OK to close the Colors dialog box.

7. If you prefer to use different fonts to display Web pages, click the Font Settings button. You can choose a fixed and proportional font, but the default settings are generally good choices.

8. Click Apply and then OK to apply any changes and close the dialog box.

If you changed the Multimedia settings, you may need to click the Refresh button to see the effects of those changes on the current Web page. You see the difference immediately if you load a new Web page.

Exercise 6: Changing the connection settings

Because most of your use of Internet Explorer is on the Internet, it's important to make certain that Internet Explorer is using the best connection settings. In this exercise you learn how to view and adjust the connection settings.

To change the Internet Explorer connection settings, follow these steps:

1. If necessary, start Internet Explorer.

2. Select View ➢ Internet Options and click the Connection tab.

3. Click the Settings button to display the Dial-Up Settings dialog box.

4. Make certain the Connect without user intervention checkbox is selected. This ensures that if you need to access a Web page, Internet Explorer uses Dial-Up Networking to connect to your ISP. You can deselect this checkbox if you're on a network that is directly connected to the Internet.

5. If you have more than one Dial-Up Networking connection defined, you can select the correct one to use for connecting to

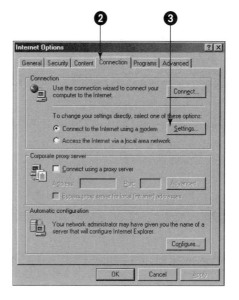

7

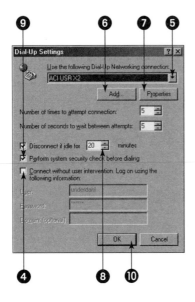

the Internet by clicking the down arrow at the right edge of the Use the following Dial-Up Networking connection list box.

6. Click the Add button to create a new Dial-Up Networking connection. You would use this option if you changed to a new ISP.

7. Click the Properties button to make a change in your current Dial-Up Networking connection, such as to change to a new phone number or to modify the IP address settings.

8. Use the up and down arrows at the right side of the Disconnect if idle for X minutes spin box to change the length of time Internet Explorer waits before disconnecting you when you haven't done anything for some time. Most ISPs automatically disconnect idle users, too, but you can use this setting to ensure you are disconnected if you forget to close Internet Explorer after a session online. You may find this setting even more beneficial if you have to access the Internet through long distance or if you use an ISP that charges for connect time.

9. Leave the Perform system security check before dialing checkbox selected to make certain there are no problems with your password.

10. Click OK to confirm your changes and return to the Options dialog box.

11. Most users won't have a need to use the Connect through a proxy server or Settings options. These options only apply if you access the Internet using a network and special software that controls that access. Your network administrator can advise you if you need to use these options.

12. Click Apply and then OK to apply any changes and close the dialog box.

You probably won't need to change the connection settings very often. If you experience difficulty establishing the connection to the Internet, you may need to adjust some of the settings for your Dial-Up Networking connection. After these settings are correct, you shouldn't need to adjust them further.

Exercise 7: Changing the navigation settings

The navigation settings control which Web page is used as your start page as well as which pages are connected to the toolbar links. These settings also control how long Internet Explorer maintains a historical record of Web pages you've visited. As a bonus, you can also quickly clear the Web page History list so other users can't find out where you've been on the Web.

To view and change the navigation settings, follow these steps:

1. If necessary, start Internet Explorer.

2. Select View ➢ Internet Options to view the General tab.

3. Enter the address for the page you want to use as your home page in the Address text box. You can click Use Current to make the currently displayed page your home page, Use Default to return to the original page, or Use Blank to use an empty home page. For example, you could visit `http://www.idgbooks.com` and assign the address to your home page.

4. Use the up and down arrows at the right edge of the Days to keep pages in history spin box to specify how often Web pages should be obsolete and no longer kept on your hard disk. It's a good idea to keep this number low to save disk space and to make certain you always are viewing the most current information. If you use the Internet quite a bit, you may want to reduce this number to seven days or less.

5. Click Clear History to remove all the stored pages. You may want to do this if you've accidentally visited Web sites that your employer may not approve, for example.

6. Click Apply and then OK to apply any changes and close the dialog box.

You can also modify the pages assigned to the Links toolbar by right-clicking a link and selecting Properties. You can do this to store addresses of Web pages you've visited. As you learn later, it's generally easier to save those page addresses in your favorites list. You may, however, want to change your start page, especially if you create your own Web site.

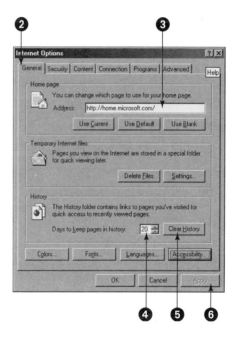

7

Exercise 8: Changing your program settings

The settings on the Programs tab of the Options dialog box control which programs are used for things like mail, news, your calendar, and your address listings. You probably won't be too concerned with these settings, but you may want to change the mail setting so that you can better organize your mail.

To view and change the program settings, follow these steps:

1. If necessary, start Internet Explorer.

2. Select View ➤ Internet Options and click the Programs tab.

3. Click the down arrow at the right side of the Mail list box to see which options are available on your system. Because Outlook Express works with your other Windows 98 programs as well as with Internet Explorer, you are able to keep all of your mail in one place if you choose Outlook Express.

4. Click the down arrow at the right side of the News list box to see which options are available on your system. Choose the option you prefer. Here, too, you probably want to choose Outlook Express so you can keep everything in one place.

5. If you wish, choose an option in the Calendar list box.

6. You probably want to select Windows Address Book as the Contact list option because the Windows Address Book also works well with Outlook Express.

7. Select the Internet Explorer should check to see whether it is the default browser checkbox. This causes Internet Explorer to verify that you haven't switched to another Web browser whenever Internet Explorer is started.

8. Click Apply and then OK to apply any changes and close the dialog box.

After you've selected your desired program settings, you probably won't need to adjust them again. Internet Explorer is able to use any newly registered file types automatically as you add new programs to your PC, without any special adjustments.

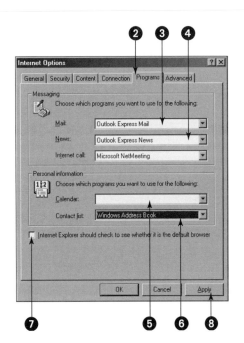

Exercise 9: Changing your security settings

The Internet can be a nasty, dangerous place to visit. Not only are there criminals who would love to steal your credit card numbers, but there are Web sites with raw adult material, and even places where your computer can easily be damaged by viruses and other dangerous programs. You can use the Internet Explorer security settings to protect yourself from most of these perils.

To adjust your security settings, follow these steps:

1. If necessary, start Internet Explorer.

2. Select View ➤ Internet Options and click the Content tab.

3. Click Enable to display the Supervisor Password Required dialog box. If you haven't set up Internet Explorer security before, you may see the Create Supervisor Password dialog box in place of the Supervisor Password Required dialog box.

4. Type the password in the Password text box. If you see the Create Password dialog box, type the same password in the Password and Confirm Password text boxes. Make certain you remember the password you type; otherwise, you won't be able to change any of the settings in the future.

5. Click OK twice to return to the Options dialog box. Then click Settings, enter your password, and click OK to continue to the Content Advisor dialog box.

6. Click one of the Category keys to display the current rating.

7. Drag the Rating slider to the right or left until you are satisfied with the setting. Continue to set each of the categories to your preference.

8. Click the General tab.

9. For the most complete protection against material you feel may be objectionable, deselect both checkboxes. Be aware, however, that many Web sites have no rating even though they do not contain anything objectionable. If you clear both checkboxes, you won't be able to visit unrated Web sites.

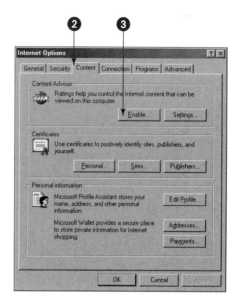

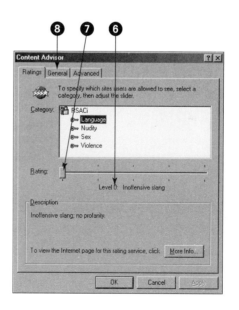

10. Click the Advanced tab. If you want to use a third-party rating system, you can specify the system you want to use. Some rating systems are continually updated by a special Web site that lists changes to Web page ratings. If you use one of these rating systems, you can specify the rating update page in the Rating Bureau text box.

11. Click Apply and then OK to apply any changes and close the dialog box.

12. You can view the current certificate settings by clicking the Personal, Sites, or Publishers button. Certificates are electronically encrypted messages that authenticate the identity of Internet users and Web sites, giving you more confidence in the integrity of businesses you encounter on the Internet.

13. Click the Security tab to view the security level settings.

14. Make certain the High radio button is selected to provide the maximum protection to your system. When you choose this setting, Internet Explorer tries to prevent programs running on Web sites you visit from doing damage to your system.

15. Click Apply and then OK to apply any changes and close the dialog box.

Remember that even the best security measures can be compromised if you're not careful. When in doubt, don't provide information or accept questionable content. This goes a long way toward keeping you and your computer safe.

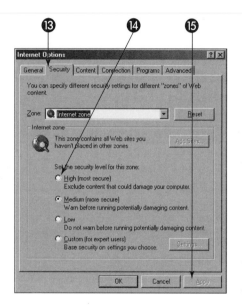

Exercise 10: Changing your advanced settings

Several remaining Internet Explorer settings are lumped together under the title advanced settings. You probably want to use the default options for most of these settings, but you find a few quite useful items here, too.

To adjust the advanced settings, follow these steps:

1. If necessary, start Internet Explorer.

2. Select View ➢ Internet Options, click the Advanced tab, and scroll down to the security settings.

3. Make certain each of the checkboxes starting with "Warn" is selected.

4. By default, the Always accept cookies radio button is selected. This setting enables Web sites to store information on your system without your knowledge. *Cookies* are text files that contain information about you and your visits to Web sites. Cookies are supposed to be available only to the Web site that stored the information on your PC, but there's no reason you shouldn't be informed before the cookie files are created. Choose Prompt before accepting cookies to select this option.

5. Click Apply and then OK to apply any changes and close the dialog box. You can leave the rest of the advanced settings set to their defaults.

Internet Explorer has many optional settings, but you've had a chance to learn about the changes you can make to improve both your speed and your security when you're browsing the Web. You can return to the Options dialog box at any time if you feel the need to further fine tune the way Internet Explorer works.

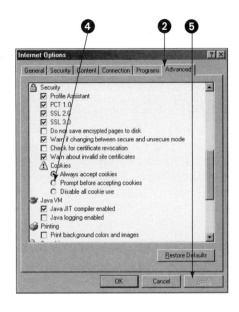

SURFING THE INTERNET

Now that you've adjusted the Internet Explorer settings, you're ready to try a little surfing. The Internet is a pretty big place, but it may not be exactly what you'd expect. You probably find many Web sites that are top quality and offer real value, but you also find many sites that aren't even worth a visit. It's pretty hard to determine in advance what you'll find, but it's pretty easy to predict that you'll find yourself heading off in directions you never imagined.

The Internet doesn't belong to anyone. Some years ago the U.S. government created an interconnection between the computer networks at government sites around the country. Eventually this interconnected group of networks expanded to include universities and other nongovernment sites, such as large companies. Standards were developed to allow all these computers to talk to each other and to make certain messages were sent to the correct destinations. In the past few years, millions of people have jumped in and made the Internet one of the hottest topics of conversation both in and out of computer circles.

Exercise 11: How do I find what I want?

At first you're bound to find the Internet a bit confusing. There aren't any road maps, and, because the Web is in a constant state of change, you may be reminded of what it's like trying to get directions to someone's house in an unfamiliar town. There are many dead ends, but there may well be several paths that lead to your destination. In this exercise you learn how to start finding your way around the Web.

NOTE *Web site addresses change faster than the weather. It's impossible to predict whether a particular Web site will be available tomorrow, much less between the time this book was written and when you're reading it. Rather than rely on specific Web site addresses you may see in the examples, treat the examples as a general guide.*

To practice finding Web sites, follow these steps:

1. If necessary, start Internet Explorer.

2. Click the Search button on the toolbar to load the search page. This page provides links to several *search engines*—services that index Web pages. These search engines provide the means for you to find Web pages based on keywords you feel identify pages you want to find. You may want to try out several of the available search engines because they don't all produce the same results.

3. Type the following text in the text box: **"IDG Books".**

When you enclose the keywords in quotation marks, most search engines treat the keywords as a single phrase rather than separate words to find. If you omitted the quotation marks, the search would look for sites that had either IDG or books, which would probably match many more sites not of interest to you.

4. Click the Search button next to the text box — not the Search button on the toolbar — to begin looking for Web pages that include the keywords. It turns out there are thousands of Web pages that include the keyword phrase "idg books" (notice that the search ignores differences in the case of the letters).

5. You can visit one of the Web pages by clicking one of the underlined links. In this case, however, it's pretty easy to guess that many of the pages are part of the same Web site, and you want to see the home page of that Web site. Because each of the links shows a *URL* — the address — for the page, you can see that several of the pages start out the same: `http://www.idgbooks.com`. To go directly to that page, type the following text in the Address text box: **http://www.idgbooks.com.**

 NOTE

*In many cases you don't have to type the entire address. For example, can can type **idgbooks** rather than **http://www.idgbooks.com**, but typing the complete address generally loads the page more quickly.*

6. Click the Close button on the Search bar to close the bar and then press Enter to go to the `http://www.idgbooks.com` Web page. It turns out this indeed is the home page for the IDG Books Worldwide Web site.

7. If you selected the Warn before accepting "cookies" checkbox, you may see security alert messages as you move to certain pages. Click Yes or No to continue. In most cases you can click No without encountering problems.

8. If you're not sure what you want to find, click the Best of the Web in the Links section of the toolbar. If you can't see any of the links, drag the separator between the Address and Links sections to expand the links section. The accompanying figure shows how the Best of the Web page may appear.

The different search engines index Web pages quite differently. As you search for Web sites, you may discover that some search engines find few pages that match your keywords, while others may

7

find so many that it's hard to know which to visit. You may want to try several different search engines to see which of them produces the best results in finding the Web sites you seek.

TIP

Web pages often include links to related sites. If you click those links you probably find other quite interesting pages that may not show up when you use one of the search engines.

Exercise 12: Keeping track of your favorite sites

You will no doubt discover Web pages that are very interesting and worth a repeat visit. You could try to remember how you got to your favorite pages, but there's a much easier way to keep track of the sites you like. You can tell Internet Explorer to remember the addresses for your favorite pages so that when you're ready for a return visit, you can simply pick out the page from your list of favorites.

To keep track of your favorite Web pages, follow these steps:

1. If necessary, start Internet Explorer.

2. Type the following text in the Address text box:
http://www.idgbooks.com.

3. Press Enter to go to the IDG Books Worldwide home page.

4. Click Favorites ➢ Add To Favorites to display the Add to Favorites dialog box.

5. Click OK to add the page to your list of favorite Web sites.

6. Click the Favorites button on the toolbar to display the list of your favorite Web sites.

7. Select Favorites ➢ Organize Favorites to display the Organize Favorites dialog box. You can create folders for your favorites, remove items from the list, or move items to different folders. You probably want to use folders to organize your favorites, perhaps by creating separate folders for different types of Web sites.

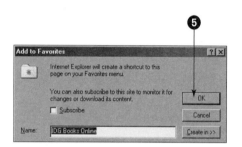

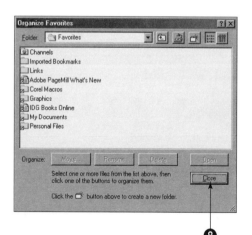

8. Click Close to close the dialog box.

The Organize Favorites dialog box includes everything in your \Windows\Favorites folder, not just your favorite Web sites. When you're organizing your favorites, you can ignore any items in the Organize Favorites dialog box that aren't related to your favorite Web sites.

CREATING A WEB SITE

What's the fun of only looking at someone else's Web pages? Windows 98 has everything you need to create and publish your own simple Web pages. In the following exercises you'll learn how you can become famous by designing your own Web page in Windows 98.

You can't learn everything about creating fancy Web sites in just a few pages, of course. But this quick overview can give you a taste of what it takes to design Web pages. If you decide you'd like to get a bit fancier, you may want to check out the many fine books by IDG Books Worldwide at your local bookstore or at http://www.idgbooks.com.

Exercise 13: Using FrontPad

FrontPad is a Web page design tool you get free with Windows 98. In this exercise you learn how to quickly create a Web page using one of the FrontPad Web page creation wizards. Once you've created a Web page, you can use FrontPad to modify the page to suit your needs.

Follow these steps to create a Web page with FrontPad:

1. Click the Start button.

2. Select Programs ➢ Internet Explorer ➢ FrontPad to open FrontPad, as shown in the accompanying figure.

3. Select File ➢ New to display the New Page dialog box.

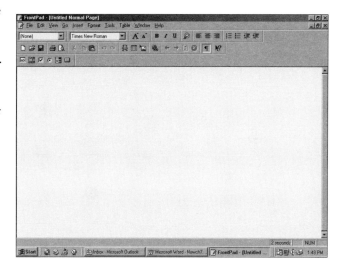

7

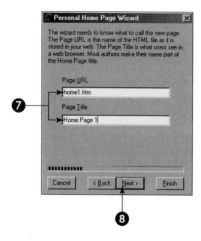

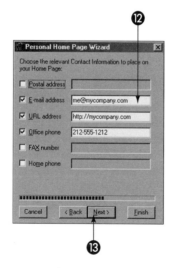

4. Select Personal Home Page Wizard as the type of page to create. You can experiment with the other types later once you've learned the basics of creating a Web page.

5. Click OK to display the Personal Home Page Wizard dialog box. You choose the basic elements of your home page in this dialog box.

6. Remove the check from Employee Information and add a check to Personal Interests.

7. Click Next to continue. You can now enter a file name (Page URL) and Page Title for your home page. For this exercise you can use the default names, but you may want to enter more descriptive names when you create Web pages in the future.

8. Click Next to continue. Since you are including a list of your favorite Web sites, you must now choose the style for the list. The default Bullet list will do just fine.

9. Click Next to continue.

10. Type the following text in the Personal Interests text box: **Windows 98**.

11. Click Next to continue.

12. Type your e-mail address and any additional personal information you'd like to include on your Web page. It's probably not a good idea to include your home telephone number unless you really like to receive calls from strange people at any hour of the day.

13. Click Next to continue.

14. If you'd like comments and suggestions about your Web page sent to you, select the Use link send e-mail to this address radio button and enter your e-mail address.

15. Click Next to continue and display the list of home page sections. If you'd like to rearrange the sections, select a section and click Up or Down to move the section. The sections appear on your home page in the order shown in this list.

16. Click Next and then Finish to create the sample home page, as shown in the accompanying figure.

17. Select File ➢ Save As and click the As File button. Click Save to save the page.

You can change the text in your Web page simply by selecting the old text and typing your new text. You can edit items by right-clicking them and selecting the appropriate options. If you wish to add images, sound, or other items, choose options from the Insert menu.

It's often better to create relatively small Web pages—at least as the top page of a Web site—and link to your more complex pages. That way users visiting your Web site won't have to endure long delays while your entire Web site loads.

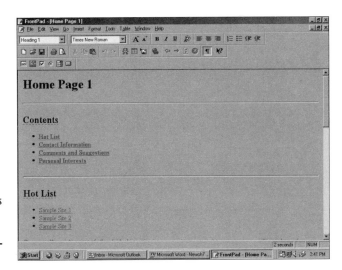

Exercise 14: Using the Web Publishing Wizard

After you've created your Web pages, you're ready to publish them on the Internet. Windows 98 includes the Web Publishing Wizard to help make this an easy project.

You need some information from your ISP before you can use the Web Publishing Wizard to publish your Web pages. You need to know where to send your files as well as any passwords necessary for access to the Web server. If you don't already have all the necessary information, ask your ISP to supply you with it to place your Web pages on the Web server.

Follow these steps to publish your Web pages using the Web Publishing Wizard:

1. Click the Start button.

2. Select Programs ➢ Internet Explorer ➢ Web Publishing Wizard to open the Web Publishing Wizard.

3. Click Next to continue.

4. Enter the name of the file or folder for your Web page. If your Web site will include multiple pages, make certain you select the folder containing the entire set of pages. If your site is contained in several folders, make certain the Include subfolders checkbox is selected. Be sure to include any graphics files or other items you've included on your Web pages, too.

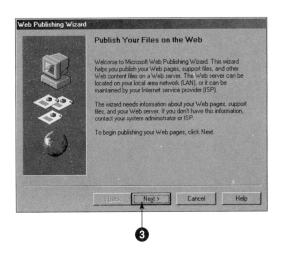

7

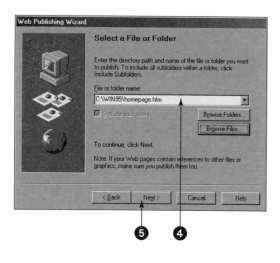

5. Click Next to continue.

6. Type a descriptive name for the Web server and click Next to continue.

7. Unless your ISP has specified otherwise, you can select Automatically Select Service Provider and click Next to continue.

8. Type the URL (address) for your Web site. Your ISP must provide this information. Click Next to continue.

9. Click Next to continue. The Web Publishing Wizard then dials your ISP and transmits your Web pages. Depending on your ISP, you may have to enter a password or some additional information to complete the process.

After you've published your Web pages, you can update them using FrontPage Express. It's a good idea to make certain your site is up-to-date; otherwise, no one will want to visit your site.

COMMUNICATING ON THE INTERNET

You can do much more on the Internet than visit Web sites. The following two exercises will give you a feel for a couple of the exciting new features of Windows 98 that enable you to communicate using both voice and video if you have the right equipment. You'll also be able to share applications and use the Internet as a secure extension of your private network.

Exercise 15: Using NetMeeting

NetMeeting takes communicating via the Internet to the limits. With the right hardware you can use the Internet as a free telephone line, as a carrier for video conferencing, as an electronic whiteboard, or even to share Clipboard objects. To use the full capabilities of NetMeeting you need a high-speed Internet connection, a video camera connected to your PC, and a few additional pieces of hardware. For this exercise, however, you don't need to go out and spend a lot of money. Instead, you see what's possible with the equipment you probably already have.

Follow these steps to try out NetMeeting:

1. Click the Start button.

2. Select Programs ➤ Internet Explorer ➤ Microsoft NetMeeting. The first time you start NetMeeting you see a series of screens that help you set up NetMeeting for use.

3. Click Next to continue. You must choose a directory server if you want people to be able to see your name and place a call to you. You should choose the same directory server selected by the people you normally call.

4. Click Next to continue. You must enter your first name, last name, and e-mail address. The remaining information is optional.

5. Click Next to continue. Choose the category for your information.

6. Click Next to display the Audio Tuning Wizard.

7. Click Next to select the type of connection you will use. Make certain you select the correct type of connection, because the connection directly affects the audio and video quality NetMeeting can provide.

8. Click Next to continue, and click Start Recording to begin testing your settings. Once you click the Start Recording button, speak into your microphone until the timer indicates the test has completed.

9. Click Next to continue. You're now ready to begin using NetMeeting.

10. Click Finish to display the NetMeeting window. Depending on the type of connection you selected, the Connection Wizard may establish a connection to the Internet.

11. Click the Call button to display the New Call dialog box.

12. Type the necessary information to reach your party in the Address text box. You can use an e-mail address, computer name, network address, or modem telephone number as appropriate.

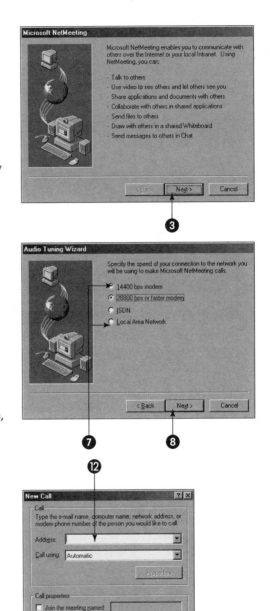

13. When you've completed your call, click the Hang Up button to disconnect.

14. Click the Close button to close NetMeeting.

If you're using NetMeeting to make a call to someone over the Internet, you may want to coordinate your call in advance by sending an e-mail telling that person when you intend to call. If you connect to the Internet using a modem, this advance scheduling is particularly important because both parties must be connected and running NetMeeting for the call to be connected.

If you're connected to a LAN (Local Area Network), you'll probably find NetMeeting even more useful than if you use NetMeeting via modems. Networks typically offer much higher data transmission rates than do modems, so you'll be able to have much higher quality audio and video on a LAN than you will over modems.

Exercise 16: Using Virtual Private Networking

Virtual Private Networking is the name Microsoft uses for a special networking protocol that enables you to access your network securely via the Internet. This special protocol is also called *Point-to-Point Tunneling Protocol* (PPTP). When you use Virtual Private Networking, you are able to access your network remotely, but unauthorized users are prevented from accessing your files.

Virtual Private Networking acts as if it were a new type of modem adapter. When you use Virtual Private Networking, your connection to the Internet and ultimately your remote network is routed first through the Virtual Private Networking Adapter and then through your modem. This extra layer provides the security to prevent unauthorized access to your network.

In this exercise you learn how to set up Virtual Private Networking so that you can access your network remotely. Your network administrator will have to add and configure the PPTP services on the network server.

To set up Virtual Private Networking, follow these steps:

1. Double-click the My Computer icon on your desktop.

2. Double-click the Dial-Up Networking icon to open Dial-Up Networking.

3. Double-click the Make New Connection icon.

4. Select Microsoft VPN Adapter (if this adapter is not shown, you need to go to the Windows Setup tab of the Add/Remove Programs dialog box and choose Virtual Private Networking from the Communications options). You can also enter a more descriptive name for the connection, but this is optional.

5. Click Next to continue.

6. You must enter the name or IP address for your network server. You may need to ask your network administrator for this information.

7. Click Next and then Finish to complete the setup.

8. To use your Virtual Private Networking connection, first open your dial-up connection to the Internet. After you're logged on to the Internet, open your Virtual Private Networking connection to establish the secure connection to your network.

Virtual Private Networking also enables you to access your server through a high speed Internet connection. This means you can connect two or more offices via the Internet and not have to worry about people stealing or damaging your files.

SKILLS CHALLENGE: USING THE INTERNET

Now it's time for a little practice. If you have trouble remembering any of the steps, go back and have another look at the exercises.

1. Open My Computer.

2. Open Dial-Up Networking.

3. Right-click the icon for your Internet connection and select Properties.

4. Check to see what phone number this connection uses.

5. Click Server Type.

6. Check your TCP/IP settings.

7. Close the Dial-Up Networking dialog boxes.

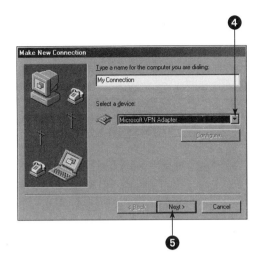

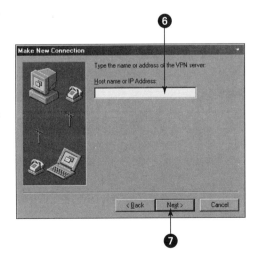

8. Connect to your ISP without first loading Internet Explorer.

 Where can you find the speed of your Internet connection?

9. Disconnect from the Internet.

10. Open Internet Explorer.

 How can you tell the URL for the current page?

11. Go to `http://www.idgbooks.com`.

12. Go back to your start page.

 How can you return to the previous page with a single click?

 How can you go back to `http://www.idgbooks.com` *with a single click?*

13. Click one of the links to go to one of the featured pages.

 How can you tell which part of the text on a page is a link?

 How can you tell which links you've already followed?

14. Check to see which program Internet Explorer uses for e-mail.

15. Search for Web pages that refer to "Area 51".

16. View your list of favorite Web sites.

17. Disconnect from the Internet.

WRAP UP

This lesson showed you how to connect to and begin using the Internet. You learned what you need to do to set up your PC for a successful connection, and you learned how to customize Internet Explorer to suit your needs. You also learned some of the basics of finding information and interesting places on the Web. With these basics you have a good foundation for continuing your explorations of the countless places you can go on the Internet.

The next lesson shows you how to use e-mail and faxes. Now that you're connected to the Internet, you can send messages virtually instantly anywhere in the world. In the next lesson you see how you can use Windows 98 applications to create and send those messages. You also find out how you can send and receive faxes right on your PC.

Problem	Solution
I can't connect to the Internet.	Check to make certain you've correctly entered your user name and password, including using the proper combination of upper- and lowercase characters. Make certain your modem is dialing the correct number. Check the IP address settings—if you aren't completely accurate, you won't be able to connect.
I can connect, but I get messages telling me none of the names I enter are valid.	Check your DNS Server settings. The DNS Server is used to convert the names you enter into valid addresses. Also make certain you're using a forward slash (/) in addresses rather than the backward slash (\) generally used on the PC.
Internet Explorer won't allow me to visit most of the Web sites I want to see.	You probably enabled the Content Advisor ratings on the Security tab of the Options dialog box and didn't adjust any of the rating levels. You need to either adjust the rating levels or disable the ratings— you need the password you entered to do so.

7

Just the Mail and Fax

GOALS

In today's world, everyone needs to communicate, and it seems like no one has the time to wait for old-fashioned mail delivery. When you need to send a message, there's no better time for the message to arrive than immediately. That's why electronic mail—e-mail—and faxes have become such a part of modern life. In Windows 98 you can send and receive e-mail and faxes right from many of your favorite programs. The primary goal of this lesson is to introduce you to using the e-mail and fax capabilities in Windows 98 and to show you how to integrate these capabilities into your everyday computing environment. You learn about the following topics:

- Configuring Windows Exchange

- Sending e-mail

- Reading your e-mail

- Sending and receiving faxes

- Creating your own address book

GET READY

For this lesson, you must have a modem that can send faxes connected to your PC. Virtually all modems manufactured in the past several years include this capability, so that shouldn't be a problem. You also need access to the Internet, but if you completed Lesson 7, that shouldn't be a problem, either. You use one practice file from the *Presenting Windows 98 One Step at a Time* CD-ROM: My file attachment.doc, which is in the Exercise folder. When you complete the exercises in this lesson, you will know not only how to send and receive e-mail and faxes, but also how to attach a file to an e-mail message and create a customized fax cover sheet.

The Windows Messaging System is used as the basis for this lesson. This Windows 98 component is sometimes called Exchange and sometimes called Windows Messaging System. It will probably show up on your desktop as *Inbox*. If you don't have Inbox on your desktop, use the Windows Setup tab in the Add/Remove Programs dialog box to install Windows Messaging System or Exchange before starting this lesson.

You may notice some small differences between your version of Windows Messaging System or Exchange and what you see in the figures in this lesson. These differences can result from a number of factors, including whether you've installed Microsoft Office 97 on your system. The basic details are quite similar regardless of any small variations you may see in the figures.

You need to know your e-mail address, and it's helpful to know someone's fax number (be sure to get permission before sending test faxes, though). You're going to send yourself some messages, and you may want to try sending faxes.

The Windows 98 beta also includes Outlook Express, which provides a slightly simpler method of sending and receiving e-mail. Unfortunately, Outlook Express does not provide fax capabilities, so it is not a complete mail and fax solution. This lesson covers Windows Messaging

System so that you can handle all your e-mail and faxes in one application.

Finally, one short exercise shows you how to incorporate CompuServe Mail into Windows Messaging System. If you don't have an account with CompuServe, you can simply skip the exercise.

CONFIGURING WINDOWS MESSAGING SYSTEM

Windows Messaging System can function as a single, central place to send and receive all of your e-mail and faxes. Whether you use the Internet, your company network, CompuServe, or faxes, Windows Messaging System can bring all your electronic messaging together so you don't have to be concerned about how the message is sent. In fact, you can even send exactly the same message to any number of different destinations without considering whether the message would go by e-mail over the Internet, by fax, or by any other service supported by Windows Messaging System.

In the following exercises you learn how to install and configure three common messaging options in Windows Messaging System: Internet Mail, CompuServe Mail, and Microsoft Fax, but there's no reason you can't add more options if necessary—Windows Messaging System is very versatile!

Exercise 1: Adding Internet Mail

Internet Mail is a Windows Messaging System option that uses your Internet e-mail account to send and receive messages over the Internet. Messages you send through Internet Mail aren't limited to simple text messages—you can send files, too. This means you can send someone a word-processing document file complete with all the formatting, a spreadsheet that includes all the formulas, or even a greeting you recorded using Sound Recorder.

 NOTE *Not all mail systems accept files attached to messages, and those that do may limit the size of file attachments. It's a good idea to make certain the recipient really can receive file attachments before you commit to sending large, important files with your messages.*

To add the Internet Mail service to Windows Messaging System, follow these steps:

1. Double-click the Inbox icon on your desktop to start the Windows Messaging System.

2. Select Tools ➤ Services ➤ Add to display the Add Service to Profile dialog box shown in the following figure. You may have a different combination of available services than shown in the accompanying figure.

3. Choose Internet Mail as the service to add.

4. Click OK to display the Internet Mail dialog box.

5. Verify that the name Windows 98 automatically entered in the Full name text box is correct. This name appears at the top of messages you send.

6. Type your e-mail address in the E-mail address text box. This should be the e-mail address provided by your ISP.

7. Type the name of the POP3 e-mail server in the Internet Mail server text box. If your ISP uses two mail servers, this should be the incoming mail server.

8. Type your user name in the Account name text box. This may be listed as your host name.

9. Type your account password in the Password text box.

10. Click the Message Format button to display the Message Format dialog box.

11. Verify that the Use MIME when sending messages checkbox is selected. This enables you to send files rather than only simple text messages. You can ignore the Character Set option for now.

12. Click OK to return to the Internet Mail dialog box.

13. If your ISP uses a second mail server to process outgoing mail, click Advanced Options to display the Advanced Options dialog box.

14. Type the name of the outgoing mail server in the Forward all outbound mail to the following mail server text box.

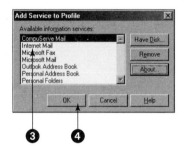

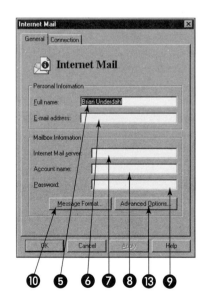

15. Click OK to return to the Internet Mail dialog box.

16. Click the Connection tab shown in the figure.

17. Select the Connect using the modem radio button (unless, of course, you're connected to a network directly connected to the Internet).

18. Open the Dial using the following connection list box, and choose the connection to your ISP. Because you've already configured this connection, you won't have to add or edit the entry.

19. Click Login As to display the Login As dialog box. Use this dialog box to specify your user name and password so Internet Mail can automatically connect without asking you for your information each time.

20. Type your user name in the User Name text box.

21. Type your password in the Password text box.

22. Click OK to return to the Internet Mail dialog box.

23. Click the Schedule button to display the Schedule dialog box. You may need to check the Work off-line and use Remote Mail checkbox to select this option.

24. Use the up and down arrows at the right edge of the Check for new messages every x minute(s) spin box to specify how often Internet Mail should automatically log on to the Internet and check for new mail. Unless you intend to send and receive a lot of e-mail, you may want to set this to 120 minutes to check every two hours. If you seldom send or receive e-mail, you might even want to use 1440 minutes to check once a day.

25. Click OK to return to the Internet Mail dialog box.

26. Click OK to continue. If you see a message similar to the message shown in the accompanying figure, click OK again.

27. As the accompanying figure shows, new services become available only after you've exited, logged off, and restarted Windows Messaging System. Click OK to confirm the message and continue.

28. Click OK one more time to return to the Windows Messaging System.

29. Select File ➢ Exit and Log Off (make certain you don't use any other method to close the Windows Messaging System).

30. Double-click the Inbox icon to restart the Windows Messaging System. Shortly after Windows Messaging System starts, Internet Mail should automatically connect to your ISP and check for new mail.

When the Internet Mail service connects to your ISP, it checks for any new mail coming to you and sends any outgoing mail that has an Internet address. If you want to check for new incoming mail or send outgoing mail, you don't have to wait for Internet Mail to make the connection. Just select Tools ➢ Deliver Now Using ➢ Internet Mail.

Exercise 2: Adding the CompuServe Mail service

Long before the Internet became as popular as it is today, online services like CompuServe provided PC users all around the world with a way to go online, download information, and send e-mail. Online services like CompuServe provide more than just the simple Internet connection you get through an ISP. They also provide content, such as forums, file-download areas, news, and much more. Millions of people still use services like CompuServe, and Windows 98 provides you a way to integrate CompuServe Mail into the Windows Messaging System.

Because CompuServe uses a proprietary mail format, it can sometimes be difficult to exchange mail between Internet mail addresses and CompuServe mail addresses, especially if you're sending a file attachment. It's often better to avoid trying to send files across the connection between CompuServe and the Internet entirely.

The following exercise shows you how to add the CompuServe Mail service to the Windows Messaging System. If you aren't a CompuServe member, you can skip this exercise.

To install the CompuServe Mail service in the Windows Messaging System, follow these steps:

1. Click the Start button.

2. Select Settings ➢ Control Panel.

3. Double-click the Mail icon.

4. Click Add to display the Add Service to Profile dialog box.

5. Choose CompuServe Mail and click OK to display the CompuServe Mail Settings dialog box shown in the accompanying figure. Your CompuServe Mail Settings dialog box may have a few differences from what you see in the next several figures, depending on the exact version of CompuServe Mail you're installing.

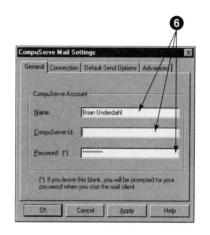

6. Type your name, account number, and password in the appropriate text boxes.

7. Click the Connection tab as shown in the accompanying figure. Your copy may lack the radio buttons shown at the bottom of the screen — the original version of CompuServe Mail lacked these options.

8. Type the CompuServe access number in the Phone Number text box.

9. Verify that your modem is shown correctly and that CompuServe is chosen in the Network list box (unless you use a different type of connection).

10. Click the Default Send Options tab. Older versions of CompuServe Mail include Payment Method options that no longer apply.

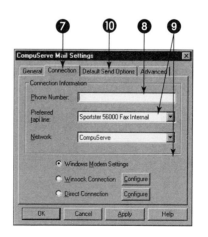

11. Make certain there are no entries in the date boxes — these options are generally not useful and could cause your messages to be delayed or lost.

12. Make certain the Send using Microsoft Exchange rich-text format checkbox is not selected. This option prevents you from sending messages to CompuServe members who are not using Windows Messaging System to retrieve their CompuServe mail.

13. Click the Advanced tab. Older versions of CompuServe Mail include an Accept Surcharges checkbox that no longer applies.

14. Remove the check from the Create Event log checkbox. Creating an event log each time Windows Messaging System accesses your CompuServe account, especially if you configure Windows Messaging System to do so automatically, results in a large number of relatively useless messages.

15. Click the Schedule Connect Times button to display the Connection Times dialog box shown in the accompanying figure.

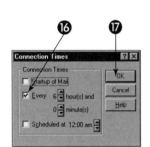

16. Select the option you prefer Windows Messaging System to use for automatically checking for mail. It's pretty handy to check several times a day — perhaps every four to six hours.

17. Click OK in each of the open dialog boxes to return to Control Panel, and then click the Close button to close Control Panel.

18. Double-click the Inbox icon to open Windows Messaging System.

19. Select Tools ➤ Deliver Now Using ➤ CompuServe Mail to verify that the service is properly installed and configured.

After you have the CompuServe Mail service installed in Windows Messaging System, sending and receiving e-mail through CompuServe is as simple as sending and receiving e-mail through the Internet. In fact, any service you add to the Windows Messaging System is easy to use because you have one central program — Windows Messaging System — handling all your e-mail.

Exercise 3: Adding Microsoft Fax

Microsoft Fax is another useful service you can add to the Windows Messaging System. Not only does this service enable you to send and receive faxes, but if the other party is also using Windows Messaging System and has the Microsoft Fax service installed, you can send and receive files with faxes, too. In addition, you can send (or receive) faxes to both other PCs and standard fax machines.

TIP

If you need to scan something but don't have a scanner, send yourself a fax from a standard fax machine. Your fax appears in electronic form on screen, as if you used a scanner to scan it in. Make certain you select the highest quality fax mode before sending the fax.

To add the Microsoft Fax service to the Windows Messaging System, follow these steps:

1. Click the Start button.

2. Select Settings ➤ Control Panel.

3. Double-click the Mail icon.

4. Click Add to display the Add Service to Profile dialog box.

5. Choose Microsoft Fax and click OK to display the Microsoft Fax dialog box shown in the accompanying figure.

6. Click Yes to display the Microsoft Fax Properties dialog box as shown in the accompanying figure.

7. Type your name, area code, and fax number in the appropriate text boxes.

8. Make certain the correct country is chosen in the Country list box.

9. Fill in any remaining text boxes as appropriate—the remaining items are optional but, if available, are used on your cover pages.

10. Click the Modem tab.

11. Choose your fax modem and click the Set as Active Fax Modem button.

12. If you're on a network and want to allow other users to send faxes through your modem, select the Let other people on the network use my modem to send faxes checkbox.

13. Click the Properties button to display the Fax Modem Properties dialog box.

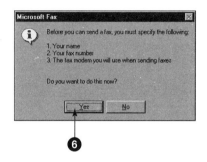

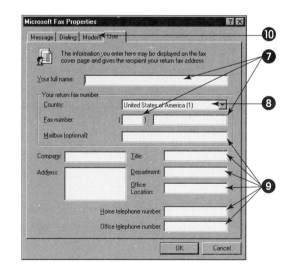

14. Select the Answer mode option you prefer:

- Select Answer after X rings if you have a dedicated telephone line for your fax modem, and select the number of rings in the list box. This enables your PC to receive faxes automatically even when you're not at your computer (as long as you leave your system on, of course).

- Select Manual to tell Windows Messaging System to display a dialog box when a call comes in. You can then choose to answer the call as a fax call if you wish.

- Select Don't Answer if you never want incoming calls answered by your PC.

15. In most cases you can leave the remaining options set to their default settings. You can always return to these settings if necessary.

16. Click the Advanced button to display the Advanced dialog box shown in the accompanying figure.

17. Select the Enable MR compression checkbox to improve the speed at which faxes are sent.

18. Select Reject pages received with errors so that your system does not accept defective pages if line noise or other problems occur.

19. Select high in the Tolerance list box. If you select a lower tolerance, your system will be overly sensitive to errors.

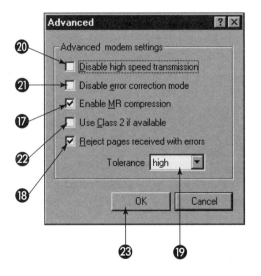

20. Make certain the Disable high speed transmission checkbox is not selected—otherwise your fax transmission speed is limited to about $2/3$ of the maximum, and more time is required to send a fax.

21. Make certain the Disable error correction mode checkbox is not selected, because error correction can improve the quality of fax transmissions.

22. Make certain the Use Class 2 if available checkbox is not selected. Class 2 fax transmissions do not allow you to send or receive file attachments.

23. Click OK to return to the Microsoft Fax Properties dialog box.

24. Click the Dialing tab.

25. In the Number of retries text box, type the number of times you'd like to try to resend faxes if the line is busy or a fax does not answer.

26. Type the amount of time to wait in the Time between retries text box.

27. Click the Message tab.

28. Select the As soon as possible radio button to send faxes as soon as you've prepared them. You can also select one of the Time to send options if you'd prefer to wait for lower-rate periods.

29. Select the Editable, if possible radio button to allow sending file attachments with faxes. File attachments can be sent only to other fax modems, and only if the receiving system is running the Windows Messaging System (or another compatible program).

30. If you want to include a cover page, select the Send cover page checkbox and select one of the available cover pages.

31. Select the Let me change the subject line of new faxes I receive checkbox so you can rename faxes to suit your needs.

32. Click OK in each open dialog box.

33. Click the Close button to close the Control Panel.

Each service you add to the Windows Messaging System can be used as needed to send messages. Microsoft Fax provides you yet another range of options in sending those messages, because you can communicate not only with other PC users, but also with standard fax machines.

SEND SOME MAIL

Now that you have your messaging services installed, you're ready to send some mail. In the following exercises you learn how to create and send e-mail messages.

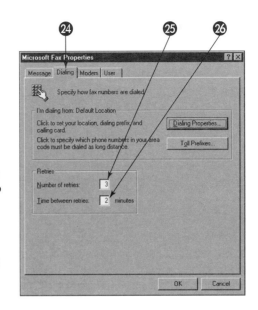

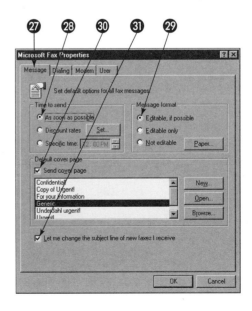

E-mail differs from ordinary mail in a number of ways. Some of the most important differences are its speed and immediacy, its capability to send more than just text in a message, and its extremely low cost. These same benefits of e-mail can work against you, however. It's pretty easy to send an angry note without considering the consequences. Once you've cooled down, it's also pretty easy to wish you hadn't hit that Send button. Just because e-mail is easy to use doesn't mean you should throw good manners out the window!

Exercise 4: Creating an e-mail message

There are many ways you can create e-mail messages. The Windows Messaging System includes a simple text editor that you can use for a quick message. You can also use WordPad or many other Windows 98 programs to create e-mail messages. In this exercise you use the most straightforward method—the Windows Messaging System text editor. If you have Microsoft Office installed on your system, Windows Messaging System may use Microsoft Word as your e-mail editor. If so, your screen may look a little different than some of the figures that follow.

NOTE *The e-mail messages you create using the Windows Messaging System text editor consist of long lines of text that Windows Messaging System automatically wraps to a new line to suit the width of the text editor window. Many other e-mail programs commonly used on the Internet don't wrap long lines of text to a new line. This can make it difficult for some people to read your e-mail messages because they have to use the horizontal scrollbar to view the complete line. In extreme cases, people not using Windows Messaging System may not be able to read your complete message if the lines are too long. If someone complains about not being able to read your complete messages, consider pressing Enter at the end of each line to place the following text on a new line.*

To create an e-mail message, follow these steps:

1. Double-click the Inbox icon to open the Windows Messaging System. The accompanying figure shows the Inbox folder of the Windows Messaging System.

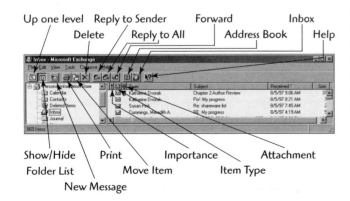

Up one level   Reply to Sender   Forward   Inbox
Delete   Reply to All   Address Book   Help

Show/Hide Folder List   Print   Importance   Attachment
New Message   Move Item   Item Type

2. Click the New Message button to display the Windows Messaging System text editor shown in the accompanying figure. Your screen may look a little different depending on the software installed on your PC. Installing Microsoft Word, for example, usually enhances the text editor by adding some of Word's formatting options.

3. Type your e-mail address in the To text box. Normally you'd type someone else's address to send that person a message, but for this exercise, you can send yourself a message.

4. Type the following text in the Subject text box: **My test message.**

5. Type the following text in the body of the message: **This is a test message I'm sending to myself to try out sending e-mail.**

6. Click the Send button to place the outgoing message in the Outbox folder as shown in the accompanying figure. Your message, of course, will contain your own e-mail address in the To column.

7. Select Tools ➤ Deliver Now Using ➤ Internet Mail to send the message.

Until it leaves your Outbox folder, you can reopen the message by double-clicking it in the Outbox folder. You may need to do this if you create a message and then discover that you forgot part of the message. You can also cancel messages that are still in the Outbox folder by selecting the message and clicking the Delete button. Once a message has left the Outbox folder, however, there's no way to stop it from being delivered.

You don't have to use Tools ➤ Deliver Now Using ➤ Internet Mail to send each message. If you configured the Internet Mail service to log on and check your mail automatically, any pending messages are sent while Internet Mail checks for incoming messages. Even if you haven't configured Internet Mail to log on and check your mail automatically, you can wait until you have several outgoing messages before logging on and delivering them.

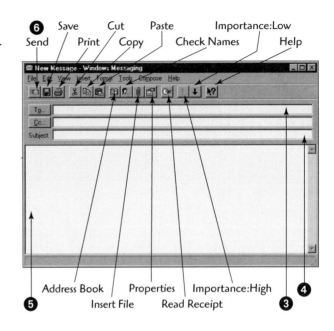

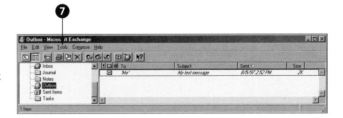

Exercise 5: Sending files

Although simple text messages probably take care of your needs most of the time, sometimes you just have to send a file, too. In Windows 98 you generally have two options for sending files. The first, which is always available, is to create a message using the Windows Messaging System text editor and *attach* a file to the message. The second method is to send a file from within an application. Each method produces the same result, although there are some minor differences between the two. For example, sending a file from within an application isn't always possible—the application must be designed for Windows 98, and it must include a File ➢ Send command.

Don't forget to check whether someone can actually receive file attachments before you spend the time to e-mail large files to them.

In this exercise you send yourself another message. This time, however, you send the message as a file attachment, so that any formatting you apply to the original document also appears in the message you receive.

To send a file along with a message, follow these steps:

1. If necessary, double-click the Inbox icon to start the Windows Messaging System.

2. Click the Start button.

3. Select Programs ➢ Accessories ➢ WordPad.

4. Type the following text: **This is an example of sending a file attached to a message.**

Or open My file attachment.doc in the Exercise folder on the *Presenting Windows 98 One Step at a Time* CD-ROM.

5. Press Ctrl+A to select the entire document.

6. Click the Italic button to format the text as italic.

7. Click the down arrow at the right edge of the Font size list box and choose 20.

8. Click the Color button and change the text to Red.

9. Click the Save button and save the file as **My file attachment.**

Your document should look similar to My file attachment.doc in the Exercise folder on the CD-ROM that accompanies this book.

10. Select File ➢ Send to display the New Message window shown in the accompanying figure. Notice that the body of the message already includes an icon for the document that you're sending as an attachment and that this New Message window looks a little different than the one you used earlier.

11. Type your e-mail address in the To text box. For this exercise you send the message to yourself as you did with the earlier message.

12. Type the following text in the Subject text box: **My text file attachment.**

13. Click the Send button to send the message.

14. Select Tools ➢ Deliver Now Using ➢ Internet Mail to send the message.

Because you're sending a message to yourself, there was no need to add additional text to the body of the message. It's a good idea, however, to include some explanation of the file attachment when you send a file to someone else. After all, would you want to open a mystery package?

In this exercise you used WordPad to create and send a file attachment. If you want to send an existing file, a file you didn't create, or perhaps multiple files in a single message, send those files as attachments to a normal message you create using the Windows Messaging System text editor. Click the Insert File button and then browse to find the files you wish to send.

READING YOUR MAIL

Reading your mail—unless it's all bills—is even more fun than sending mail. In the following exercises you learn how to read and reply to

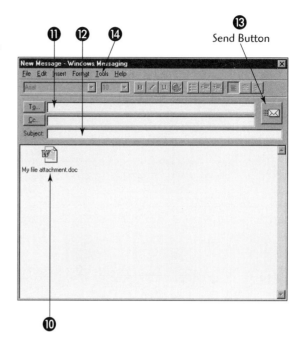

Send Button

e-mail messages. You also learn how to handle files attached to messages you receive.

Exercise 6: Reading your e-mail messages

Because the Windows Messaging System collects all your messages in one place—the Inbox—you only have to look in the Inbox to find your messages. In this exercise you learn how to read one of the messages you sent yourself earlier.

TIP

You may want to use Sound Recorder to create a voice message to attach to the New Mail Notification event to tell you when you have new messages. Double-click Sounds in Control Panel to add your voice message to an event.

To read your e-mail messages, follow these steps:

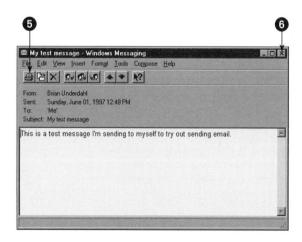

1. If necessary, double-click the Inbox icon on your desktop to open the Windows Messaging System.

2. Select Tools ➢ Deliver Now Using ➢ Internet Mail to check for new messages. The messages you sent earlier may already be in your Inbox, but there's no harm in checking to see if you have any additional messages.

3. If necessary, click the Inbox folder icon to see any messages. As the accompanying figure shows, new messages that you haven't read are shown in bold type, while messages you have read are shown in normal type.

4. Double-click the new message to open it, as shown in the accompanying figure.

5. Click the Print button to print a copy of the message. Notice that your printed copy of the message includes a header with information about the message to help you keep track of your messages.

6. Click the Close button to close the message.

It doesn't matter whether a message was one you sent to yourself or whether it was sent by someone halfway around the world. When you use Windows Messaging System, it's just as easy to read any message, regardless of its origin.

Exercise 7: Replying to and forwarding messages

One thing that sets e-mail apart from old-fashioned, hand-delivered mail is the ease with which you can reply to an e-mail message or forward a copy of the message to someone else. In this exercise you learn how to reply to an e-mail message and see how to forward a copy when necessary.

To reply to an e-mail message, follow these steps:

1. Double-click the message entitled "My test message" to open the message again.

2. Click the Reply To Sender button to open the reply window shown in the accompanying figure. Notice that the To text box and the Subject text box are already filled in, and a copy of the original message is included in the body of the message. The copy of the original message is indented to show that it is the copy.

3. Type the following text in the message body: **This is my reply**.

4. Click the Send button to place your reply in the Outbox.

5. Select Tools ➢ Deliver Now Using ➢ Internet Mail to connect to your ISP and send your reply.

Forwarding a message is almost as simple as replying to a message. Rather than clicking the Reply To Sender button, you click the Forward button. When you forward a message, you must choose the recipient. Also, the message subject line begins with FWD rather than RE to indicate that the message is a forwarded message and not a reply to a message.

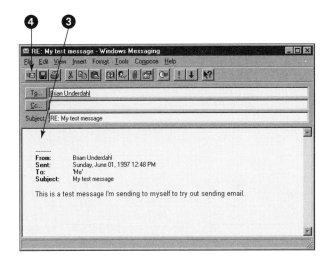

Exercise 8: Saving file attachments

E-mail messages that contain file attachments require slightly different handling than simple text messages. In most cases you probably want to save the attached file for future use. In the following exercise you learn how to view and save file attachments in your e-mail messages.

To view and save file attachments, follow these steps:

1. Double-click the message entitled "My text file attachment" to open the message.

2. Right-click the icon for My file attachment.doc in the message body to display the menu shown in the accompanying figure.

3. Select Open to open the attached document. Notice that all of the character formatting you added to the original document remains in the document.

4. Click the Close button to close WordPad (or Word, if you have Word installed on your PC).

5. Right-click the icon for My file attachment.doc and select Save As to display the Save As dialog box.

6. Click the down arrow at the right edge of the Save in list box and select the folder in which you want to save the file. Be sure you know where the file is saved — it's easy to forget where you saved a file attachment.

7. Click Save to save the file.

8. Click the Close button to close the message.

It's a good idea to be a little cautious about saving file attachments if you don't know the person who sent the message, or if you're not certain of the origin of the file. File attachments could contain computer viruses, and once they're saved on your hard disk, they're free to damage your system.

WE WANT THE FAX

Fax machines were around long before PCs and were the original method of instantly sending a copy of a document to someone a long distance from you. Faxes remain popular because they're inexpensive, convenient, and fast. In recent years PC modem manufacturers have added the capability to send and receive faxes through your modem. It really doesn't matter whether one end of a fax transmission has a fax machine and the other end has a PC — they're totally compatible.

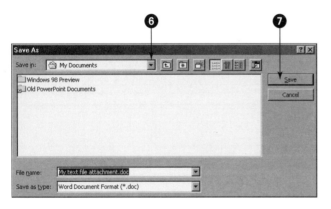

8

If you've ever received a fax, you probably noticed that most faxes sent from fax machines leave something to be desired. Faxes can be hard to read and are often blurred or distorted. Faxes sent from PCs usually don't have these problems; they are much cleaner and easier to read. The big reason for this is that fax machines have to scan a document before sending it. If the paper goes through the scan a little crooked, the fax is a little crooked, too. When you send a fax from your PC, however, you're using the receiving fax machine as a printer, getting the best possible quality from that printer.

Exercise 9: Faxing a message

Although you can use the Windows Messaging System text editor to create a fax message, it's more likely you want something a little fancier. Because Windows 98 prints an outgoing fax message as if it were connected by a very long cable to a printer called a fax machine, you send most faxes by selecting Microsoft Fax as a printer. This means that your fax arrives at its destination looking just about like it does on your screen. If you use fancy character formatting in your document, the fax includes the fancy formatting, too.

TIP

If both the sending and receiving ends are PCs using Windows Messaging System, you can include a file attachment with a fax you send from your PC, just as if you were sending a file attachment with an e-mail message. You may want to use this option if you need to send a file to another PC user who doesn't have an e-mail account, or whose e-mail account won't accept file attachments. Because the entire message is sent using fax protocols, this is one of the easiest methods of sending someone a file. Unfortunately, it's also one of the slowest because the transmission speed is limited to the highest fax speed, which is about half the speed of most modern modems.

To send a fax from a Windows 98 application, follow these steps:

1. If necessary, start Windows Messaging System by double-clicking the Inbox icon on your desktop.

2. Click the Start button.

3. Select Programs ➤ Accessories ➤ WordPad.

4. Type the following text: **This is my test fax**.

5. Select File ➤ Print to display the Print dialog box.

6. Click the down arrow at the right edge of the Name list box, and choose Microsoft Fax.

7. Click OK to display the Compose New Fax dialog box.

8. Type the name of the recipient in the To text box.

9. Type the area code and fax telephone number in the Fax # text box, and then click Next to choose a cover page.

10. Select the Yes radio button to use a cover page. You may not want to use a cover page if you are faxing someone a letter and your letterhead provides your complete contact information, but a cover page is a good idea when the purpose of the document may not be completely clear.

11. Choose Generic and then click Options to display the Send Options for this Message dialog box. You can use this dialog box to override your default fax options for the current fax. For example, if you normally hold faxes until discount calling rates go into effect, you might choose to send a local fax immediately.

12. Click OK and then Next to continue. As the accompanying figure shows, you can now enter a subject line and a note for the cover page.

13. Type the following text in the Subject text box: **This is a test fax**.

14. Click Next to continue to the final screen.

15. Click Finish to send the fax.

After you've clicked Finish to send the fax, Windows 98 processes the fax and places it in the fax queue. If you've chosen to send the fax immediately, the fax will be sent within a few minutes of clicking Finish. If there is a problem such as a busy signal, your system tries again as many times as you specified in the Microsoft Fax

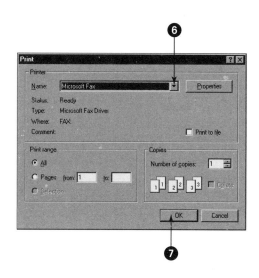

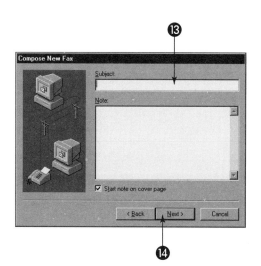

Properties dialog box. You may need to increase the number of retries if you frequently send faxes to a busy fax machine.

Exercise 10: Reading faxes

When you receive a fax, the fax appears in your Windows Messaging System Inbox folder just like any other messages you receive. In this exercise you learn how to view faxes you receive, so it would be handy if you asked someone to send you a quick fax before you begin the exercise. It doesn't matter whether they send the fax from another PC or from a standard fax machine. All you need is a quick note so you can get the feel for reading faxes you've received.

 NOTE *Windows Messaging System must be running for you to receive a fax. Be sure you start the Windows Messaging System before someone tries to send you a fax.*

To view an incoming fax, follow these steps:

1. Double-click the new fax in the Windows Messaging System Inbox folder to display the message window shown in the accompanying figure. Faxes are stored in a special format; you cannot view their contents directly.

2. Double-click the fax icon in the message window. This opens the fax in the Fax Viewer as shown in the accompanying figure.

3. Click the Fit to Width button to zoom in so you can read the message. You can also use the Zoom In and Zoom Out buttons or the Predefined Zooms list box to choose 25%, 50%, or 100% zoom.

4. If the fax was transmitted upside down, click the Rotate Left or Rotate Right button twice to invert the image.

5. Click the Print button to print a copy of the fax.

6. Click the Close button to close Fax Viewer.

7. Click the Close button to close the message window.

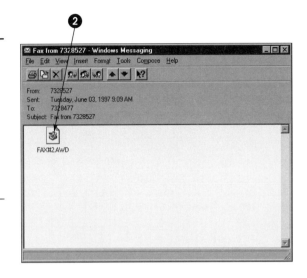

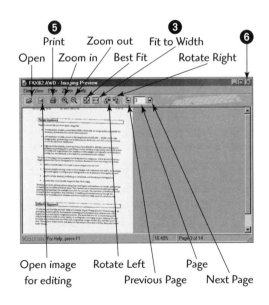

Faxes you receive remain in the Inbox until you delete them. You can reply to a fax or forward a fax just like any other message you've received, but the recipient must be using Windows Messaging System to view a fax you've forwarded.

Exercise 11: Creating a fax cover page

Cover pages are extra sheets you send at the beginning of a fax. You include information so that the fax is routed to the correct person, the recipient knows the subject of the fax, and the recipient knows how to contact you with a response. Many times a cover page is unnecessary, especially if you're faxing a letter using your letterhead.

Windows 98 includes several cover pages you can use as is, or you can create your own cover page using the cover page editor. If you like, you can even modify one of the existing cover pages. In this exercise you learn how to use the cover page editor to slightly modify one of the existing cover pages.

To use the cover page editor, follow these steps:

1. Click the Start button.

2. Select Programs ➤ Accessories ➤ Fax ➤ Cover Page Editor.

3. Select File ➤ Open.

4. Double-click Urgent!.cpe to open the Urgent! cover page as shown in the accompanying figure.

5. Click {Sender's Address} to select the dotted box containing the field for your address. Items on a fax cover page enclosed in brackets are fields filled in when the fax is sent using information you supplied when you set up Microsoft Fax, or that you supply when you send a fax.

6. Click the Cut button to remove this field from the cover page.

7. Select the {Sender's Company} field.

8. Click the down arrow at the right edge of the Font Size list box and choose 16 to increase the point size.

9. Right-click the {Sender's Company} field.

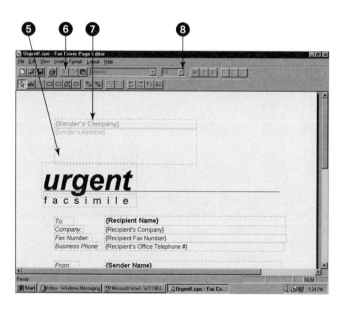

10. Select Line, Fill and Color to display the Line, Fill and Color dialog box.

11. Select the Draw border/line checkbox, choose 5 in the Thickness list box, and choose Black in the Color list box to add a thick border around your company name.

12. Select the Color radio button and choose Dark Gray in the Color list box to fill the box with a dark gray pattern.

13. Choose White in the Text color list box to make the text print as white. Your dialog box should now look like the accompanying figure.

14. Click OK to return to the Cover Page Editor.

15. Click the Center button to center your company name in the box.

16. Drag the borders of the {Sender's Company} field to make a larger box as shown in the accompanying figure.

17. Select File ➢ Save As and type the following text in the File name text box: **My urgent.**

18. Click Save to save the modified cover page. Your final document should look similar to the final document, My urgent.cpe, located in the Exercise folder on the book's CD-ROM.

19. Click the Close button to close the cover page editor.

You can add plain text, objects, or fields to a cover page. To add text or objects you draw, use the buttons on the Drawing toolbar. To add fields, use the options on the Insert menu to select a field to add. It's probably not a good idea to add most images to fax cover pages, however, because many fax machines are rather poor at printing any type of graphic.

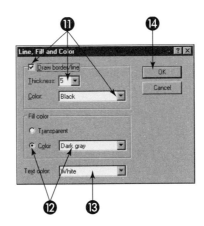

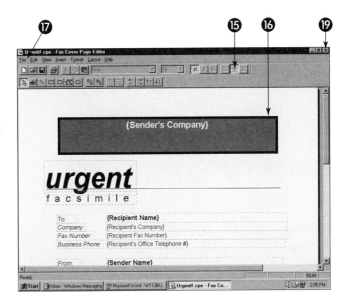

CREATE YOUR OWN ADDRESS BOOK

It can be a little inconvenient always entering the e-mail address or fax number whenever you want to send a message. It's much easier to save the addresses and phone numbers in the Windows Messaging

System Address Book, and then select the recipient from the list when you want to send a message.

Exercise 12: Adding names to your Address Book

You probably use a telephone that stores some of the phone numbers you frequently call. When you want to call one of these stored phone numbers, just push a button or two and your telephone dials the number for you. The Windows Messaging System Address Book provides a similar capability for your e-mail and fax messages. In this exercise you learn how to add people to your Address Book.

To add information to your address book, follow these steps:

1. If necessary, double-click the Inbox icon to start the Windows Messaging System.

2. Click the Address Book button to display the Address Book shown in the accompanying figure. Your Address Book probably won't have any entries yet.

3. Click the New Entry button to display the New Entry dialog box. If you haven't installed CompuServe Mail, you probably won't have some of the options shown in the accompanying figure.

4. Choose Internet Mail Address as the type of address you wish to add. You can add other types of addresses by choosing the proper type from the Select the entry type list box.

5. Click OK to display the New Internet Mail Address Properties dialog box.

6. Type the name of the person in the Display Name text box. The name you type doesn't have to be the person's real name—you can use an easy-to-remember nickname if you like.

7. Type the person's e-mail address in the E-mail Address text box. This is something like someone@somecompany.com.

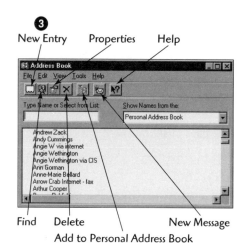

New Entry   Properties   Help

Find   Delete   New Message

Add to Personal Address Book

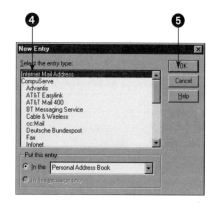

8. Click OK to add the new entry to your Address Book. If you like, you can add more information on the other tabs of the New Internet Mail Address Properties dialog box before you close the dialog box, but the two entries you've added are all that is required.

9. Click the Close button to close your Address Book.

| TIP | *Right-click the sender's name when you receive e-mail, and select Add to Personal Address Book to quickly add new entries to your Address Book.* |

Adding a fax number or CompuServe address to your Address Book is as simple as adding an Internet address, but when you add fax numbers, you probably want to add more of the optional information. When you send a fax using a cover page, Microsoft Fax can include information fields from the Business tab to make the cover page more complete.

Exercise 13: Using your Address Book names

After you've added names to your Address Book, it's much easier to send messages. Rather than typing out the complete e-mail address, you can simply type the person's name or choose an entry from your address book.

To use names from your address book, follow these steps:

1. If necessary, double-click the Inbox icon to start Windows Messaging System.

2. Click the New Message button to begin creating a new message.

3. Type the name of the recipient in the To text box. You should type the same name you added to the Display Name text box when you created the Address Book Entry.

4. If you're not certain you entered the name correctly, click the Check Names button. If more than one possibility exists, this displays the Check Names dialog box shown in the accompanying figure. If the name you entered is correct, the Check Names

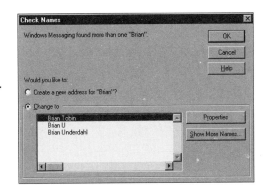

dialog box won't be displayed, but the name is underlined to show that it is correct.

5. If the Check Names dialog box is displayed, choose the correct name and click OK to add the underlined name to the To text box.

6. To add additional names to either the To or the Cc text boxes, type the additional names separated by a semicolon (;). If you're not certain of the correct names, click the To or the Cc buttons and choose names from the Address Book.

7. Complete your message and click the Send button.

TIP *To send a blind carbon copy—a copy that the other recipients don't know about—select View ➤ Bcc Box and add the additional recipient in the Bcc text box.*

You may find that you have multiple Address Book entries for some people. You might, for example, have an Internet e-mail address and a fax number for certain people. To make it easier for you to select the correct Address Book entry for these people, you might want to include something like "- e-mail" or "- fax" when you create the related entries.

SKILLS CHALLENGE: USING MAIL AND FAX

Now it's time to try out the skills you've learned in this lesson.

1. Start Windows Messaging System.

2. Determine which messaging services are available.

 How can you tell whether the same mail server provides both incoming and outgoing mail delivery to your PC?

3. Determine how often the Windows Messaging System checks for new Internet mail.

How can you tell *Windows Messaging System* not to check for Internet mail automatically?

4. If you have CompuServe Mail installed, check to see how often *Windows Messaging System* automatically looks for CompuServe Mail.

5. Determine the name of your fax modem.

6. Determine how many rings you'll hear before your fax modem answers a call automatically.

 What setting can you use so that your fax modem only answers calls with your approval?

 How can you determine how many times your system retries sending a fax?

7. Check to see which fax cover page is set as your default.

8. Check to see if you have any new mail in your Inbox.

 How can you tell if a message includes an attachment?

9. Send yourself a message with a file attachment.

10. Create a new message in WordPad.

11. Send the WordPad message to yourself.

 How can you send the same message to both an e-mail address and a fax machine without sending the message twice?

12. Open the Generic cover page in the Cover Page Editor.

13. Change the Sender's Company field to white text on a black background.

14. Add your e-mail address to your Address Book.

Problem	Problem
I can receive but not send e-mail over the Internet.	Check to make certain your ISP uses the same mail server for incoming and outgoing mail. You may need to use the Advanced settings in Internet Mail to specify a different outgoing mail server.
My modem stopped answering fax calls.	You probably installed new modem drivers or made some other change to your modem settings. Whenever you change modem settings, Microsoft fax may decide to change back to the Don't answer setting. Go back to the fax modem properties dialog box and reset the answer settings.

 How can you quickly add someone who sent you a message to your Address Book without actually opening your Address Book?

15. Send yourself a message using your name rather than your e-mail address.

WRAP UP

This lesson showed you how to use e-mail and faxes. Now you can send messages virtually instantly anywhere in the world. You learned you can use Windows 98 applications to create and send those messages. You learned how you can send and receive faxes using your PC as well as how to manage all your e-mail addresses and fax numbers in your Address Book.

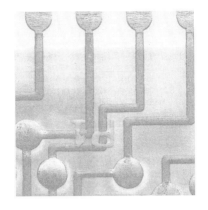

Installing Windows 98 Beta

60 MINUTES

If you buy a new PC after Windows 98 is released, your PC will likely come with Windows 98 already installed. If you upgrade to Windows 98, you'll find it's pretty easy to install it yourself. In this appendix you learn what you need to do to prepare for installing Windows 98 beta, and then actually proceed with the installation.

PREPARING TO INSTALL WINDOWS 98 BETA

Here are a few steps you need to follow before you install Windows 98:

1. Make sure your computer is compatible with Windows 98. Basically, it must have an 80386, 80486, Pentium, Pentium Pro, Pentium II, or compatible processor; 8MB of memory; and about 50MB or more of free disk space. You'll be much happier if you don't try to run Windows 98 on a 386, and even most 486 systems will be pretty slow. You're also much better off with at least 16MB of memory and 100MB of free disk space.

2. Make sure you don't have any unresolved hardware problems or conflicts. If something doesn't work correctly before you install Windows 98, it won't work afterwards, either.

3. Back up any critical files. Installing Windows 98 shouldn't cause any data to be lost, but why take the chance?

4. Make sure you have a blank, high-density diskette available.

5. If you're connected to a network, make certain you have a list of your user names and passwords.

INSTALLING WINDOWS 98 BETA

You'll need about an hour to install Windows 98 — maybe longer if you encounter any problems or have a slow system. When you're ready, follow these steps:

1. Place the Windows 98 Beta CD-ROM in your CD-ROM drive (or the first Windows 98 diskette in drive A).

2. If you're running Windows 3.x, select File ➢ Run.

3. Type the following text (if your CD-ROM drive is not drive D or if you are installing from diskettes, use the correct drive letter): **d:\setup.**

4. Follow the prompts and click the Next button when necessary.

5. If the setup program prompts you to choose a directory, choose the option to install Windows 98 in the same directory as your existing version of Windows — otherwise you have to reinstall all of your programs.

6. At one point the Setup program directs you to create a startup disk. You can use this diskette to start your PC in case there's a problem with your hard disk.

7. Continue to follow the prompts and finish the installation. Be sure to remove any diskettes before allowing the system to restart.

If Windows 98 has any problems restarting, wait a few minutes before you do anything. Remember that it may take an hour or so to complete the installation.

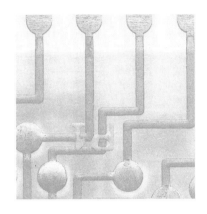

Answers to Skills Challenge Questions

■ Bonus Question 1.1

How do you create a shortcut that opens Windows Explorer with the C:\Windows\Start Menu\Programs\Accessories folder visible in the contents pane?

Open the Windows Explorer, point to the C:\Windows\Start Menu\Programs\Accessories folder icon in the left pane, hold down the right mouse button, and drag the pointer onto your desktop. (If the Windows Explorer window is covering the entire desktop, click the Restore button to reduce the size of the Windows Explorer window so you can see your desktop.) Click Create Shortcut(s) Here.

■ Bonus Question 1.2

How do you create a shortcut that opens Windows Explorer with the contents of your CD-ROM drive visible?

Open the Windows Explorer, point to the icon for your CD-ROM drive, hold down the right mouse button, and drag the pointer onto your desktop. (If the Windows Explorer window is covering the entire desktop, click the Restore button to reduce the size of the Windows Explorer window so you can see your desktop). Click Create Shortcut(s) Here.

■ Bonus Question 1.3

How can you add WordPad as an option to the Send To command?

Create a shortcut to WordPad in the \Windows\SendTo folder.

■ Bonus Question 1.4

What can you do to make it easy to copy files to a specified folder using the right-click menu?

Create a shortcut to the specified folder in the \Windows\ SendTo folder.

■ Bonus Question 1.5

What do you do to make Windows Explorer run automatically whenever you start Windows 98?

Create a shortcut to Windows Explorer in the \Windows\Start Menu\Programs\StartUp folder.

■ Bonus Question 1.6

How do you find files created during June, 1997?

Specify 6/1/97 in the "between" and 6/30/97 in the "and" text boxes on the Date Modified tab of the Find dialog box. Then select the Find all files created or modified radio button before you click Find now.

■ Bonus Question 1.7

How can you find out which files were created or modified by a program you installed today?

Select the during the previous X days radio button, select 1 in the spin box, and select the Find all files created or modified radio button on the Date Modified tab of the Find dialog box before you click Find now.

■ Bonus Question 1.8

How can you find a document file someone created on your computer yesterday if you don't know the name or location of the file?

Although you can simply select 2 in the during the previous X days spin box and perform the search, you may want to set both the "between" and "and" text boxes to yesterday's date and use that option to limit the search.

■ Bonus Question 1.9

How do you find and open the help file called Backup.hlp?

Click the New Search button, type **Backup.hlp** in the Named text box, click Find Now, and then double-click Backup.hlp in the results panes.

■ Bonus Question 2.1

How do you change to the High Contrast White (Extra Large) color scheme?

Right-click a blank space on the desktop, select Properties, click the Appearance tab, and choose High Contrast White (Extra Large) in the Scheme list box.

■ Bonus Question 2.2

How do you increase the size of the on-screen text to five times normal so that a vision-impaired user can read the Windows 98 screen?

Right-click a blank space on your desktop, select Properties, click the Settings tab, click Custom, and specify 500% in the Scale fonts to be X of normal size text box.

■ Bonus Question 2.3

How do you make a picture into wallpaper that covers your entire desktop?

Choose the picture in the Wallpaper list box on the Background tab of the Display Properties dialog box, and then select the Tile radio button.

■ Bonus Question 2.4

What can you do to protect your privacy when you step away from your desk?

Select a screen saver and a password on the Screen Saver tab of the Display Properties dialog box, and set the screen saver Wait time to a very short time.

■ Bonus Question 2.5

How can you hide the titlebar text?

Select Active Title Bar in the Item list box of the Appearance tab of the Display Properties dialog box, and set the font color to the same color as the titlebar.

■ Bonus Question 2.6

How do you find out where someone hid the Taskbar?

Move your mouse off each edge of the screen. If the Taskbar is hidden at that edge, it will appear after a short delay.

■ Bonus Question 2.7

How do you make it easier for someone with limited physical abilities to double-click the mouse?

Double-click the Mouse icon in Control Panel, and set the Double-click speed to the slowest setting.

■ Bonus Question 2.8

What do you do to make the mouse pointer easier to find for someone who's never used a mouse before?

Select the Show pointer trails checkbox on the Motion tab of the Mouse Properties dialog box.

■ Bonus Question 2.9

What two settings can you use to make the keyboard easier to use for someone just learning to type?

Set the Repeat delay and Repeat rate settings in the Keyboard Properties dialog box.

■ Bonus Question 3.1

What is the one step you must always remember to do before saving a find files search if you want Windows 98 to remember any date specification you entered?

You must make certain Options ➢ Save Results is selected, and that you've selected Find Now before you select File ➢ Save Search.

■ Bonus Question 3.2

What is the fastest way to find the first item that starts with W in the Windows Explorer contents pane?

Press W to jump to the first item beginning with W.

■ Bonus Question 3.3

How can you remove one item from a selection?

Hold down Ctrl while you click the item you want to remove.

■ Bonus Question 3.4

How can you add an option to open the Text Document file type with WordPad in addition to keeping the default action?

Open Windows Explorer and select View ➢ Options. Then click the File Types tab, select text, click Edit, select New, and type **Open** in the Action text box and **WordPad** in the Application used to perform action text box.

■ Bonus Question 4.1

What format option can you use to make certain a diskette doesn't contain any bad sectors?

Make certain the Full format type radio button is selected.

■ Bonus Question 4.2

What can you do to prevent a diskette from being formatted and destroying any data it contains?

Slide the write-protect tab open.

■ Bonus Question 4.3

How can you copy a file on your desktop to a diskette without using Windows Explorer?

Right-click the file icon, select Send To, and choose the diskette as the destination.

■ Bonus Question 4.4

How can you specify an exact amount of free space rather than a percentage?

Click the Start button and select Programs ➢ Accessories ➢ System Tools ➢ DriveSpace. Then select the icon for the drive, select Drive ➢ Adjust Free Space, and enter an exact value in either the compressed drive or the host drive free space text box.

■ Bonus Question 4.5

What setting checks for file system errors without doing a surface scan?

Select the ScanDisk Standard type of test rather than the Through type of test.

■ Bonus Question 4.6

How can you specify that you want to check all of your disk drives for errors in one operation?

Select all of the drives in the Select the drive(s) you want to check for errors list box before you click Start.

■ Bonus Question 4.7

What setting is necessary to keep ScanDisk from stopping and showing a summary report if there are no errors?

Click the Advanced button and select Only if errors found.

■ Bonus Question 5.1

How can you tell the length of a sound file without playing the file?

Right-click the sound file, choose Properties, and look on the Details tab.

■ Bonus Question 5.2

What artist created the Microsoft Sound?

Right-click the sound file, choose Properties, and look on the Details tab to see that the artist was Brian Eno.

■ Bonus Question 5.3

How can you quickly mute all sounds from your PC?

Click the speaker icon on the Taskbar and choose Mute.

■ Bonus Question 5.4

How can you create the effect of having an echo occur before the sound?

Use the Sound Recorder Effects ➢ Reverse command to reverse the sound. Then use Effects ➢ Add Echo. Finally, use Effects ➢ Reverse again.

■ Bonus Question 5.5

How can you remove all changes from a sound recording?

Select File ➢ Revert.

■ Bonus Question 5.6

How can you play the songs on an audio CD in reverse order of the way they appear on the CD?

Edit the play list and add the songs starting from the end of the titles.

■ Bonus Question 5.7

How can you make the same set of songs play several times in a row?

Either click the Continuous Play button, or add the songs to the play list several times.

■ Bonus Question 5.8

How much disk space does the lowest-quality PCM format audio recording require for each second of recording?

8 Hz, 8-bit mono requires 8K per second.

■ Bonus Question 6.1

How can you tell whether a program you installed can be uninstalled using Add/Remove Programs?

If a program can be uninstalled, it will appear on the Install/Uninstall tab of the Add/Remove Programs dialog box.

■ Bonus Question 6.2

Which folder generally holds shared program components?

C:\Windows\System

■ Bonus Question 6.3

How can you find the configuration files used by old Windows programs?

Look for files with an INI extension.

■ Bonus Question 6.4

How can you find out what additional program is needed to run the MS-DOS Help program?

If you try to run the help program you'll see a message `Can not find file QBASIC.EXE`, which tells you that Help.COM needs QBASIC.EXE.

■ Bonus Question 6.5

How can you run Wolf.com and then run another MS-DOS command in one MS-DOS session?

Click the Start button and select Programs ➤ MS-DOS Prompt. Then run the programs from the command line.

■ Bonus Question 6.6

How can you print a list of filenames without first copying the list into WordPad?

When you're at the MS-DOS Prompt command line, redirect the output of the DIR command to the printer by adding **> PRN** to the end of the command line.

■ Bonus Question 6.7

What do you need to include in an MS-DOS command if you want to use a long filename that includes spaces?

Enclose the long filename in quotes.

■ Bonus Question 7.1

Where can you find the speed of your Internet connection?

Double-click the modem icon on the Taskbar.

■ Bonus Question 7.2

How can you tell the URL for the current page?

Look in the Address text box.

■ Bonus Question 7.3

How can you return to the previous page with a single click?

Click the Back button.

■ Bonus Question 7.4

How can you go back to `http://www.idgbooks.com` *with a single click?*

Display the History list using the down arrow at the right edge of the Address text box, and click `http://www.idgbooks.com`.

■ Bonus Question 7.5

How can you tell which part of the text on a page is a link?

It will be underlined and a different color.

■ Bonus Question 7.6

How can you tell which links you've already followed?

They will be in a color different than the other links.

■ Bonus Question 8.1

How can you tell whether the same mail server provides both incoming and outgoing mail delivery to your PC?

Look in the Advanced Options dialog box. If your ISP specifies both a POP3 and an SMTP mail server, the POP3 server is incoming, and the SMTP server is outgoing.

■ Bonus Question 8.2

How can you tell the Windows Messaging System not to check for Internet mail automatically?

Select the Work off-line and use Remote Mail checkbox.

■ Bonus Question 8.3

What setting can you use so that your fax modem only answers calls with your approval?

Select the Manual Answer Mode radio button.

■ Bonus Question 8.4

How can you determine how many times your system will retry sending a fax?

Look on the Dialing tab of the Microsoft Fax Properties dialog box, and check the setting in the Number of retries text box.

■ Bonus Question 8.5

How can you tell if a message includes an attachment?

Look for the paper clip icon.

■ Bonus Question 8.6

How can you send the same message to both an e-mail address and a fax machine without sending the message twice?

Just specify both addresses in the To text box.

■ Bonus Question 8.7

How can you quickly add someone who sent you a message to your Address Book without actually opening your Address Book?

Right-click that person's name and select Add to Address Book.

What's on the CD-ROM

The CD-ROM in the back of the book includes the exclusive *One Step at a Time On-Demand* software. This interactive software coaches you through the exercises in the book's lessons while you work on a computer at your own pace.

The CD-ROM also includes an electronic version of the book in Adobe Acrobat PDF format. You can read the complete version of the book's text and figures on your computer's display while you run Windows 98 beta.

USING THE ONE STEP AT A TIME ON-DEMAND INTERACTIVE SOFTWARE

One Step at a Time On-Demand interactive software includes the exercises in the book so that you can search for information about how to perform a function or complete a task. You can run the software alone or in combination with the book. The software consists of the following three modes:

- **Concept** mode displays an introduction to each exercise.

- **Demo** mode provides a movie-style demonstration of the same steps that are presented in the book's exercises, and works with the sample exercise files that are included on the CD-ROM in the Exercise folder.

- **Teacher** mode simulates the software environment and permits you to interactively follow the exercises in the book's lessons.

■ Installing the software

The *One Step at a Time On-Demand* software can be installed on Windows 3.1, Windows 95, the beta version of Windows 98, and Windows NT 4.0. To install the interactive software on your computer, follow these steps:

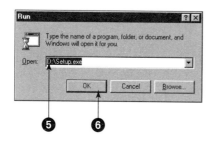

1. Place the *Presenting Windows 98 One Step at a Time* CD-ROM in your CD-ROM drive.

2. Launch Windows 3.1 (if you haven't already). The Program Manager appears.

3. Choose File.

4. Select Run. The Run dialog box appears.

5. Type **D:\Setup.exe** (where D is your CD-ROM drive).

   Note: Alternatively, for Windows 95, Windows NT 4.0, or Windows 98 beta users, click the Start menu, select Run, and type **D:\Setup.exe** (where D is your CD-ROM drive) in the Run dialog box to begin installing the software.

6. Click OK to run the setup procedure. The On-Demand Installation dialog box appears.

7. Click Continue. The On-Demand Installation Options dialog box appears.

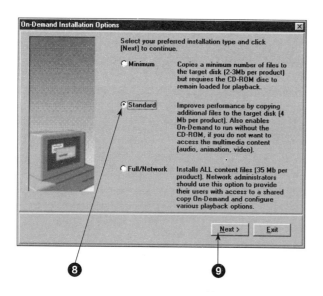

8. Click the Full/Network radio button (if this option is not already selected).

9. Click Next. The Determine Installation Drive and Directory dialog box appears.

10. Choose the default drive and directory that appears, or click Change to choose a different drive and directory.

11. Click Next. The Product Selection dialog box appears, which enables you to verify the software you want to install.

12. Click Finish to complete the installation. The On-Demand Installation dialog box displays the progress of the installation. After the installation, the User Registration dialog box appears.

13. Enter information in the User Registration dialog box, including a password.

14. Click OK. The Password Verification dialog box appears.

15. Type the password again.

16. Click OK. The On-Demand Installation dialog box appears.

17. Click OK to confirm the installation has been successfully completed.

■ Running Concept, Demo, or Teacher mode

Once you've installed the software, you can view the text of the book and follow interactively the steps in each exercise. To run Concept mode, Demo mode, or Teacher mode, follow these steps:

1. Launch Windows 3.1 (*if you haven't already*). The Program Manager appears.

2. Double-click the IDG Books icon that appears on your desktop. The IDG Books window opens.

3. Double-click the One Step at a Time icon. The *Presenting Windows 98 One Step at a Time* cover appears.

4. Click the start button.

5. The Interactive Training dialog box appears.

Note: Alternatively, for Windows 95, Windows NT 4.0, or Windows 98 beta users, click the Start menu, select Programs ➢ IDG Books ➢ One Step at a Time. A small On-Demand toolbar appears on the desktop. Click the icon of the professor. The Interactive Training dialog box appears.

6. Select the Contents tab. A list of the lessons appears, divided into four modules.

7. Click the plus icon next to the lessons you want to explore, or click the Lessons radio button. A list of the lessons appears.

8. Click the plus icon next to the lesson you want to explore, or click the All Topics radio button. A list of topics appears, which correspond to the exercises in the book.

9. Double-click a topic of your choice. A menu appears.

10. Select Concept, Demo, or Teacher.

11. Follow the onscreen prompts to use the interactive software and work through the steps.

Note: In Concept mode, to return to the Lesson Selection dialog box, click the yellow text box, or press the Enter key. In Demo mode, you only need to perform actions that appear in red. Otherwise, the software automatically demonstrates the actions for you. All you need to do is read the information that appears on screen. (Holding down the Shift key pauses the program; releasing the Shift key activates the program.) In Teacher mode, you need to follow the directions and perform the actions that appear on screen.

STOPPING THE PROGRAM

To stop running the program at any time, press Esc to return to the Interactive Training—Lesson Selection dialog box. Press Esc again to close the software, or click Exit. The On-Demand toolbar reappears.

To exit the program, click the icon on the On-Demand toolbar that displays the lightning bolt image. A menu appears. Choose Exit. The On-Demand—Exit dialog box appears. Click Yes to exit On-Demand.

A

alignment Positioning of text relative to the left or right margin.

anchor position The beginning of the object or selection.

animated cursor A mouse pointer that includes movement.

argument A piece of additional information controlling how a program runs. Also known as a *parameter*.

attach To include a file with a message.

Audio Visual Interleave *(AVI)* Windows 98 video files in which the audio and video portions are both included interleaved in the same file.

B

bitmap An image file in which all objects are part of a single object.

Blind carbon copy (Bcc) A copy that the other recipients don't know about.

boot disk A disk you can use to start Windows 98.

Boss key The key that quickly hides 3D Pinball, the Esc key.

bounding box An imaginary rectangular box as wide and as high as the object being drawn.

bullets Markers often seen at the left of a list of summary points.

C

cascading menu A menu that appears and offers additional choices when a menu item that has an arrow is selected.

Clipboard A Windows 98 tool you can use to cut, copy, and paste objects.

combo box A list box that includes a list box and a text box.

command-line interface The MS-DOS window where you type commands. Also known as the *prompt*.

compound documents Documents containing data from a number of sources.

Compressed Volume File (CVF) A special file used by DriveSpace to create additional space on a disk by storing everything in a single, compressed file.

cookie A text file that contains information about a Web surfer's visits to Web sites.

cover page An extra sheet sent at the beginning of a fax.

cross-linked Multiple files that seem to be using the same disk space. At least one of each pair of cross-linked files will probably be unusable.

D

desktop theme A special collection of color schemes, wallpaper, animated cursors, and sounds in Plus!

destination disk The target disk.

Distribution Media Format (DMF) Diskettes specially formatted to prevent them from being copied.

downloading Receiving files.

dragging Holding down the left mouse button while moving a selected object.

draw program A program that creates objects that can be stretched or moved independently of any other objects in the image.

dropping Releasing an object by letting up on the mouse button.

E

ellipsis Three periods that follow a menu command indicating that a dialog box will appear when the command is selected.

embedding Placing an OLE object in a document.

error-correcting file transfer protocol A method of breaking up files into relatively small pieces and verifying that each of those pieces is received properly to ensure that files are transferred properly.

event Something that can be assigned a sound, such as

starting Windows 98, opening a menu, or closing a program.

F

file transfer protocol A method ensuring that files are transferred properly.

focus The dotted outline showing which dialog box element is currently active.

formatting The process of creating the electronic marks that allow your disk drives to write in the right places on a disk.

fragmented Stored in several noncontiguous pieces on a disk.

G

Graphical User Interface, or GUI ("gooey") The Windows 98 visual-style interface. In contrast, MS-DOS uses a *command-line interface,* or *prompt.*

H

host drive The drive letter used to access the physical drive rather than the compressed drive.

hotkey Alt + the underlined character, which activates a menu command.

I

icon A small picture that represents a program or document.

indent Extra distance between the document margin and the paragraph margin.

in-place editing A temporary appearance change that allows use of a source application's toolbars so that an object can edited without leaving the document.

insertion pointer The slowly blinking vertical line where new text will appear.

Internet service provider (ISP) A company that provides access to the Internet.

invert A special effect in which each color is replaced by its complement.

L

link A connection to another Web page.

linking Placing a reference to an OLE object in a document.

lost file fragments Leftover pieces of files taking up space even though the file was deleted.

M

margin The distance printing begins from the edge of the paper.

MS-DOS mode The operating mode in which your entire system is dedicated to running an MS-DOS program.

MS-DOS prompt The MS-DOS command line you use to issue DOS commands.

Musical Instrument Digital Interface (MIDI) A method of generating music using a synthesizer.

N

Null modem cable A special cable that enables two PCs to talk directly to each other.

O

Object Linking and Embedding (OLE) A way to share data that allows you to create *compound documents.*

OLE client A program that can receive drag-and-drop information.

OLE server A program that can send drag-and-drop data.

P

paint program A graphics program that creates *bitmap* images.

parameter A piece of additional information that controls how a program runs. Also known as an *argument*.

password A secret word that allows access to a resource such as a folder.

pica A typographic measurement approximately one twelfth of an inch.

pixel A unit of measure of screen resolution. Short for picture element.

point A typographic measurement. There are approximately 72 points in an inch.

polygon A multisided object.

R

Registry A special database Windows 98 uses to keep track of important information about your system. If the Registry is damaged, you may not be able to use your computer.

restore The process of making backed-up files available for use.

root directory The ultimate parent of all the folders on a disk.

ruler The measurement line just above the text window in a word processor.

S

sampling rate The number of times per second sound is recorded.

scrap A piece of a document saved on the desktop.

search engine A service that indexes Web pages.

shortcut A copy of an icon used to access a program or document.

skewing Leaning a selection at an angle.

source disk The original disk used in a copy operation.

stretching Making a selection grow or shrink by a percentage.

T

tabs Fixed points used to specify precise text positioning.

terminal program A program that makes your PC into a communications terminal so that you can upload and download files.

toggle A command that changes states from selected to deselected, or deselected to selected, each time the command is selected.

Tooltips Hints that appear when the mouse pointer is held over Toolbar buttons.

TrueType fonts Scalable fonts.

U

Uniform Resource Locator (URL) The address for a Web page.

uploading Sending files.

V

virtual desktop An area larger than the actual monitor display provided by some display adapters.

W

wave files Windows 98 sound files that are simply a digital recording of sounds.

Web browser A program that enables a Web surfer to view the contents of pages on the *World Wide Web*, the graphical portion of the Internet.

word wrap The action used to display lines longer than the width of the window.

World Wide Web The graphical portion of the Internet. Often simply called the *Web*.

write-protect slider A small plastic rectangle on the diskette that prevents your PC from writing anything on this diskette until you move the slider back to cover the hole.

(continued)

(continued)

Save $10 on your next purchase of On-Demand Interactive Learning!

The Interactive Simulation included on the CD-ROM is a special version of *On-Demand Interactive Learning*, a revolutionary new desktop learning tool from PTS Learning Systems. This version has been specifically designed for use with the One Step at a Time exercises. PTS Learning Systems also offers different versions of On-Demand Interactive Learning that provide the same great interactive support and learning.

As a special bonus to One Step at a Time customers, you can receive $10 off any purchase on On-Demand Interactive Learning! To place an order, please call 1-800-387-8878.

Also, you may install live modules of On-Demand Interactive Learning and find out more about PTS Learning Systems by using the CD-ROM in this book. If you have a browser (Internet Explorer or Netscape Navigator), please do the following:

1. Start your browser.
2. Select File from the menu.
3. Select Open.
4. Type D:\info\welcome.htm.
   (where D is the letter of your CD-ROM drive)
5. Click OK to view the contents.

For more information about PTS and our products, please visit our Web site at www.ptsls.com.

PTS Learning Systems currently offers On-Demand Interactive Learning for the following:

- Windows 3.1
- Windows 95
- Windows NT
- Microsoft Word
- Microsoft Excel
- Microsoft PowerPoint
- Microsoft Internet Explorer
- Microsoft Office
- Lotus SmartSuite
- Lotus Notes

Receive $5!

When Purchasing any of the Following Books:

Windows® 98 One Step at a Time	0-7645-3184-0
Access 97 One Step at a Time	0-7645-8027-2
Excel 97 One Step at a Time	0-7645-3139-5
Microsoft® Internet Explorer 4 One Step at a Time	0-7645-3104-2
Office 97 One Step at a Time	0-7645-3050-X
Outlook™ 97 One Step at a Time	0-7645-3128-X
Word 97 One Step at a Time	0-7645-3129-8

Just follow the instructions on the card below.
Offer Good Through May 31, 1998

 **Get $5 Back!**

on Your Next Purchase of a *One Step at a Time* Book.

To receive your rebate, please send a copy of the cash register receipt dated January 1, 1998 thru May 31, 1998 with the UPC number written on the back of the cash register receipt and mail to:

 One Step Rebate, P.O. Box 8006, Walled Lake, MI 48391-8006

In Canada, to receive your $7 CAN rebate, please send a copy of the cash receipt dated January 1, 1998 through May 31, 1998 and mail to:

 One Step Rebate, P.O. Box 6120, Paris, ON, N3L 3W6

Which book(s) did you buy?

Name

Address

City   State/Prov.   Zip/Postal Code

IDG BOOKS WORLDWIDE, INC.
END-USER LICENSE AGREEMENT

READ THIS. You should carefully read these terms and conditions before opening the software packet(s) included with this book ("Book"). This is a license agreement ("Agreement") between you and IDG Books Worldwide, Inc. ("IDGB"). By opening the accompanying software packet(s), you acknowledge that you have read and accept the following terms and conditions. If you do not agree and do not want to be bound by such terms and conditions, promptly return the Book and the unopened software packet(s) to the place you obtained them for a full refund.

1. **License Grant.** IDGB grants to you (either an individual or entity) a nonexclusive license to use one copy of the enclosed software program(s) (collectively, the "Software") solely for your own personal or business purposes on a single computer (whether a standard computer or a workstation component of a multiuser network). The Software is in use on a computer when it is loaded into temporary memory (RAM) or installed into permanent memory (hard disk, CD-ROM, or other storage device). IDGB reserves all rights not expressly granted herein.

2. **Ownership.** IDGB is the owner of all right, title, and interest, including copyright, in and to the compilation of the Software recorded on the disk(s) or CD-ROM ("Software Media"). Copyright to the individual programs recorded on the Software Media is owned by the author or other authorized copyright owner of each program. Ownership of the Software and all proprietary rights relating thereto remain with IDGB and its licensers.

3. **Restrictions On Use and Transfer.**
   (a) You may only (i) make one copy of the Software for backup or archival purposes, or (ii) transfer the Software to a single hard disk, provided that you keep the original for backup or archival purposes. You may not (i) rent or lease the Software, (ii) copy or reproduce the Software through a LAN or other network system or through any computer subscriber system or bulletin-board system, or (iii) modify, adapt, or create derivative works based on the Software.
   (b) You may not reverse engineer, decompile, or disassemble the Software. You may transfer the Software and user documentation on a permanent basis, provided that the transferee agrees to accept the terms and conditions of this Agreement and you retain no copies. If the Software is an update or has been updated, any transfer must include the most recent update and all prior versions.

4. **Restrictions On Use of Individual Programs.** You must follow the individual requirements and restrictions detailed for each individual program in Appendix C: "About the CD-ROM" in this Book. These limitations are also contained in the individual license agreements recorded on the Software Media. These limitations may include a requirement that after using the program for a specified period of time, the user must pay a registration fee or discontinue use. By opening the Software packet(s), you will be agreeing to abide by the licenses and restrictions for these individual programs that are detailed in Appendix C: "About the CD-ROM" and on the Software Media. None of the material on this Software Media or listed in this Book may ever be redistributed, in original or modified form, for commercial purposes.

5. **Limited Warranty.**
   (a) IDGB warrants that the Software and Software Media are free from defects in materials and workmanship under normal use for a period of sixty (60) days from the date of purchase of this Book. If IDGB receives notification within the warranty period of defects in materials or workmanship, IDGB will replace the defective Software Media.
   (b) **IDGB AND THE AUTHOR OF THE BOOK DISCLAIM ALL OTHER WARRANTIES, EXPRESS OR IMPLIED, INCLUDING WITHOUT LIMITATION IMPLIED WARRANTIES OF MERCHANTABILITY AND FITNESS FOR A PARTICULAR PURPOSE, WITH RESPECT TO THE SOFTWARE, THE PROGRAMS, THE SOURCE CODE CONTAINED THEREIN, AND/OR THE TECHNIQUES DESCRIBED IN THIS BOOK. IDGB DOES NOT WARRANT THAT THE FUNCTIONS CONTAINED IN THE SOFTWARE WILL MEET YOUR REQUIREMENTS OR THAT THE OPERATION OF THE SOFTWARE WILL BE ERROR FREE.**
   (c) This limited warranty gives you specific legal rights, and you may have other rights that vary from jurisdiction to jurisdiction.

6. **Remedies.**
   (a) IDGB's entire liability and your exclusive remedy for defects in materials and workmanship shall be limited to replacement of the Software Media, which may be returned to IDGB with a copy of your receipt at the following address: Software Media Fulfillment Department, Attn.: *Presenting Windows 98 One Step at a Time*, IDG Books Worldwide, Inc., 7260 Shadeland Station, Ste. 100, Indianapolis, IN 46256, or call 1-800-762-2974. Please allow three to four weeks for delivery. This Limited Warranty is void if failure of the Software Media has resulted from accident, abuse, or misapplication. Any replacement Software Media will be warranted for the remainder of the original warranty period or thirty (30) days, whichever is longer.
   (b) In no event shall IDGB or the author be liable for any damages whatsoever (including without limitation damages for loss of business profits, business interruption, loss of business information, or any other pecuniary loss) arising from the use of or inability to use the Book or the Software, even if IDGB has been advised of the possibility of such damages.
   (c) Because some jurisdictions do not allow the exclusion or limitation of liability for consequential or incidental damages, the above limitation or exclusion may not apply to you.

7. **U.S. Government Restricted Rights.** Use, duplication, or disclosure of the Software by the U.S. Government is subject to restrictions stated in paragraph (c)(1)(ii) of the Rights in Technical Data and Computer Software clause of DFARS 252.227-7013, and in subparagraphs (a) through (d) of the Commercial Computer—Restricted Rights clause at FAR 52.227-19, and in similar clauses in the NASA FAR supplement, when applicable.

8. **General.** This Agreement constitutes the entire understanding of the parties and revokes and supersedes all prior agreements, oral or written, between them and may not be modified or amended except in a writing signed by both parties hereto that specifically refers to this Agreement. This Agreement shall take precedence over any other documents that may be in conflict herewith. If any one or more provisions contained in this Agreement are held by any court or tribunal to be invalid, illegal, or otherwise unenforceable, each and every other provision shall remain in full force and effect.

CD-ROM INSTALLATION INSTRUCTIONS

The CD-ROM includes the interactive *One Step at a Time On-Demand* software. This software coaches you through the exercises in the book while you work on a computer at your own pace. *One Step at a Time On-Demand* interactive software includes the text of the book, so that you can search for information about how to perform a function, how to complete a task, or make use of the software itself.

You can run the software in *Concept* mode, *Demo* mode, or *Teacher* mode. Concept mode introduces you to the topic being demonstrated, while Demo and Teacher mode simulate the software environment and permit you to interactively follow the steps in each exercise. The software can be used alone or in combination with the book.

■ Installing the Software

The *One Step at a Time On-Demand* software can be installed on Windows 3.1, Windows 95, the beta version of Windows 98, and Windows NT 4.0. To install the interactive software on your computer, follow these steps:

1. Place the *Presenting Windows 98 One Step at a Time* CD-ROM in your CD-ROM drive.

2. Launch Windows 3.1 (if you haven't already). The Program Manager appears.

3. Choose File.

4. Select Run. The Run dialog box appears.

5. Type **D:\Setup.exe** (where D is your CD-ROM drive).

   Note: Alternatively, for Windows 95, Windows NT 4.0, or Windows 98 beta users, click the Start menu, select Run, and type **D:\Setup.exe** in the Run dialog box (where D is your CD-ROM drive) to begin installing the software.

6. Click OK to run the setup procedure. The On-Demand Installation Dialog box appears.

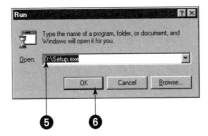

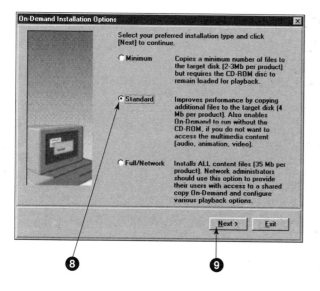

7. Click Continue. The On-Demand Installation Options dialog box appears.

8. Click the Full/Network radio button (if this option is not already selected).

9. Click Next. The Determine Installation Drive and Directory dialog box appears.

10. Choose the default drive and directory that appears, or click Change to choose a different drive and directory.

11. Click Next. The Product Selection dialog box appears, which enables you to verify the software you want to install.

12. Click Finish to complete the installation. The On-Demand Installation dialog box displays the progress of the installation. After the installation, the User Registration dialog box appears.

13. Enter information in the User Registration dialog box, including a password.

14. Click OK. The Password Verification dialog box appears.

15. Type the password again.

16. Click OK. The On-Demand Installation dialog box appears.

17. Click OK to confirm the installation has been successfully completed.

Please see Appendix C, "What's on the CD-ROM," for information about running the *One Step at a Time On-Demand* interactive software.